SUSTAINABLE
GLOBAL COMMUNITIES
IN THE
INFORMATION AGE

Recent Titles in
Praeger Studies on the 21st Century

SUSTAINABLE GLOBAL COMMUNITIES IN THE INFORMATION AGE

Visions from Futures Studies

Edited by Kaoru Yamaguchi

Praeger Studies on the 21st Century

Westport, Connecticut

Published in the United States and Canada by Praeger Publishers,
88 Post Road West, Westport, CT 06881.
An imprint of Greenwood Publishing Group, Inc.

Printed in the United States of America

(∞)™

The paper used in this book complies with the
Permanent Paper Standard issued by the National
Information Standards Organization (Z39.48–1984).

10 9 8 7 6 5 4 3 2 1

English language edition, except the United States and Canada,
published by Adamantine Press Limited, Richmond Bridge House,
417-419 Richmond Road, Twickenham TW1 2EX, England.

First published in 1997

Library of Congress Cataloging-in-Publication Data

Sustainable global communities in the information age : visions from
  futures studies / edited by Kaoru Yamaguchi.
       p.   cm.—(Praeger studies on the 21st century, ISSN
  1070–1850)
     Includes bibliographical references and index.
     ISBN 0–275–96063–3 (alk. paper).—ISBN 0–275–96062–5 (pbk. :
  alk. paper)
     1. Community development.   2. Sustainable development.
  3. Economic development.   4. Environmental policy.   I. Yamaguchi,
  Kaoru.   II. Series.
  HN49.C6S87   1997
  307.1′4—dc21   97–11602

Library of Congress Catalog Card Number: 97–11602

ISBN: 0-275-96063-3 Cloth
       0-275-96062-5 Paperback

Copyright © 1997 by Adamantine Press Limited

Contents

Part IV. Sustainable Community Projects in Awaji Island

Preface

Never doubt that a small group of thoughtful, committed citizens can change the world; indeed, it's the only thing that ever has.   Margaret Mead[1]

The Information Age is absolutely different from the Industrial Age. Accordingly, socioeconomic systems in the information age should not be the same as those of the industrial age, based on capitalist market economies and socialist planned economies. Those systems turned out to be neither sustainable nor community-based. Therefore, we have to look for new socioeconomic systems that are not only suitable for information and global communications technology in the information age, but also *sustainable* and *community-based.*

The failure of the industrial age is partly due to the education system peculiar to the industrial age, which only values highly fragmented specialists, without questioning the interrelationships of professions and fragmented viewpoints. Therefore, to create new socioeconomic systems in the information age, it becomes absolutely necessary to establish a new type of higher-education system that focuses on holistic viewpoints by unifying fragmented professions. This, of course, does not exclude traditional professional analyses at all. Such research is desperately needed for the advancement of high technology by the human mind. At the same time, we need a research programme that will evaluate both the positive and negative feedback of those fragmented professions and search for a holistic viewpoint leading to the balanced development—of humankind and of the entire environment of all living beings—in the future. New sustainable and community-based socioeconomic systems will be envisioned and created in the process of establishing these new types of higher institution in the information age.

To put these ideas and visions into action, a small group of people gathered on Awaji Island, Japan, from 16 to 19 August 1993 to hold the First World Futures-Creating Seminar under the main theme 'Renewing Community as Sustainable Global Village'. Their professional backgrounds were diverse: science, medicine, neurobiology, economics, political science, psychology, history, communications, comparative cultures, futures studies, and local and international governmental administration, to name but a few. The reader is referred to Chapter 20 for a detailed explanation of the nature of the seminar and its later evolution.[2]

[1] Dr Theodore J. Voneida, Chair of the Department of Neurobiology, Northeastern Ohio Universities College of Medicine, who represented Dr Roger Sperry, Nobel Laureate, and read his lecture paper on his behalf on the first day of the seminar (16 August 1993), encouraged the seminar participants with this quotation in his own closing remarks.

[2] Further information is provided on the Network University homepage at the World-Wide Web site http://www.bekkoame.or.jp/~k_yama/.

This book is the initial joint product of the small group who presented the material at the first seminar. It is our great honour that two Nobel Laureates, Dr Jerome Karle and Dr Roger Sperry, supported our future-oriented visionary research and contributed their own deep and thoughtful views on the future of our planet. The future-oriented perspective enabled us to place the visions of these multidisciplinary professionals within the unifying framework of this book: Sustainable Global Communities in the Information Age.

However, more than three-and-a-half years have passed since the first seminar. I am to be blamed for having taken such a long time to complete my editorial work in this fast-moving information age. Yet, the contents of the book, some parts of which have been updated, are still fresh and worth sharing, I believe, because they are mostly concerned with future-oriented visionary perspectives and fundamental issues that will be relevant to those navigating their way through an information overload.

This project has been realised with the help of many people. My first thanks go to Mistugu Saito, former mayor of Goshiki-cho town, who made the future-oriented decision to sponsor this research project, and to Hisao Onoe, professor emeritus of Kyoto University, whose participation in the seminar as a vice-chairman and whose consistent support for the project have been a major source of encouragement to me. My gratitude next has to be offered to Mitsuhiro Nishida, Shosuke Morinobe and members of the staff of the Department of Planning and Information, Goshiki-cho: without their devoted work, this project would not have been such a success. Moreover, I am proud of the townspeople of Goshiki-cho and congratulate them for having hosted this challenging global project. I would also like to thank Kazuki Nishioka, Richard J. Sadowsky and other home-stay volunteers in Awaji Island who kindly offered warm welcomes, delicious feasts and comfortable overnight accommodation to the seminar participants. Finally, I am deeply indebted to Jeremy Geelan, who encouraged me constantly and took great pains to help this book materialise as an Adamantine Study on the 21st Century.

Dr Roger Sperry

An envelope still remains with me and will remain undelivered forever—a sealed envelope dated 18 April 1994 and addressed to Dr Roger Sperry, Division of Biology, 156-29, California Institute of Technology, Pasadena, California 91125, USA.

I happened to come across the news of Dr Sperry's sudden death in the evening newspaper on 19 April, just a day before I was planing to deliver the first draft of this book to all contributors. It was unbelievable to me: I had corresponded with him several times in those days concerning the publication of his paper in this volume. To be specific, I had received two faxes signed by Dr Sperry himself on 15 February and 21 March 1994, and a fax signed by his assistant, Mary Jeffries, on 5 April 1994. He seemed fine in this correspondence. Hence I have no words to express my sadness, but just my respectful condolences.

Dr Sperry encouraged me very much from the beginning, when I was first planning to initiate the seminar and a higher-education project on Awaji Island. In a letter dated 26 April 1993, he wrote to me:

I am most pleased and deeply honored to accept your kind invitation to participate in your First World Futures-Creating Seminar, and yes, I will start very soon to gather thoughts in preparation for a lecture along the lines you suggest for presentation by Professor Voneida. Hopefully I'll be able to send a version, or at least a gist, by mid-July.

Also, should there be anything further I might do—(in a background role)— that might be of any help in your laudable effort, please do not hesitate to let me know.

With thanks and appreciation, and continuing best wishes for your most important project.

In my last fax to him, on 3 April 1994, I wrote as follows:

Your search for the integration of religion and science within a single consistent world-view is also our consistent search under the future-oriented interdisciplinary project.

Two days later, on 5 April, he sent me a floppy diskette of his paper, which convinced me that he would indeed support our project consistently. Now I am making a promise to him that we will carry on his messages in our project. With this in mind, I have decided, with the approval of all contributors, to dedicate this book to Dr Sperry, with a memorial paper by Dr Voneida in the following pages.

K.Y.

Goshiki-cho town
Awaji Island, Japan
March 1996

Roger Sperry's Views on Mind, Consciousness, and Human Values: A Challenge to the World Community

THEODORE J. VONEIDA

I first met Roger Sperry in 1958, when I spent a summer in his laboratory as a visiting graduate student from Cornell University. I returned in 1960 as a Cal-tech Postdoctoral Fellow, and remained for the following three years, during which time I not only began my own scientific career, but also had the very great opportunity to work with and learn from a man whose ideas about brain function, mind, consciousness and human values were to have a worldwide impact. I shall attempt, in the following few pages, to place some of Sperry's long-term views on the mind as an emergent property of brain function in a broader perspective, which includes some of his thinking about the relationships between the mind and human values, and his very deep concerns for the future of humankind.

One doesn't have to look very far these days to discover yet another opinion about the mind or consciousness. It has indeed become not only acceptable, but also quite fashionable to discuss this aspect of brain function, and nearly everyone seems to be doing it.[1] This was certainly not the case when Sperry began thinking and writing about the subjective properties of brain processes during the mid-1950s. In 1958, for example, as part of the discussion at the Josiah Macy Conference on the Central Nervous System and Behavior, he stated:

I have never been entirely satisfied with the materialistic or behavioristic thesis that a complete explanation of brain function is possible in purely objective terms with no reference whatever to subjective experience, i.e., that in scientific analysis we can confidently and advantageously, disregard the subjective properties of the brain process. I do not mean we should abandon the objective approach or repeat the errors of the earlier introspective era. It is just that I find it difficult to believe that the sensations and other subjective experiences per se serve no function, have no operational value and no place in our working models of the brain. (Sperry 1958)

And again, in his 1965 paper 'Mind, Brain and Humanist Values', he wrote:

Any model or description (of the brain) that leaves out conscious forces . . . is bound to be sadly incomplete and unsatisfactory. . . . This scheme is one that puts mind back over

---

[1] Crick and Koch 1990; Edelmann 1987, 1989; Flanagan 1991, 1992; Hale 1989; Jaynes 1976; McGinn 1991; Oakley 1985; Ornstein 1986; Penfield 1975; Popper and Eccles 1977; Searle 1992; Strawson 1994; Thomas 1978.

matter, in a sense, not under or outside or beside it. It is a scheme that idealizes ideas and ideals over physical and chemical interactions, nerve impulse traffic, and DNA. It is a brain model in which conscious mental psychic forces are recognized to be the crowning achievement of some five hundred million years or more of evolution.

Thus, while many neurobiologists were busily engaged in studies related to the question of 'right brain, left brain' function, based on Sperry's own earlier work with the 'split-brain' preparation, Sperry himself had already moved on to questions of mind and consciousness, which required a 'reunification', so to speak, of hemispheric function. This was very typical of Sperry's style—to open an area with several brilliant strokes, then to leave the details to others, while he was already moving on to a consideration of new problems. The 1965 paper referred to above was his first major paper in this area. In it he proposed that subjective experience plays a primary role in brain function, and that behaviourism, which views consciousness as non-existent, and reductionism, which reduces it to physico-chemical events, must both be replaced by a more holistic view of consciousness based on the concepts of 'emergence' and 'downward causation'. The concept of emergence, according to Sperry, 'occurs whenever the interaction between 2 or more entities, be they subparticles, atoms or molecules, creates a new entity with new laws and properties formerly nonexistent in the universe'. He pointed out the parallel with quantum physics, in which 'interactions among subatomic particles result in emergent properties which in no way resemble the particles from which they arose'. It is important to emphasise that Sperry did not see this as dualism, which treats the mind as a separate entity outside the brain, and capable of existing independently of it. Nor did he accept the term 'psychophysical interaction', as suggested by Popper and Eccles (1977).

Thus, in Sperry's view, although consciousness is generated from neural activity and is therefore fully dependent upon it, it is none the less separate from it. Consciousness is seen to emerge from the activity of cerebral networks as an independent entity. It is, as Trevarthen (1990) pointed out, 'a special instance of a general principle, "macrodeterminism", in which the higher, more evolved forces throughout nature exert control over their lower components'. This newly emerged property, which we have chosen to call *the mind* or *consciousness*, continually feeds back into the system from which it has emerged, resulting in a highly dynamic process of emergence, feedback (downward causation), newly emergent states, further feedback, and so on. The enormous power and unique nature of these newly emergent phenomena disappear when they are reduced to their previous state of individual components.

Sperry elevated this concept of emergence from the individual to the global level, stating (1972) that 'the new paradigm affirms that the world we live in is driven not solely by mindless physical forces but, more crucially, by subjective human values. Human values become the underlying key to world change.' Value systems, then, may be viewed as the emergent properties of many minds, working together over fairly long periods of time to effect changes in society, and hopefully, to feed back into it to bring about a better world—one that will result in a greater quality of life and species survival, rather than a reduction in quality and possible extinction. Sperry (1993) contended that this view, integrating macro- with microdeterminism and the causal reality of mental states, is a more valid foundation for all science, not just psychology, with 'endless humanistic implications for philosophy, religion and human values'.

By introducing the issue of human values, Sperry moved beyond the specifics of mind and consciousness to urge that these very unique and powerful forces be directed towards improving and preserving the quality of life on our planet, rather than the reverse. He made an especially strong appeal to the scientific community to turn its efforts towards these goals. In his 1972 paper 'Science and the Problem of Values', for example, he argued that:

> the social value factor be more generally recognized as a powerful causal agent in its own right and something to be dealt with directly as such. No more critical task can be projected for the 1970's than that of seeking for civilized society a new, elevated set of value guidelines more suited to man's expanded numbers and new powers over nature, a frame of reference for value priorities that will act to secure and conserve our world instead of destroying it.

Again, in 1986, in 'The Human Predicament: A Way Out?', he issued a direct challenge to science by pointing out that, in the past, science had done little, if anything, to remedy the root causes of worsening world conditions, and urged a philosophical change in direction towards a 'new, reformed "macro-determinist" science [which] includes consciousness and subjective values . . . provides common universal ethical foundations on which all nations could work to build a World Government or at least a World Security System to help control nuclear developments and other global threats that require international collaboration'.[2]

Sperry's thinking about subjective experience, consciousness, the mind and human values makes a powerful plea for a new scientific examination of ethics in the workings of consciousness. These ideas were crystallised in his paper 'The Impact and Promise of the Cognitive Revolution', which I had the honour of delivering for him at the centennial meeting of the American Psychological Association (Sperry 1993). It was his great hope, and his sincere belief, that our very survival depends upon our ability to put our collective minds together and to use the enormous emergent power that they are capable of generating.

His urgent plea has begun, finally, to be heard by the scientific community. In response, and under the able leadership of his long-term friend and colleague Rita Levi-Montalcini, an international conference was convened at the University of Trieste in November 1992 to discuss these ideas in greater detail. The plan was to work towards the creation of a strong statement of duties, emanating from the academic community but speaking to every 'mind' willing to listen, that might represent a corollary to the United Nations 'Declaration of Human Rights'. I was privileged to represent Sperry at the first meeting of this group,

---

2 For a more complete discussion of Sperry's views on the mind and human values, see Erdmann and Stover 1991.

which included ten Nobel Laureates and numerous others, representing disciplines ranging from neurobiology, chemistry, physics and economics to theology. After much discussion a draft version of what was then called 'The Magna Carta of Human Duties' was generated. Subsequent meetings resulted in a final version, entitled 'A Declaration of Human Duties', which was forwarded to the United Nations and is presently under consideration for possible adoption.

This conference volume represents another legacy of Sperry's views on the mind and human values, and it is appropriate that it be dedicated to him. Indeed, Kaoru Yamaguchi's inspiration for calling and organising the conference is directly located in the impact of Sperry's ideas on his own thinking. The long-term goal of this and future conferences is to work towards the establishment of a Network University of the Green World, in which students from all over the world can communicate with faculty and with each other on topics related to human values, both through direct contact at summer workshops and through global computer networking. The theme of this conference, 'Sustainable Global Communities in the Information Age', with presentations by a wide variety of scholars and students from various parts of the globe, is based in part on Sperry's thesis that consciousness itself is a kind of community, emerging from a great interactive network of individual parts, upon which it is dependent for its being, but from which it is also separate, independent and unique.

This brief account represents but a small portion of the impact and the promise of Roger Sperry's ideas on mind and consciousness as emergent properties of brain function, and their virtually unlimited potential for generating value systems that guide and determine human behaviour. I have presented only a few examples of the far-reaching, global effects of the thinking of one man. Indeed, the tremendous energy generated by the mind of this quiet man with a wry smile is perhaps the best testimony of all to his concept of mind as an emergent property of the brain. The physico-chemical events, the neurotransmitters, the circuitry of Sperry's brain were probably quite similar to those of most other human brains. Yet, the mind that emerged from those interactions was truly unique: it not only inspired and stimulated the minds of those of us who were privileged to know him and work with him; it will also continue to stimulate and generate ideas from minds yet to emerge.

References and Further Reading

Crick, F. and Koch, C. (1990). 'Towards a Neurobiological Theory of Consciousness', *Seminars in the Neurosciences* 2: pp. 263–75.

Edelmann, G. (1987). *Neural Darwinism*, New York: Basic Books.

—— (1989). *The Remembered Present: A Biological Theory of Consciousness*, New York: Basic Books.

Erdmann, E. and Stover, D. (1991). *Beyond a World Divided*, Boston, Mass.: Shambhala.

Flanagan, O. (1991). *The Science of the Mind*, 2nd edn., Cambridge, Mass.: MIT Press, Bradford Books.

—— (1992). *Consciousness Reconsidered*, Cambridge, Mass.: MIT Press, Bradford Books.

Hale, M. (1989). *The Mind: Its Origin, Evolution, Structure and Functioning*, Pittsburgh, Pa.: Hale-van Ruth.

Jaynes, J. (1976). *The Origin of Consciousness in the Breakdown of the Bicameral Mind*, Boston, Mass.: Houghton Mifflin.

McGinn, C. (1991). *The Problem of Consciousness*, Oxford: Blackwell.

Oakley, D. (ed.) (1985). *Brain and Mind*, London: Methuen.

Ornstein, R. (1986). *The Psychology of Consciousness*, New York: Penguin.

Penfield, W. (1975). *The Mystery of the Mind*, Princeton, N.J.: Princeton University Press.

Popper, K. and Eccles, J. (1977). *The Self and its Brain*, New York: Springer.

Ryle, G. (1966). *The Concept of Mind*, London: Penguin.

Searle, J. (1992). *The Rediscovery of the Mind*, Cambridge, Mass.: MIT Press, Bradford Books.

Sperry, R. (1955). 'On the Neural Basis of the Conditioned Response', *British Journal of Animal Behaviour* 3(2): pp. 41–4.

—— (1958). Discussion in M. A. B. Brazier (ed.), *Josiah Macy Conference: The Central Nervous System and Behavior*, New Jersey: Madison Print.

—— (1965). 'Brain and Humanist Values', in J. R. Platt (ed.), *New Views of the Nature of Man*, Chicago, Ill.: University of Chicago Press.

—— (1972). 'Science and the Problem of Values', *Perspectives in Biology and Medicine* 16: pp. 115–30.

—— (1986). 'The Human Predicament: A Way Out?', *Contemporary Philosophy* 11(6): pp. 2–4.

—— (1993). 'The Impact and Promise of the Cognitive Revolution', *American Psychologist* 48: pp. 878–85.

Strawson, G. (1994). *Mental Reality*, Cambridge, Mass.: MIT Press, Bradford Books.

Thomas, S. (1978). *The Formal Mechanics of Mind*, Sussex: Harvester.

Trevarthen, C. (1990). 'Roger W. Sperry's Lifework and our Tribute', editor's preface to *Brain Circuits and Functions of the Mind: Essays in Honor of Roger W. Sperry*, Cambridge: Cambridge University Press.

Voneida, T. (1993). 'Performance of a Visual Conditioned Response in Split-Brain Cats', *Experimental Neurology* 8: pp. 493–504.

Contributors

Dirk A. Ballendorf is Professor of Micronesian Studies, Micronesian Area Research Center, University of Guam, USA. He received his Ed.D. and M.A. in history from Harvard University. He began his academic career as an instructor at Boston University in 1970. As a foreign service reserve officer, he served in the Peace Corps in the Pacific, the Middle East and Washington. In 1977 he was named President of the Community College of Micronesia at Pohnpei in the Eastern Caroline Islands. He has been in his current position since 1979, and was Director of the centre for five years. He has been a visiting professor, scholar and lecturer at universities in Australia, New Zealand, Germany, France, Russia and the USA. He has also been the editor of *GLIMPSES MAGAZINE*, a regional quarterly published in Guam, and a historical features journalist on radio and television in Guam.

Ingrid Burkett is a Ph.D candidate at the University of Queensland, Australia. She received a B.Soc.Wk. (Hons) from the University of Queensland and an M.Bus. (Comm) from Queensland University of Technology. She has worked as a social worker, trauma counsellor and research assistant. Her Ph.D work is entitled 'Thinking, Acting, Linking Globally from the Local Community: A Community Development Response to Globalisation'. In this work she is exploring the emerging nexus between local and global processes influencing community development work.

Yoon-Jae Chung is an associate professor in the Department of Political Science and International Relations, Chungbuk National University, Republic of Korea. He received his Ph.D. in political science from the University of Hawaii, and his B.A. and M.A. from Seoul National University. His research interests are focused on the political leadership approach to development and democracy. He recently published a paper entitled 'A Reevaluation of President Park Chung Hee's Modernization Leadership', and is now co-authoring a book on the nature of political leadership in Korea in the future, while teaching theories of 'global utopia' and world governance for the twenty-first century. In 1995 he served as Director of the research committee of politics and society for the Korean Political Science Association. He is a member of the World Futures Studies Federation (WSFS).

Jim Dator is a professor and Head of the Alternative Futures Option in the Department of Political Science, University of Hawaii, and Director of the Hawaii Research Center for Futures Studies. He received a Ph.D. in political science from the American University and a M.A. in political science from the University of Pennsylvania. He served as Secretary-General and then President of the World Futures Studies Federation (1983–1993). Dr Dator has three major areas of specialisation. They are futures studies (especially the design of new political institutions, and the future of law, education, and technology); the political–economic futures of North America, East Asia, and the Pacific Islands; and media production and the politics of media. He has consulted with state futures commissions for Florida, Hawaii, Oregon and Illinois, and has been a planning consultant to the state judiciaries of Hawaii, Virginia, Arizona, Massachusetts, Illinois and Kansas and the Federated States of Micronesia. He has lectured to several thousand general, professional, governmental and business, as well as futurist, audiences worldwide.

Nandini Joshi is Managing Trustee of the Foundation for Constructive Development, Ahmedabad, India. She received her Ph.D. in economics from Harvard University. She taught at the Indian Institute of Management, Ahmedabad, was appointed Director of the Birla Institute of Scientific Research and worked with the Council of Scientific and Industrial Research as well as with the United Nations Conference on Trade and Development, Geneva. She is active in grassroots work in villages and at the moment strongly committed to the implementation of the *charkha* or spinning wheel at the grassroots level. Countering arguments that the *charkha* is neither viable nor practical, she believes that this simple implement can be profitable, practical and implementable, and in fact could carry the world into the twenty-first century; in other words, the *charkha* can usher in a non-violent revolution, the consequences of which could accumulate in the form of prosperity, freedom and peace. She says it is from the poor, simple people that practical lessons in economics can be learned. Though economics tells you how to make profits, it does not teach you to alleviate unemployment and tackle the root cause of unemployment (from 'Meet Nandini Joshi', *The Times of India*, Ahmedabad, 23 December 1992).

Jerome Karle works at the Laboratory for the Structure of Matter, Naval Research Laboratory, Washington, D.C., USA. He was born in Brooklyn, New York, on 18 June 1918 into a family with strong artistic traditions, several of whom had careers in the fine and commercial arts. Dr Karle received a Ph.D. in physical chemistry from the University of Michigan. He has served as President of the International Union of Crystallography and has been Chairman of the Chemistry Section of the National Academy of Sciences. For a number of years, he was a professorial lecturer at University College, University of Maryland. He was also a visiting professor at the University of Kiel in Germany. His research has been concerned with diffraction theory and its application to the determination of the atomic arrangements of substances in various states of aggregation. In 1985, he was awarded the Nobel Prize for Chemistry.

Michael LaFontaine is Director of the Community Land Trust Project, New Hampshire Community Loan Fund, Concord, New Hampshire 03302–0800, USA. He received his Law degree from Boston University and his A.B. (with

honors) from Boston College. The New Hampshire Loan Fund is a regional off-
shoot of the Institute for Community Economics, from which the Community
Land Trust model originated. The fund has developed and preserved over 1,250
units of housing. He works closely with seven Community Land Trusts in New
Hampshire, assisting in the growth of new organisations, providing training and
technical assistance on the wide range of issues facing maturing organisations,
and developing a supportive public and institutional context in which to sustain
the Land Trust model. He serves on the faculty of the annual Conference of
Community Land Trusts throughout the USA.

Takamaro Matsuura is Director of the Goshiki-cho Health and Welfare Center,
and Vice-Chairman of the Kinki District Medical Facilities Council of the National Health Insurance. He received his M.D. from Osaka Medical School, and
was a part-time lecturer at the school. Dr Matsuura worked at Osaka Medical
School Hospital in 1972, and Saku General Hospital in Nagano Prefecture
between 1972 and 1982, where he served as Head of the Health Management
Department in 1982. In 1983 he was invited to the Goshiki-cho Health and
Welfare Center as a director. He played a crucial role in the initiation of such
advanced medical information systems in Goshiki-cho as medical IC cards and
the home-care support system using a two-way CATV network. IC cards
facilitate the efficient health management of townspeople through the medical
information that they store, while medical network systems enable real-time, interactive audio-visual communication between doctors in hospitals and patients
at home. Dr Matsuura's pastimes are the literary arts and travelling.

Chuck Matthei is President of the Equity Trust, Inc., Voluntown, Connecticut
06384, USA. He has been a community development practitioner for over twenty
years. He was previously Executive Director of the Institute for Community
Economics (ICE), which pioneered the community loan fund model. During his
tenure at ICE (1980–90) its revolving loan fund granted more than $16 million
in loans to 250 projects in thirty states. He has assisted in the development of
twenty regional loan funds nationwide and organised the National Association
of Community Development Loan Funds, which currently includes forty-two
member funds managing $165 million in assets.

Kazuo Mizuta is a professor at the School of Liberal Arts, Kyoto Sangyo University. He received his Ph.D. in comparative culture from Pacific Western
University, and his M.A. in English literature from Western Michigan University. He was formerly a teaching assistant in the Department of East Asian
Languages, University of Wisconsin, Madison. This experience has influenced
his later research towards comparative studies of the cultures of the USA and
Japan.

San San Myint received a B.Sc. (Hons) from the Rangoon Arts and Science
University, Burma, and a M.Bus. (Comm) from the Queensland University of

Technology, Australia. She has worked at the Rangoon Arts and Science University, the United States Information Service (Burma) and the Asian Mass Communication Research and Information Center (Singapore). She is currently working on a Ph.D. in the Department of Government at the University of Queensland.

Hiroyuki Niwa is a professor at Nagoya Cultural College, Japan, where he began work in 1992. He received his M.A. in economics from Nagoya City University. He was Chief Correspondent at the Mainichi newspaper, and covered many community development projects in the Tokai region of central Japan in his later career.

Belden Paulson is Professor of Public Policy, University of Wisconsin, Milwaukee. He received his Ph.D. and M.A. in political science from the University of Chicago. During the last fifteen years he has been teaching on various dimensions of futures studies. Much of his futures work has related to innovations in learning. Fifteen years ago his wife, Lisa, and he co-founded the High Wind Association, an international community in Wisconsin, which has focused on solar buildings, sustainable agriculture and alternative lifestyles. Three years ago they co-founded, with several representatives of other universities, Plymouth Institute, a centre for sustainable development based on 292 acres of land. Two of its major projects are the creation of an eco-village, which is becoming an R&D centre for sensitive land use, homes employing renewable energy sources and biological sewage treatment, and governance combining private and community ownership; and a field-experience campus committed to whole-systems, sustainable futures-thinking in a practical, hands-on setting. Over the years his research and writings on Italy, Brazil, China, America's inner cities and international communities have focused on various aspects of life in a sustainable community. During 1994–6 he served on the Education Working Group of the President's Council on Sustainable Development.

Qin Linzheng is a research professor at the Chinese Academy of Social Sciences. He was a postdoctoral researcher at Harvard University, and in 1991 was awarded the title of Returning Scholar of Outstanding Contribution in China. He is interested in doing interdisciplinary research on social change, social development and the information society; global problems; and the cross-impact of science, technology and society. He conducts project research for academic institutions, government organisations and such international bodies as UNESCO and UNDP. He acts as scientific researcher, policy analyst, enterprises consultant, educator in training programmes and as honorary editor or adviser of domestic journal, newspaper and other publications. He works as a counsellor with the World Futures Studies Federation and the International Association Futuribles, and as an international advisory board member on the journal *Futures*. He was also the founder, and is now the executive vice-president and the secretary-general, of the Chinese Society for Futures Studies.

Mitsugu Saito is a former mayor of Goshiki-cho. After experience as a town councilman and deputy mayor, he was elected town mayor in July 1979 and served four consecutive terms, until July 1995. As mayor he consistently built a progressive health- and culture-oriented town for the benefit of local residents. In 1985 he established the Goshiki-cho Kenmin Kenko Mura health centre, which three years later introduced an IC health-card system to store individual health and medical care information, the first system of its kind in Japan. In April 1994 the town began operation of a CATV system with interactive capabilities. This cutting-edge system is now used by doctors and nurses visiting the homes of elderly patients to send IC health-card information and receive video images from a central clinic for use in medical treatment. Park Facilities, which was completed in April 1995, serves as a centre for cultural exchange among people from across Japan and the world. It was created in honour of the historical figure Takataya Kahei, a man from Goshiki known for developing a new sea-trading route via Japan's northern territories in the late eighteenth century. Mayor Saito enjoys sports and travel.

Albert Sasson is Assistant Director-General of the Bureau of Studies, Programming and Evaluation (including also the Division of Statistics), UNESCO. Dr Sasson received a Doctor of Natural Sciences degree in microbiology from the University of Paris in 1967. After a career at the Faculty of Science in Rabat (Morocco) from 1954 to 1973 (as Dean of the faculty from 1963 to 1969), he joined UNESCO in 1974. As a member of the Division of Ecological Sciences, he participated in the activities of the Programme on Man and the Biosphere (MAB), notably those concerning arid and semi-arid zones, and prepared major state-of-knowledge reports on the tropical forest and grazing land ecosystems of the world (*Tropical Grazing Land Ecosystems*, 1979). From 1979 to 1985 he participated, within the Bureau of Studies and Programming of the Directorate-General of UNESCO, in the elaboration of the biennial programmes and the Medium-Term Plan of the organisation in science and technology. From 1985 to 1987 he was Director of the Central Evaluation Unit of the Directorate-General of UNESCO. In 1988 he was appointed Director of the Bureau of Programme Planning within the Office for Planning, Budgeting and Evaluation, and in August 1990 Director of the Bureau of Studies, Programming and Evaluation.

Roger W. Sperry worked in the Division of Biology, California Institute of Technology. Dr Sperry received his bachelor's degree in English literature from Oberlin College in 1935, and his M.A. in psychology from the same institution in 1937. He received a Ph.D. in zoology from the University of Chicago in 1941. He held fellowships at Harvard from 1941 to 1946, where he worked in the Yerkes Laboratories of Primate Biology, and performed military service from 1942 to 1945 by taking part in the OSRD Medical Research Project on Nerve Injuries. He taught as an assistant professor in the University of Chicago's Department of Anatomy until 1952, then in 1952–3 served as an associate professor of psychology at the same school and simultaneously as the section chief for neurological diseases and blindness at the National Institute of Health. In 1954 he became the Hixon Professor of Psychobiology at Caltech, where he remained until his retirement in 1984. In addition to sharing the Nobel Prize in Physiology and Medicine in 1981 with David H. Hubel and Torsten N. Wiesel, he also received the National Medal of Science in 1989 from President George Bush, the Wolf Prize in Medicine and the Albert Lasker Medical Research Award in 1979, and the California Scientist of the Year Award in 1972.

Tony Stevenson specialises in the futures of communication and the way emerging communications technologies and local–global tensions can change the way we live, learn and work in the next century. He is Associate Professor and Director of the Communication Centre at the Queensland University of Technology, Australia, and Secretary-General of the international non-governmental organisation the World Futures Studies Federation. Prior to becoming an academic in 1985 he was a journalist and a consultant in organisational communication and issues-management. He is a partner in a project to develop a community in the rainforest at Gheerulla, near his favourite beach at Noosa on the Sunshine Coast, north of Brisbane.

Brian Tokar is a faculty member in Social Ecology at Goddard College in Plainfield, Vermont, USA. He received an M.A. in biophysics from Harvard University and a B.S. in biology and physics from MIT. He is the author of *The Green Alternative: Creating an Ecological Future* (San Pedro, CA: R.&E. Miles, 1987; rev. edn. Philadelphia: New Society Publishers, 1992), which is also available in Japanese as *Midori no Mō Hitotsu no Michi* (Tokyo: Chikuma Shobo, 1992). He has written and lectured widely on Green politics and emerging ecological movements, with articles appearing regularly in *Z Magazine* (a Boston-based political monthly), *The Ecologist* and many other publications. His new book, *Earth for Sale*, will be published by South End Press in Boston in the spring of 1997. For twenty years he has been an activist in the peace, anti-nuclear and environmental movements, and he has been a consultant to community groups across the USA on issues of food safety, biotechnology, environmental health and Green political organising.

Cesar Villanueva is Director of BALAYAN, the Community Development and Volunteer Formation Office of the University of St. La Salle, Bacolod City 6100, the Philippines. He is also a full-time faculty member of the university, teaching Community Development Economics. He received his A.B. Economics from Ateneo de Manila University and is an M.A. candidate in Extension Administration at Silliman University. He is presently a member of the Executive Council of the World Futures Studies Federation, the National Vice-Chair of the Philippine Partnership for Support Services Agencies, Visayas Committee Chair of the Philippine–Canadian Joint Committee for Human Resource Development and a member of the Program Advisory Committee of the

Philippine–Australian Community Assistant Program. He is also a founding member of the Negros Caucus and Visayas Network of Development NGOs.

Theodore J. Voneida is a professor and Chairman of the Department of Neuro-biology, Northeastern Ohio Universities College of Medicine, Rootstown, Ohio, USA. Dr Voneida was born in Elbridge, New York, and has lived in Ohio since 1962. Upon completing his master's degree in science education at Cornell University in 1953, he was drafted and sent to the Walter Reed Army Institute of Research, where he worked for two years in Walle Nauta's laboratory. It was during that time that he met and married Swanny Bekkedahl, an occupational therapist. They returned to Ithaca, New York, in 1956, and he completed his Ph.D. in 1960. He then spent three years in Roger Sperry's laboratory at the California Institute of Technology. In 1962 he joined the faculty of the Case Western Reserve College of Medicine, where he went from assistant to full professor. In 1976 he was invited to join the newly established Northeastern Ohio Universities College of Medicine, where he became Professor and Chair-man of the first Neurobiology Department in the USA. He has been an activist in the peace and environmental movements since the early 1960s, and was invited by President Carter to the White House for the historic signing of the federal strip-mine bill. He has recently completed an animated, interactive computerised textbook of neuroanatomy, and has published extensively in the area of learning and memory.

Kaoru Yamaguchi is a professor at Osaka Sangyo University, Japan. He received his Ph.D. in economic theory from the University of California at Berkeley, and his M.A. in mathematical economics from Kobe University. At the invitation of Jim Dator, he joined the World Futures Studies Federation in 1987, while he was teaching at the Economics Department, University of Hawaii. Since then he has been actively involved in futures studies, presenting his integrated economic theories at the world conferences in Beijing (1988), Budapest (1990) and Barcelona (1991). In June 1992, he was invited to attend the UNESCO seminar on 'Teaching about the Future' in Vancouver, where he emphasised the need for a higher institution for future-oriented studies and proposed a series of future-oriented interdisciplinary seminars on Awaji Island, Japan, as a first step.

Zhang Zerong is a professor and Director of the Economic Research Institute, Sichuan Academy of Social Sciences. He received his B.A. in Economics from the Northwest Finance and Economics College in China. In 1988, he was invited to the tenth world conference of the World Futures Studies Federation, Beijing. Since then he has been actively involved in futures studies.

Part I

Environmental Issues and Futures Studies

1 Some Remarks on the Human and Planetary Condition

JEROME KARLE

1.1 Introduction

The past few hundred years of human history have witnessed remarkable developments in science and technology. Man's profound scientific understanding and his technological facility have expanded very rapidly. At the present time, they continue to accelerate, affecting greatly almost all aspects of people's activities in all but the least developed areas. Medical diagnostics, treatments, pharmaceuticals and appliances, and transportation and communications facilities are examples of the ongoing scientific and technological revolution that greatly affect individual lives on a daily basis. The advances in health, comfort, convenience and personal well-being are most evident.

Despite these inspiring accomplishments, the future is more and more threatened with a deterioration of the quality of life and the proliferation of social inequities. It is therefore imperative that societies make planning for the future a high-priority consideration. Appreciation of this need is increasing, having become much more widespread in recent years as people find the various manifestations of the pressing problems part of their own life experience. In looking towards the future, it is incumbent on us to consider our past and present circumstances in order to establish key issues, priorities and necessary action. In this way, the impact of the threats may be minimised, and cultural, ethical and humane values may not only prevail but even be enhanced. Many individuals and organisations have already devoted much effort to these questions. Much still needs to be done to bring societies and governments to effective action. It is my intention here to present some impressions obtained from a number of the studies that have been made already while emphasising the degree to which many of the current and potential problems are interconnected.

The objective is to identify major factors that contribute to or generate the conditions that threaten our planet. Such factors must be controlled so that their harmful effects may be minimised or reversed. Failure to do so could lead to great harm to the earth and to the life upon it. When we think of problem areas, we think of the environment, of human violence and warfare, of the many failings of human character, of the failings of leadership, of the interactions of economics, population and human psychology, and of health and food supply, and we wonder about the extent to which many of these problems are interconnected and whether the interconnections can be sorted out so that there may be some hope of dealing with the problems effectively.

1.2 Environment

In the literature of organisations dedicated to preserving a healthful and humane environment, much discussion has appeared concerning the many human activities that have severely degraded it. These activities threaten the habitability of major portions of the earth and perhaps all of it. How far do we have to look to find examples? Polluted air, waterways and oceans, ravaged lands, erosion, desertification, deforestation, and radioactive and chemical wastes are by now either common experience or common knowledge. Even the more esoteric threats, which may not be as broadly appreciated or sensed, such as the depletion of the ozone layer and the accumulation of greenhouse gases, have been brought to our attention. At what point does the damage become irreversible? How great an insult can the earth take and still bounce back? Have we already passed the point of no return with some of these issues? Possibly; possibly not. It would be prudent, nevertheless, to take immediate steps to minimise the effects of the various threats. This requires no less than global co-operation among societies as well as their governments. Can this be achieved?

There is another aspect of a proper environment that it is important to consider, namely, quality of life. This means different things to different people, but it may be broadly described as an aspect of life that goes beyond the minimal requirements of subsistence, shelter and basic health needs. For many of us, quality of life involves artistic, aesthetic and intellectual components, human decency, high standards of behaviour, peace, trust, kindly interactions among peoples with a respect for human dignity, and sufficient space in which to dwell. The amount of space for comfort may vary considerably among us, but I believe that most of us need room for privacy, thought and contemplation. This is not to be found readily in the congested cities and living conditions associated with high population densities.

High-density population impacts profoundly on the environment and all aspects of the quality of life. It is difficult to imagine an environmental problem that would not be improved by a decrease in population and made worse by an increase in population. Since the current trend is towards an explosion of population in many parts of the world, it is clear that this factor in environmental problems demands immediate attention.

Nature's Storehouse

There are many reasons for not destroying such huge ecological areas as the rainforests. A major one is the fact that such areas are vast biological storehouses of substances that have important potential to benefit humans. This derives from the fact that living organisms, including both flora and fauna, develop chemical mechanisms that protect them from hostile environments, predators, infectious agents and disease. Such problems have been solved in nature in a great variety of ways, most of which are yet to be discovered. The compounds involved have the potential to serve humanity in many ways—as antibiotics, insecticides, herbicides, fungicides, preservatives, drugs such as anticancer agents and anti-malarials, heart drugs and many other types of physiologically active substance. Destruction of ecological systems destroys forever the opportunity to learn their secrets.

1.3 Sustainable Economy

Economics and War

The earth is finite and the number of people the earth can support is finite, under the best of circumstances. As a consequence, people have developed the concepts of a sustainable economy and a sustainable earth. Rarely is the expression 'sustainable economy' heard. The term economic growth predominates. Certainly activities that replace other ones can grow and, to an extent, new activities can grow. Growth can also be associated with a raising of the average quality of life in the world. There are limits, however, and the limits arise from limits on natural resources, limits on need and demand, limits generated by environmental considerations, and constraints on total population. This statement provides a clear indication that future economic policy must be in harmony with the finiteness of resources and population, and the requirements for a wholesome environment.

Economic competition is often enhanced by limited resources and markets. In the extreme case, it leads to warfare. A major component of many wars has been economic competition. There have been, of course, additional issues, but it seems fair to say that economic motivation has predominated. Economic competition should not be expected to cease when warfare ceases. The experience of the period after the Second World War, for example, is testimony to the fact that the underlying aspects of economic competition never disappeared, but simply took on another form. If and when the major players in industrialised states decide to confront economic reality by supporting and developing their human, humane and industrial capacities in a manner consistent with the broad concepts of sustainability and a large measure of self-sufficiency, they may be able to save their countries and future generations from severe economic hardship, if not destruction.

There is not much to say about warfare *per se*. It is enormously destructive, it dehumanises and brutalises survivors, damages the environment, wastes resources and may leave legacies of great potential harm to future generations. Nevertheless, warfare has been all too common a phenomenon in this century. Societies must find other, non-violent ways to deal with their economic stresses and other perceived inequities. Certainly, pouring arms into those societies that are most likely to use them offensively does not help matters. The large and apparently irresistible profit motive in the selling of arms makes control very difficult. The economic gain may be short range but the harm can be major and long lasting. There is not likely to be a net gain for any society in the long run.

There are other circumstances in which perceived short-term economic gains motivate inappropriate behaviour and result in net economic loss and harm to society. Industrial pollution is an example. From my contacts with the various news media in Europe, I have the impression that it is rather popular to blame chemists for pollution because some sort of 'chemicals' are often involved. Although there may on occasion be a chemist sufficiently high in industry to do so, chemists as a class have not been in a position to make decisions that determine how environmentally safe a manufacturing plant will be. In fact, in very many cases, chemists know what to do to protect the environment but have no way to implement their knowledge. Pollution often occurs because industry makes short-range economic decisions, or because appropriate legal regulations are not in place or are not enforced. I have made a point of this not simply to exonerate chemists but, more importantly, to emphasise that economic and environmental problems require clear thought on the part of all concerned. The problems that threaten the world involve everyone. Solutions to the problems may require expert help but the implementation of the solutions involves us all; societies and governments must be strongly involved and come together.

Gainful Employment in the Age of Automation

I recall reading an article several years ago that characterised a current economic dilemma, namely, that a new revolution is taking place in manufacturing without an accompanying reduction in the working week. One of the main causes of this revolution is automation, with its attendant efficiencies. The author asserted that this is the first time a major manufacturing advance in efficiency has not been followed by a reduction in the working week. The consequence of this is that advanced societies are becoming remarkably incapable of providing meaningful employment for a large fraction of their citizenry. Expanding populations can certainly add to the problem. In the present economic climate in many developed countries, the industrial response to monetary problems is to dismiss large numbers of employees and overwork others. This does not lead to economic stability for society as a whole. Manufacturers must be prepared to anticipate rather than simply respond to dwindling supplies of raw materials and rapidly changing markets.

It would be most appropriate for societies to analyse the social and economic implications of the rapidly developing technologies, changing markets in the world economy and other powerful forces that affect the quality of life in their communities. The problems are not insoluble. It seems that successful societies would need to have a sustainable plan in which all the population has the opportunity to make a contribution and thereby earn enough compensation to enjoy what most people would recognise as a decent standard of living. Can this be achieved in the atmosphere of competition that has characterised the industrial revolution up to this time? Is it possible to achieve sustainable economies and decent living standards without inhibiting the various aspects of individual initiative and creativity? There is a myriad of questions that societies may consider. The world, however, cannot possibly benefit from continued procrastination in facing these issues or wait for the results of endless debate and deliberation. Too much debate and little testing is as bad for societies as it is for science.

What needs to be done, were governments willing, is to take a careful look at resources, human and otherwise, set goals on the basis of high and presumably workable ideals and implement them. There is a need for flexibility, so that, in learning from experience, corrections could be made in a stepwise process. This requires governments to be composed of, or advised by, people of the highest intelligence and personal standards and whose greatest satisfactions would derive from the good results that they could achieve. This is not as difficult to secure as it may seem. There are many such people. The important step is for governments to be open to accepting well-motivated, well-thought-out plans and to make difficult, selfless decisions for the good of society, unencumbered by parochial considerations.

A view of the history of the twentieth century suggests that the world is more than ready but ill-prepared for such high-minded developments. That certainly seems to be broadly true. Nevertheless, there are a few countries that have renounced war and appear to have pursued, for long periods, steps toward a humane society. It is very important for those who would have high-minded thoughts concerning the future of world societies to realise that there is little chance of accomplishing very much without the help of senior government leaders, who would have the decision-making power to proceed with new approaches.

There have, in recent years, been some attempts to bring nations together, largely with the purpose of enhancing progress in the developing nations. One of the hopes has been for a decrease in the population explosion as the general quality of life increases, a phenomenon that has been observed in the more developed nations. A quite recent large-scale effort was the United Nations Conference on Environment and Development, which took place in Rio de Janeiro during June 1992. Will this UN conference be a useful effort in the attempt to place societies on a rational and humane basis? Only time will tell.

There is an aspect to these efforts that I do not understand. This concerns the concept that developed nations would provide help—conceptual, financial and technical—to developing nations to enhance their progress. As indicated elsewhere in this chapter, developed countries have a long way to go to achieve environmentally sound, sustainable economies in their own countries. They must counter the trend towards larger discrepancies between the richer and poorer members of their societies and, in the age of automation, find useful and productive roles for an increasing number of their citizens. It is legitimate to wonder, under the present circumstances, just what it is that developed nations would be exporting to developing ones.

Multicomponent Participation

Many of the problems associated with a deteriorating environment can be readily corrected by scientific and technological applications. Examples are the replacement of current energy sources by renewable ones that do not add to the carbon dioxide burden in the atmosphere, and technologies and processes that minimise pollution. Science and technology also continue to make major contributions to the health and well-being of people, as well as enhancing many other aspects of the quality of life. With all the wonders of science and technology that have developed over the past few centuries and are currently appearing at an accelerating pace, the fact remains that science and technology are not enough to solve all the world's problems. There are matters of ethics, government leadership, economics and social philosophy that must also play an active role in addition— a truly multicomponent participation.

The question arises as to whether high levels of technology should be the goal of all societies on this earth. It is a rather difficult question, if for no other reason than the fact that high levels of technology are currently very remote from the lifestyles of many areas. In such areas, perhaps present goals should be to assure sustainable, humane and healthful communities consistent with current levels of development.

There is a feature of the effects on society of science and technology that is a cause for special concern. As societies depend more and more on complex technology, it takes only one individual to commit an error or one component to break down to jeopardise the functioning of a major portion of a community. An extreme case is a deliberate act of terrorism or sabotage in which individuals take advantage of products of technology to cause harm and destruction. Thus, modern technology can enable a very few people to cause highly disabling events to occur, intentionally or otherwise.

1.4 Ethics and Education

It is important that young people be trained from an early age to question contemporary concepts and the ideas that swirl around them. They should be taught how to think and draw rational conclusions. Alongside this, the development of high ethical standards needs to be emphasised in the educational process. Although such standards should come from the home as well as the school, if they do not come from the home, they must come from the school. The learning of purely factual material is, of course, indispensable, but education obtained in the absence of fine-tuned reasoning and an ethical sensitivity is probably a major contributor to current societal ills.

A valuable leadership quality is the ability to apply sound intellectual power to problems and to use the results in an ethical fashion. It is to be expected that an educational system that emphasises such qualities in general would raise the standards and the quality of life for society as a whole. In addition to teaching how to think, another very worthwhile feature of an educational system is for it to be broadly based. Everyone who attended my liberal arts college was required to study mathematics (including calculus), attend a 'science survey' course, take a particular science course of their choice, attend courses on such subjects as government and history, public speaking, English literature, music appreciation and hygiene, and develop language skills. There were undoubtedly other requirements that I do not recall. Other courses taken by the students were at the students' choice. High standards and broad requirements were also maintained in elementary and high schools. Ethics *per se* was not taught, but there was a no-nonsense, respectful atmosphere in which the business of the schools was conducted. In elementary school there were two report cards, one for scholastic accomplishments and one for personal behaviour. Although I attended college (all male and free of charge) during the height of the depression years of the 1930s, students attended classes as respectable gentlemen, generally dressed in suits.

An educational system such as the one I was fortunate to attend, the New York City system, provided students with a broad education and literacy in many intellectual areas, and prepared them to go into the world with heightened insights and understanding. The graduates were clear about their choices for further, specialised studies, confident about their own capabilities and, by and large, good citizens. Many have had outstanding careers. The school system also served people well who did not go to college or preferred to learn a trade while in high school. I attended school in New York City during the 1920s and 1930s. Perhaps there are historical records extant that could serve as a worthwhile model. There may be many individuals in the field of education who would argue that there have been some advances in education since the 1930s that would surpass such a model. This is perhaps so and should also be considered. I look, however, at the challenges and the discipline that I faced as a student compared with those broadly followed in many locations at present, and I must conclude that the older system was, in general, the more successful. My experience as a participant and observer is largely confined to the USA. Readers in other countries may perhaps see some similarities to their own views and experiences.

The thought that there should be special graduate institutions to train the leaders of the future in the main subjects of critical importance is a very fine one (Yamaguchi 1992). It may even be said that such institutions ought to be regarded as indispensable. Subjects of critical importance have been discussed in many publications during previous decades. Their urgency has become increasingly recognised and publicised, so that many of the issues have become part of public knowledge. Perhaps we may hope that, in the future, training in the proposed graduate institutions will be a prerequisite to appointment to high political office and that the students will be among the finest graduates of an educational system that promotes broad scholarship combined with ethical principles. The world can always benefit from great leaders with impeccable standards who have broad intellects and a good sense of what may be achieved in practice.

Character

It is evident that a society comprised of people who had high ethical standards, avoided antisocial behaviour and had a deep regard for human dignity and self-respect that was based on high personal standards would have the potential to exceed by far current experiences. The actual level of character and morality in present-day societies is a matter of concern. Antisocial behaviour at all levels can defeat attempts to raise the average standard of living, solve economic and environmental problems and achieve humane and cultured civilisations through-out the world. There are many areas of our world in varying degrees of strife and otherwise sorry states.

The serious implication is that it is not possible to assume that governments and societies are necessarily ready to correct the problems of the world or to try to do so within a thoughtful, rational and humane framework.

We are told by behavioural scholars that it is important to start to instil character into children at a very young age; otherwise, in general, the process is not particularly successful. This is a subject that merits careful consideration, since it seems to be vital for the achievement of more humane and ethical societies in the future. In addition to building character, it is important to teach young people to have enquiring minds and well-ordered priorities. They must learn to think, gather information and draw rational conclusions based on the information. A common impediment in reaching people is their tendency to draw conclusions based on emotion or other motivations, rather than informa-tion and analysis. They will often proceed by trying to justify the conclusions and insist on their validity in the absence of careful thought. Societies' pre-occupation with trivia and self-endangering behaviour reflects questionable value systems. Such value systems are, however, a mark of the twentieth century. Considering the threats to future existence, it is self-defeating to persist in maintaining many of our current societal priorities and values. There need to be, of course, flexibility and respect for a variety of opinions, but when ethical standards, for example, are quite low, it should be possible to decide on which standards should be raised and in what way. We make laws to try to correct or prevent unacceptable behaviour. It is much better when people's ethics, humane principles and self-respect make laws unnecessary.

1.5 Summary Remarks

Interconnections

There are a number of issues concerning the interactions of humans with the earth and with each other that have been briefly noted. Some of the more im-portant ones are listed in alphabetical order below:

- Economic matters
- Education

- Environment
- Ethical, humane and wholesome behaviour
- Finiteness of resources
- Health care
- Population
- Priorities and values
- Quality of life
- Sustainability

These issues are far from independent of each other. They are, rather, grossly interdependent. This interdependence leads to the concept of 'indispensables', namely, those issues that are indispensable to the achievement of widespread improvements in the human condition. In fact, without proper handling of the indispensables, the attempt to achieve improvements in a broad sense by appropriate treatment of the other issues has little chance of success.

Indispensables

Population control is an indispensable. I am in agreement with many others who have indicated that unless population is brought under control, it will not be possible to enhance the human condition on a broad scale. Any progress will be eliminated by the huge numbers of people who must be supported if the unbridled increase in overall population persists. Population control must be achieved. A second indispensable is sustainability. The concept of sustainability must be brought into the handling of environmental problems. Activities that degrade the environment can no longer be tolerated. Renewable energy sources, for example, must replace the burning of fossil fuels. Economic decisions impact greatly on the sustainability of the environment and, in fact, on the viability and sustainability of an economy. It was pointed out in a talk that I heard recently that the inhabitants of Easter Island, located off the west coast of South America, used up all the resources of the island to the extent that they did not have enough food to subsist and did not have enough wood to build boats on which to escape from the island.

Proper human behaviour is an indispensable. The sheer animosity of various groups towards their neighbours in many areas of the world is a serious impediment to progress. The ease with which seemingly cultured societies can be transformed to behave in a barbaric fashion is another sad lesson of the twentieth century. Such threats of unbridled hostility and violence must be curtailed if a proper environment for peace and stability is to be achieved.

Barriers

There are various barriers that can interfere with the broad attainment of a quality existence. The problems that need to be overcome are formidable. They are manifold and extensive. Great leadership in the world is required to overcome societal indolence, selfish motives, lack of character, perverse priorities and values, widespread unwholesome lifestyles, lack of co-operation, extreme poverty, educational limitations, violence and the lack of suitable mechanisms to settle disputes peacefully, exploitation of the earth and of people, and a population explosion that is out of control.

Societies whose survival is marginal cannot readily give much attention to the issues that are raised in this chapter. It is very difficult for societies or individuals on the edge of survival to change the patterns of their lives. Many marginal societies are overpopulated, are under severe economic pressures, and have low levels of health care.

As recent history shows, large portions of the world can be brought into war by extremely antisocial governments. Considering the number of such governments, it seems to be all too easy for them to form. In order to achieve any semblance of world order, it is necessary to prevent, or at least largely minimise, such occurrences. Could some form of world government with a world constitution be capable of achieving this with perhaps a number of other benefits? Further study is merited.

Concluding Question

We live in a world in which there are major inequities within societies and among societies. It is also a world whose future is greatly threatened. Do we want nature to take its course—a path that is often extremely harsh—or will the world's population and its leaders be willing and able to take the major courageous steps required to mitigate nature's harshness, preserve the earth and generate a more equitable and humane future?

Reference

Yamaguchi, Kaoru (1992). Creating a Higher Institution for Future-Oriented Studies, *Teaching about the Future*, Proceedings of the seminar organised jointly by UNESCO and the Canadian Commission for UNESCO, ed. by Richard A. Slaughter, Vancouver, Canada, 21–23, June 1992.

2 The Impact and Promise of the Cognitive Revolution

ROGER W. SPERRY

2.1 Advance Overview

Reflecting on a century past, with an eye to the future, what I have to say is coloured in no small part by a concern long shared with the late B. F. Skinner, namely 'Can APA [the American Psychological Association], or any other organization, count on another hundred years?' Skinner's answer became increasingly less optimistic, especially in his last decade. He concluded, 'The more we learn about human behavior, the less and less promising appear the prospects.' Reflecting a similar vein of increasing concern, I see a possible ray of hope in psychology's cognitive revolution and what it could mean in bringing new perspectives, beliefs, and values—in short, new mind-sets and a new way of thinking—which are much needed if humanity is to survive the next century.

During the past hundred years of the APA, psychology is said to have gone through three major revolutions. In addition to the recent shift to cognitivism, there were the two earlier revolts, which were associated with J. B. Watson and Sigmund Freud. I believe that, of the three, the current so-called 'cognitive', 'mentalist' or 'consciousness' revolution is the most radical turnaround; the most revisionary and transformative.

A main theme I want to stress concludes that the cognitive revolution in psychology is leading the way among the sciences to a new and improved—that is, a more comprehensive, adequate, and valid—conceptual foundation for scientific as well as for all causal explanation and understanding. Any perceived paradox here is indeed quite real. Psychology, after having been put down for decades by the so-called 'hard' sciences as not being really a science, is now turning the tables. It is, in effect, asserting that reductive physicalism or microdeterminism, the traditional explanatory model of science (including behaviourism), has serious shortcomings and is no longer tenable.

This chapter is a slightly revised version of Roger Sperry's paper 'The Impact and Promise of the Cognitive Revolution', *American Psychologist*, August 1993: 878–85. Several minor changes have been made by the editor since the sudden death of the author on 17 April 1994. Although these changes were never formally approved by the author, on 15 February 1994 the editor received a fax from Roger Sperry saying 'Yes, you have my permission to use the [Impact] article in any way you wish (that is, in full, abbreviated, edited), however you think most appropriate.' The editor respectfully expresses his condolences.

Other disciplines, even physics, are beginning to agree and join in, discovering and adopting the new antireductive and emergent insights. These other disciplines include, for example, computer science, neuroscience, biology, anthropology, evolutionary and hierarchy theory, general systems theory, and, of course, quantum theory, among others.[1] Each discipline, however, appears to have a different version of how these innovations came about, and each finds the origins within its own particular field.

I strongly believe that, in the long run, history will show that, among the sciences, psychology was actually the first discipline to overthrow its traditional mainstream doctrine in favour of the new paradigm. By the early 1970s, mainstream psychology had already adopted the new outlook,[2] whereas the other fields came to it later, especially during the 1980s. In effect, most have just been following and developing varied forms and applications of what, in essence, is the same basic new core concept. At least that is the conclusion I have come to and wish to support.

First, it will help to review quickly some of the salient features of the cognitive revolution as I see it: the essence of this revolt, what it means, some of its consequences and future implications. Most importantly, the cognitive revolution represents a diametric turnaround in the centuries-old treatment of mind and consciousness in science. The contents of conscious experience, with their subjective qualities, long banned as being mere acausal epiphenomena, or just identical to brain activity or otherwise in conflict with the laws of the conservation of energy, have now made a dramatic comeback. Reconceived in the new outlook, subjective mental states become functionally interactive and indispensable for a full explanation of conscious behaviour. Traditional microdeterminist reasoning that brain function can be fully accounted for in neurocellular–physiochemical terms is refuted, as too are former assumptions that traditional materialism provides, in principle, a complete coherent explanation of the natural world. The cognitive–consciousness revolution thus also represents a revolt against the long-time worship of the atomistic in science. Reductive microdeterministic views of personhood and the physical world are replaced by a more holistic, top–down view in which the higher, more evolved entities throughout nature, including the mental, vital, social, and other high-order forces, gain their due recognition along with physics and chemistry.

It is important to stress, however, that the cognitive changeover from behaviourism to the new mentalism does not carry on all the way from the previous extreme to its opposite, that is, to a mentalistic dualism. Rather, the shift is to a quite new heterodox position that integrates and blends aspects of prior opposed solutions into a novel unifying synthesis (Natsoulas 1987). The new position is mentalistic, holding that behaviour is mentally and subjectively driven. This,

[1] See e.g. Blakemore and Greenfield 1987; Campbell 1974; Checkland 1981; Gell-Mann 1988; Gleick 1987; Goodwin 1978; Greenberg and Tobach 1988; Grene 1987; D. R.Griffin 1981; D. Griffin 1988; Laszlo 1972; Piaget 1970; Popper and Eccles 1977; Stapp 1982; Wasow 1989.

[2] Dember 1974; Matson 1971; Palermo 1971; Pylyshyn 1973; Segal and Lachman 1972.

however, does not mean that it is *dualistic*. In the new synthesis, mental states, as dynamic emergent properties of brain activity, become inseparably interfused with and tied to the brain activity of which they are an emergent property. Consciousness in this view cannot exist apart from the functioning brain.

A new reciprocal form of causal control is invoked that includes downward as well as upward determinism. This bidirectional model applies not only to control of the emergent *mental* over the *neuronal* in the brain, but also to the emergent control by holistic properties in general throughout nature. Accordingly, it has also been gaining ground in other sciences. What started as an intradisciplinary revolution within psychology is thus turning into a major revolution for all science. As a consequence, scientific descriptions—not only of behaviour, cognition, the self and so on, but for all physical reality—are being vastly transformed, with wide humanistic, philosophical and epistemological, as well as scientific, implications. Like the Darwinian and Copernican revolutions, to which some authors now compare it, the cognitive revolution leads to a combined *ideological revolution*, as defined by Karl Popper (1975). Alternative beliefs emerge about the ultimate nature of things, and a changed cosmology brings a new set of answers to some of humanity's deepest questions.

To many psychologists, such claims for the cognitive revolution seem a lavish, even fanciful, overstatement. I believe, however, that firm substantial backing can be found for each of these assessments, plus many more extensions yet unmentioned. Towards a preliminary understanding of why the impacts should be so profound and far-reaching, consider the fact that the cognitive revolution, as conceived here, involves radical changes in not just one but in two core concepts, *consciousness* and *causality*, both of which have extremely wide, almost ubiquitous application to everything we experience and try to understand. In view of this alone, it is obvious that the paradigmatic shift to cognitivism–mentalism, following centuries of rigorous materialism, is bound to have numerous far-reaching consequences.

Among further effects, this turnabout in the causal status of consciousness abolishes the traditional science–values dichotomy. The fact that we are in a new era today with respect to values is well recognised (Edel 1980). Thus, the cognitive revolution, from an ethical standpoint, might equally well have been called a *values* revolution. The old, value-free, strictly objective, mindless, quantitative, atomistic descriptions of materialist science are being replaced by accounts that recognise the rich, irreducible, varied and valued emergent macro and holistic properties and qualities in both human and non-human nature. Subjective human values, no longer written off as ineffectual epiphenomena or reduced to microphenomena, become the most critically powerful force shaping today's civilised world, the underlying answer to current global ills and the key to world change (Sperry 1972, 1991*a*).

In addition, a different approach is opened and a resolution offered for that age-old enigma, the free will–determinism paradox. Blending previous opposites in a heterodox middle-way position, the new cognitivism retains both free will and determinism, each reconceived in a modified form and integrated in a way that preserves moral responsibility (Deci 1980; Libet 1992; Sperry 1964, 1970). Volition remains causally determined but no longer entirely subject to the inexorable physiochemical laws of neurocellular activation. These lower-level laws are supervened by the higher-level controls of the subjective conscious self in which they are embedded (just as, introspectively, it seems to be). The implications become critical for a scientific treatment of personal agency and social interaction (Bandura 1989; Smith 1983). Overall, we still inhabit a deterministic universe, but it is ruled by a large array of different types, qualities, and levels of determinism. In retrospect, we would not want it otherwise; in particular, we would not want to live in an indeterminate, non-causal, and thus random, chaotic universe, totally unpredictable and with no reliability or rational higher meaning.

In sum, the type of reality and worldview upheld by science is thoroughly transformed, greatly enriched and more appealing, as well as more credible. A fundamentally changed picture of ourselves and the world gives scientists an entirely new outlook on existence, a whole new story (Augros and Stanciu 1984) plus a higher social role and enhanced public image. The vast gulf of mutual incompatibility that has long separated the world of science from that of the humanities is abolished and replaced by a congenial continuum (Jones 1965; Snow 1959). Most important, perhaps, for the growing number among us who, like Skinner, see real cause for concern about the prospects for another hundred years, these renovations of the cognitive revolution provide a new way of knowing and understanding, a unifying new vision, in which some see a rational solution to our global predicament in the form of more realistic guiding beliefs and values to live and govern by.

Perspectives that Need to Be Clear

Before going further, I need to clarify some frequent misconceptions. First, at a time when it seems to be open season on personal theories of consciousness, it is important to recognise that what we are dealing with here is not just personal, obscure or even minority theory or opinion but rather the actual working conceptual framework and dominant doctrine for the past two decades of the whole discipline of science that specialises in mind and behaviour and thus best speaks for science as a whole on these matters (Baars 1986; Gardner 1985). Also, my main focus here is not on the philosophical abstractions, such as whether mentalism or reductionism may ultimately prove correct, but on the recorded fact of a turning-point in the history of science and its cause.

Second, when I speak of behaviourism here, I mean behaviourism *per se*, in the sense of an overriding paradigm, metatheory or working conceptual framework for psychology in general. The reference is not to any of the various subordinate theories, practices and approaches to behaviour, learning, or brain function that may incidentally have become associated with it by coming into vogue during the half-century reign of behaviourism. It is the overriding conceptual paradigm itself that the cognitive revolution has overthrown, especially the renunciation (in common with the other natural sciences) of mental or subjective factors as valid constructs for causal explanation.

Third, my concern throughout is not with any esoteric, radical or other, recent fringe development but with the central working premises of the solid scientific mainstream. The history of science, what it stands for, its principles, conceptual foundations, applications, and implications—science viewed as a whole—are what shape the present position and treatment. The remaining, adamant behaviourists represent a respected minority challenging the new principles, but they no longer represent mainstream psychology.

Fourth, in view of salient misconceptions,[3] it is worth repeating that the type of mentalism upheld here is not dualistic in the classical philosophical sense of two different, independent realms of existence. In our new macromental or holo-mental synthesis, mental states as dynamic emergent properties of brain states cause behaviour but are not dualistic, because they are inextricably interfused with their generating brain processes. Mental states in this form cannot exist apart from the active brain. At the same time, mental states are not the same as brain states. The two differ in the way a dynamic emergent property differs from its component infrastructure. It is characteristic of emergent properties that they are notably novel and often amazingly and inexplicably different from the components of which they are built. The recognised methodological difficulties posed by the use of introspection, however, are not remedied.

Furthermore, my reasons for bypassing quantum theory, the most frequently cited source of the new worldview, in favour of mind–brain theory needs a brief mention. In the present view, quantum mechanics, as a conceptual framework, fails to give a complete, coherent account of events at macro levels; nor does it subsume classical Newtonian laws as commonly inferred from the mathematical equations. Both quantum and Newtonian theory fail, in our present view, to cover adequately an important key principle, namely, that the collective spatio-temporal patterning *per se* of physical masses—or of particles, energy sources, or other mass–energy entities—exerts causal influence *in and of itself*. To explain and understand the macroworld with its endless different entities and relations, one does not even expect in this scheme to find the answers in quantum mechanics (the ultimate reduction) or in any 'superstring' theory or other such 'Theory of Everything'. These subatomic features are the same for any macro entity, be it a great cathedral or a sewage outlet. Furthermore, these universal common subatomic elements are supervened and superseded in the two-way causation model through the downward control exerted by the higher-level components in which they are embedded. Again, what counts are the different spatiotemporal patternings of the components at all levels and between levels—their one- to four-dimensional gestalts. As a rule, this space–time causality, or 'pattern factor', prevents the reduction of macro- to lower-level microphenomena. It also rules out the transposition of subatomic properties upward to the macroworld.

---

[3] e.g. Bunge 1980; Chezik 1990; Peterson 1990; Pirolli and Goel 1990; see also Natsoulas 1991; Sperry 1992.

Overall, none of this applies, of course, with respect to most radiation phenomena. Also it is important to keep in mind that the new paradigm does not dispose of either quantum or Newtonian theory. It merely supplements them by adding the supervening, irreducible but highly critical space–time factors.

2.2 Contested Historical Aspects

Now, some twenty years since the cognitive revolution marked a major turning-point in the history of science, we still lack any satisfying consensus as to its exact nature and source, its driving rationale or its precise meaning for the future. Within psychology itself, different subfield interest groups continue to vie over these and related questions.[4] If the overall impact and potential implications are anything like those inferred here, it becomes crucial to understand the true nature and essence of the cognitive revolution better.

The story of this revolt, as I interpret it, was not one of finding new positives to support the important role of cognition, since many of them had already been evident for some time. Rather, the story is one of discovering an alternative logic by which to refute the seemingly incontestable reasoning that had previously required science to ostracise mind and consciousness. How the discovery of this new logic came about is most easily explained in terms of the historical context out of which the new reasoning arose. Throughout the behaviourist–materialist era, extending well up into the 1960s, the age-old riddle of the mind–brain relationship involved a contradictory paradox. On the one hand, it seemed obvious from common experience that our behaviour is *mentally* driven. On the other hand, from the standpoint of neuroscience, it seemed equally obvious that a complete account of brain function, including the brain's entire input–output performance, could be provided in strictly objective neuronal–biophysical terms. In the explanatory system of neuroscience, absolutely no place could be found to include the likes of conscious or mental forces, and the same applied for behaviourist psychology. Behaviourism as a philosophy of science made the science of mind consistent with that of neuroscience and the other natural sciences (Skinner 1964). On this basis, the antimentalist tenets of behaviourism seemed irrefutable throughout behaviourism's heyday. As humanist Andrew Bongiorno (1991), now in his nineties, recalled, 'For half a century behaviorism reigned supreme in academe. To overthrow behaviorism would require an overthrow also of the conceptual foundations of neuroscience and of science in general.' What, then, led to its downfall? Or, to put it another way: What made cognitivism suddenly rise in its own right—no longer under the restrictive dictates of a reigning behaviourism, as in the earlier days of Edward Tolman, but as a new and independent positive paradigm predicating a worldview and tenets of its own that stood opposed to the long-dominant doctrine of the behaviourist–

---

[4] e.g. Amsel 1989; Baars 1986; Bevan 1991; Bolles 1990; Chezik 1990; Keil 1991; Kendler 1990; Lamal 1990; Natsoulas 1987; Simon 1991; Sperry 1980, 1991*b*; Wasow 1989.

materialist era? Whatever caused this turnabout, it came with a startling suddenness, described in the early 1970s by Pylyshyn (1973: 1) as having 'recently exploded' into fashion. It was as if the floodgates holding back the many pressures of consciousness and subjectivity were suddenly opened. What caused this abrupt turnabout has continued to puzzle many leaders in the field (Boneau 1992).

Mind-Sets in 1964

As late as 1964, there still was no incipient sense of the impending turnabout, as is clear from various conferences, books, and articles of and about the period.[5] Within psychology, the debates between phenomenologists and behaviourists were going on as before, without shaking the dominant reign of the behaviourist doctrine (Koch 1963; Wann 1964). In 1964, humanist Carl Rogers, who had searched during his long career for a scientific foundation for what he called 'subjective knowing', was still summarising the situation in terms of volition being 'an irreconcilable contradiction' and 'deep paradox' with which we just have to learn to live (Rogers 1964: 40). In September of the same year, the eminent neurophysiologist John Eccles reaffirmed at the Vatican Conference on Consciousness his reasoned conviction as a scientist, in line with physiological tradition, that consciousness is totally superfluous from the standpoint of neuroscience. But then, expressing what many of us nevertheless felt, he added, 'I do not believe this story, of course, but I do not know the logical answer' (Eccles 1966: 248). The discovery of this logical answer was close at hand and was to be the key factor in making possible the cognitive revolution as well as Eccles's own notable campaign, which he embarked on shortly afterwards, extolling 'psychophysical interaction'.

By 1971 it already was clear that many psychologists had come to recognise that their discipline was in the process of a major paradigm shift, in which behaviourism was being replaced by an opposing new mentalism or cognitivism (Matson 1971; Palermo 1971; Segal and Lachman 1972). Thus, the revisionary concepts of the new paradigm—those concepts that finally broke the materialist logic in which science had been locked for more than 200 years—must by then not only have been introduced but also have become sufficiently clear and convincing to cause mainstream psychology to start switching its support to the new mentalism. During the period 1964–71, therefore, something must have happened to reveal the long-sought logical answer to the baffling impasse over consciousness and its role in science.

Key Factor

What happened, I believe, was the discovery that the traditional logic by which

---

[5] e.g. Bertalanffy 1968; Eccles 1966; Feigenbaum and Feldman 1963; Feigl 1967; Hook 1960; Koch 1963; Manicas and Secord 1983; Nagel 1971; Simon 1962; Smythies 1965; Wann 1964.

consciousness had been excluded from scientific explanation and which was supposedly closed, complete and incontestable, was in fact basically flawed or incomplete and that this inadequacy could be rectified through a different form of causal explanation. An alternative (bidirectional, top–down as well as bottom–up) form of causal determinism was perceived that put mind and consciousness in a functionally interactive, non-reductive, and ineliminable causal role, thus breaking the long-standing impasse and irreconcilable contradiction of the mind–brain paradox (Popper 1972; Sperry 1964, 1965).

The reason why this particular attempt to legitimise consciousness succeeded, where innumerable others had failed, lies in the use of a quite different approach. Previous efforts had stayed within the traditional reference frame, attempting to insert consciousness into the chains of causation already covered in the brain-behaviour sciences—at synaptic junctions between brain cells, for example (Eccles 1953). By contrast, the successful effort preserved intact the lower-level chains of causation already dealt with in science and simply encompassed or embedded them in a higher-level (yet-to-be-described) cognitive system of cerebral processing. In this way, *subjectively experienced conscious qualities*, viewed as irreducible emergent dynamics of brain processing, could be given objective interactive causal influence without contradicting the earlier gains of science. In other words, success was attained only by changing the rules of the game, by inventing a different paradigm for scientific causal explanation.

Notably, this same seven-year period is also marked by a second extraordinary polar shift in the prevailing mainstream view. This shift related to another age-old controversy, the debate over holism and reductionism. After various ups and downs from the late nineteenth century on, reductionism rose to a new high in the mid-1960s. Referred to in historical perspective as a 'reductionist euphoria' (Nagel 1971), this rise was bolstered especially by successes in molecular biology (Crick 1966). This wave of extreme reductionism soon gave way, however, to a new outburst of holism. There was an acceptance of the concept of the irreducible whole that still continues today in what appears to be an all-time high for holism in the long history of this polemic (Checkland 1981).

In my present analysis, these two shifts, to mentalism and to holism, are interlinked with, tied to and dependent on the revised model for causal determinism. Both depend on the causal reality of irreducible emergent phenomena that interact as wholes at their own macro level and in the process carry their embedded constituents along a space–time course determined by emergent interaction at the higher level. Subjective agency may thus be viewed as a special instance of downward control, a special case of emergent causality in the reciprocal up–down paradigm for causal control.

Faced with the question of which of the two alternative views of causation might be the more valid—the old one-way or the new two-way model—mainstream psychology, in a move involving hundreds or thousands of critical specialist minds viewing the issue from all different subdisciplinary angles, chose collectively to switch from the traditional one-way tenets of behaviourism to the bidirectional views of the new mentalism. Without going into detail, many reasons supporting this choice can now be seen that add up to the fact that much is gained and nothing is lost (since traditional microdeterminism *per se* is preserved). In the briefest possible terms, the new two-way model combines traditional bottom–up microdeterminism with novel principles of emergent, top–down macro and mental causation.[6]

A strengthened concept of the irreducible whole is provided, including the demonstration that the spacing and timing of infrastructural components is in itself causative. In any but perhaps the most ultra-simple of hierarchic systems, immense space–time complexities (same-level, as well as multinested interlevel pattern factors) rule out reduction to lower-level laws—even in principle. This, the additional factor of the relativity of reference frames and other details have been reviewed elsewhere (Sperry 1991*b*). Illustrated in simple physical examples, such as the space–time trajectory of a molecule within a rolling wheel, a flowing eddy, wave action, and a flying plane, the existence and importance of downward causation for an adequate description of the natural world order seems obvious (see Popper and Eccles 1977: 209).

Psychology in the Lead?

The fact that the conceptual developments that legitimised consciousness also apply to emergent, macro, and holistic properties in general is fast becoming recognised in other disciplines. Following the mentalist changeover in psychology, which started in the 1960s and was established by the early 1970s, the new paradigm began to gain ground in other fields. Never before in the history of science has there been such an outburst of new sciences, new world-views, new visions of reality, new epistemologies, ontologies, and so on. The 1980s, especially, might well be called the decade of emerging new paradigms. We soon had the new 'systems view of the world' (Laszlo 1972), the new 'Worlds 2 & 3' of Popper (1972), the 'Tao of physics' (Capra 1977), the cognitive view of biology and the new science of qualities (Goodwin 1978), the 'aquarian conspiracy' (Ferguson 1980), the new view of animal awareness (D. R. Griffin 1981), the new dialogue with nature (Prigogine and Stengers 1984), the new story of science (Augros and Stanciu 1984), the new philosophy of science (Manicus and Secord 1983), the new evolutionary epistemology (Greenberg and Tobach 1988) and the reenchantment of science in a postmodern era (e.g. D. Griffin 1988; Toulmin 1982)—and the list goes on.

All of these developments share one central thrust, the rejection of traditional reductive (or microdeterminist) physicalism, previously accepted as a seemingly incontestable, complete and coherent working paradigm for science, time-tested over centuries. Thus, in the final analysis, all of the above recent visions, out-

---

[6] Dewan 1976; Natsoulas 1987; Popper and Eccles 1977; Ripley 1984; Rottschaefer 1987; Sperry 1964, 1991*a,b*.

looks, sciences, philosophies and so on depend on the presumed existence of some newly perceived flaw, incompleteness or inadequacy in the traditional microdeterminist reasoning. We yet know of only one such flaw that would qualify, namely, the one corrected by the concept of emergent determinism, since it was invoked in changing the causal status of consciousness. Microdeterminist reasoning in itself is not rejected, only the long-time assumption that it gives a complete and sufficient account. The day-to-day practice, methodology and previously proven potentials of science are little changed. Nothing is lost and a whole new outlook on existence is gained.

2.3 Towards a High-Quality Sustainable World

The second part of my thesis, the promise, calls for a change of mind-set. We go back to Skinner's concern about making it to another centennial. Most of the foregoing is dwarfed by the question of survival, which is fast becoming the overriding imperative of our times, 'a cause of all causes which, should it fail, all others go with it'. Nothing in science today is of more basic importance than the effort to save science and all the other hard-won legacies of aeons of evolution.

By now it is widely agreed that what is needed to remedy our present self-destructive course will involve major changes on a global scale in human thinking and behaviour. What discipline is in a better position or better qualified professionally than behavioural science to point out what has basically gone wrong and provide sound remedial proposals—especially given psychology's new worldview? For the first time, the cognitive–mentalist paradigm now makes possible a science-based approach to such Global Forum-type questions as what kind of world we want and what must we do to get there. We can see a new approach to such ultimate moral issues as which ideals best guide existence on planet Earth and what constitutes the highest measure for right and wrong and social justice. What follows illustrates some of the answers that might logically flow from the new outlook, along with corresponding logistics for a possible way out of our global predicament. The language in which they are expressed here is not so much for fellow scientists as for the informed public, and religious and political leaders whose understanding is needed most. Any directives in this realm are always debatable. At least, however, they give a possible start, providing a target to aim at.

The bottom-line message is as follows: *We can now look to science to save the world, not through new improved technology, green revolutions and the like (which only stave off and thereby magnify the eventual downfall) but instead by providing more realistic and sustainable beliefs and values to live and govern by.* This message is not new, but it received rather short shrift from both scientists and ethicists when voiced initially (Sperry 1972) in opposition to the then-prevailing science–values antithesis (Bixenstein 1976; Edel 1980). The value–belief arguments still hold, however, and current ambient attitudes seem more receptive.

Science, Values and Survival

Today's mounting global ills will not be cured merely by applying more or better science and technology. Despite their marvels and apparent successes, their gains are typically offset by the expanding demands of a growing population. Amid rising population pressures, almost anything that enables more people to fare or thrive better—a new energy source, an aqueduct, another mass-transit system, or even environmental reform— inevitably has as a long-term result a further escalation in our collective problems. Until population is stabilised, this paradox means that many seemingly desirable innovations with obvious short-term benefits just serve in the long run to put us deeper and deeper into a no-win position. Thus, slowly but surely, our civilisation becomes ever more deeply enmeshed in a vicious spiral of mounting population, pollution, energy demands, environmental degradation, urban overcrowding and associated crime, homelessness and hopelessness. With one thing reinforcing another, we become more and more firmly entrapped year by year.

What is needed to break this vicious spiral is a basic revision worldwide in human lifestyles, aims and attitudes, redirecting social values and policy towards more long-term priorities that will preserve an evolving quality of life for future generations. A major reconception of the human venture is called for, a higher overarching perspective including ultimate goals and values, or, as Einstein put it in reference to atomic power, 'We need a new way of thinking if mankind is to survive' (Clark 1972).

The new way of thinking, spawned by the cognitive–consciousness revolution, shows strong promise in this direction. Reversing previous doctrine in science, the new paradigm affirms that the world we live in is driven not solely by mindless physical forces but, more crucially, by subjective human values. Human values become the underlying key to world change (Sperry 1972, 1991a). The 'battle to save the planet' becomes, in large measure, a battle over values.

The reason conventional values are not working today and have been driving our entire ecosystem towards collapse is that the initial assumptions are wrong for modern times. Human values are not absolute; they are not immutably pre-fixed by natural law or divine ordination. Human values are, by nature, evolutionary, interrelated and conditional on the context in which they evolve (Pugh 1977). To cling to unchanging values in a rapidly changing world can be fatal.

For centuries it has been the starting assumption that because human life is special, even sacred, the more people the better. 'Go forth and multiply and take dominion' was morally good at the time the Scriptures were written. Two thousand years later, however, with the global situation reversed and an exploding world population with its multiform side-effects threatening to destroy everything we value, it follows that because human life is precious, even sacred, *less is better*. 'Retract and multiply less' becomes today's prime imperative. Such an inescapable reversal in our basic starting assumptions overturns an entire complex of long-revered, centuries-old tradition. Today's world calls for a whole new, higher outlook, with moral convictions that can override long-cherished value systems of the past, including long-esteemed traits deeply inherent in human nature itself but evolved without regard for the projected effects in today's kind of world. A more far-sighted vision is required for what it means to be humane.

Considering the massive carryover and long-term momentum in world population growth, and assuming that ecologic irreversibilities plus social-system breakdowns are bound to occur well in advance of the final crunch, there may be much less time than we think. Twenty-five years ago we could still see a choice: either adopt new, more sustainable values by foresight or have them forced by the mounting intolerabilities in living conditions (Sperry 1972). Today, almost everywhere we turn, the signs of overload, overcrowding and intolerability are showing. Rising demands for subsistence in a direly depleted, degraded ecosphere are not the sole concern. In numerous subtle and unsubtle ways overpopulation tends to desensitise humanity and increasingly devalue the individual person. Our sense of the specialness of human life, its meaning, singular worth, dignity and wonder undergoes an insidious, unobtrusive but inexorable erosion to which our inherent human nature is particularly vulnerable. The process is so slow and the habituation capacity of the human brain so great that the adverse trends, spread over decades or even generations, tend to taken for granted.

Instead of our long-time social evasion of sensitive population issues, we need intensive study and open debate aimed at creating informed views of what the optimal population levels might be, regionally and globally, and *what ideals to strive for in an overall guiding plan for existence on planet Earth*. We urgently need bright new utopian goals we can at least aim for, instead of drifting further with outdated guidelines of a distant past.

It is important to remember that the more rarity, diversity and contrast in our lives and the world we live in, the greater the value and meaning. A world designed to maximise, equalise and homogenise the 'human carrying capacity' automatically degrades and demeans human life. We all tend to adjust to our own personal 'baseline of happiness', below which life is depressing and above which it is rosy. Our baselines do not need to be identical; the proven benefits of biodiversity do not stop at the human social order.

The overall immensity and the many facets of the global rescue effort we now face, environmentally and in social and moral priorities, not to mention the international legislation needed to implement and secure the various reforms, add up to a most formidable task. When we add in the urgency now required to ensure a decent viable ecosphere, the hurdle seems almost insurmountable.

We are well past the point at which we can leave to the next few generations the type of ecosphere that they deserve or that we inherited. The increasingly hard choices ahead will further pit growing human needs against the rest of nature. Decisions not to have additional much-desired children, to forego lucrative industrial profits or to abandon cherished livelihoods, for example, might all come more readily were they reinforced by the pressure of a public moral sense, backed by the power of a quasi-religious commitment. In short, a non-catastrophic outcome to what has seemed a losing battle would appear to demand nothing short of a rapid conversion of all humankind to a changed sense of the sacred, a changed sense of ultimate value and the highest good. Such a shift at the very top would then condition the entire hierarchy of social values and thus tend to drive all the other reforms.

Guidelines Consistent with Science

Aside from the urgency factor, some of us see a possible ray of hope in the outlook now emerging from the consciousness–cognitive revolution in science. A new way of thinking and perceiving that integrates mind and matter, facts and value, religion and science brings more realistic insights into the kinds of forces that made and move the universe and created humankind. A deep moral basis is provided for environmentalism, population balance and other measures that would preserve and enhance our world instead of destroying it. Humanity's creator becomes universalised in the grand orderly design of all evolving nature with special focus on our own biosphere. The cosmic forces of creation become inextricably interfused with creation itself. Evolution, driven from above downward, by emergent and subjective dynamics, as well as from below upward, becomes a gradual emergence of increased directedness, purpose and meaning among the forces that move and govern living things.

The highest good is seen in an ever-evolving quality of existence, with a continuing open-ended future as a *sine qua non* for preserving higher meaning. The sanctity of human life is perceived in a framework in which the very definition of human rights includes and depends on the rights and welfare of coming generations (Sperry 1991*a*). Perspectives of this kind, based in the credibility and universality of science and taken as a common core for human value–belief systems, might prove an acceptable foundation at the United Nations on which to build a unifying system of world law and justice and at the same time help to arouse a deep sense of outrage at what modern humanity is doing to itself and its future.

The promise of the cognitive revolution is multiform, but in the context of today's global ills and our imperilled future it may be seen to rest in its bringing to science a higher role and level of meaning, one that uses the emergent properties of specialised brain processes to offer new beliefs and value systems for the twenty-first century.

References

Amsel, A. (1989). *Behaviorism, Neobehaviorism, and Cognitivism in Learning Theory: Historical and Contemporary Perspectives*, Hillsdale, N.J.: Erlbaum.

Augros, R. M. and Stanciu, G. N. (1984). *The New Story of Science*, New York: Bantam.

Baars, R. J. (1986). *The Cognitive Revolution in Psychology*, New York: Guilford.

Bandura, A. (1989). 'Human Agency in Social Cognitive Theory', *American Psychologist* 44: pp. 1175–84.

Bertalanffy, L. von (1968). *General Systems Theory*, New York: Braziller.

Bevan, W. (1991). 'A Tour Inside the Onion', *American Psychologist* 46: pp. 475–83.

Blakemore, C. and Greenfield, S. (1987). *Mindwaves: Thoughts on Intelligence, Identity and Consciousness*, Oxford: Basil Blackwell.

Bixenstein, E. (1976). 'The Value–Fact Antithesis in Behavioral Science', *Journal of Humanistic Psychology* 16(2): pp. 35–57.

Bolles, R. C. (1990). 'Where Did Everybody Go?', *Psychological Science* 1: pp. 112–13.

Boneau, C. A. (1992). 'Observations on Psychology's Past and Future', *American Psychologist* 47: pp. 1586–96.

Bongiorno, A. (1991). The work cited here by Sperry could not be traced in a literature search.

Bunge, M. (1980). *The Mind–Body Problem*, New York: Pergamon Press.

Campbell, D. T. (1974). 'Downward Causation in Hierarchically Organized Biological Systems', pp. 139–61 in F. J. Ayala and T. Dobzhansky (eds.), *Studies in the Philosophy of Biology*, Berkeley, Calif.: University of California Press.

Capra, F. (1977). *The Tao of Physics*, East Lansing, Mich.: Shambhala.

Checkland, P. (1981). *Systems Thinking, Systems Practice*, New York: Wiley.

Chezik, D. D.(1990). 'Sperry's Emergent Interactionism', *American Psychologist* 45: p. 70.

Clark, R. W. (1972). *Einstein: The Life and Times*, New York: Avon.

Crick, F. (1966). *Of Molecules and Men*, Seattle, Wash.: University of Washington Press.

Deci, E. L. (1980). *The Psychology of Self-Determination*, Lexington, Mass.: Heath.

Dember, W. N. (1974). 'Motivation and the Cognitive Revolution', *American Psychologist* 29: pp.161–8.

Dewan, W. N. (1976). 'Consciousness as an Emergent Causal Agent in the Context of Control System Theory', pp. 179–98 in G. G. Globus, G. Maxwell and I. Savodnik (eds.), *Consciousness and the Brain*, New York: Plenum Press.

Eccles, J. C. (1953). *The Neurophysiological Basis of Mind: The Principles of Neurophysiology*, Oxford: Clarendon Press.

—— (ed.) (1966). *Brain and Conscious Experience*, New York: Springer.

Edel, A. (1980). *Exploring Fact and Value*, vol. 2, New Brunswick, N.J.: Transaction Books.

Feigenbaum, E. A. and Feldman, J. (eds.) (1963). *Computers and Thought*, New York: McGraw-Hill.

Feigl, H. (1967). *The 'Mental' and the 'Physical'*, with 'Postscript after Ten Years', Minneapolis, Minn.: University of Minnesota Press.

Ferguson, E. S. (1980). *The Aquarian Conspiracy*, Los Angeles, Calif.: Tarcher.

Gardner, H. (1985). *Mind's New Science: A History of the Cognitive Revolution*, New York: Basic Books.

Gell-Mann, M. (1988). 'Simplicity and Complexity in the Description of Nature', *Engineering and Science* 51(3): pp. 2–9.

Gleick, J. (1987). *Chaos: Making a New Science*, New York: Viking.

Goodwin, B. C. (1978). 'A Cognitive View of Biological Process', *Journal of Social and Biological Structures* 1: pp. 117–125.

Greenberg, G. and Tobach, E. (1988). *Evolution of Social Behavior and Integrative Levels*, T. C. Schneirla Conference Series vol. 3, Hillsdale, N.J.: Erlbaum.

Grene, M. (1987). 'Hierarchies in biology', *American Scientist* 75: pp. 504–10.

Griffin, D. (1988). *The Reenchantment of Science*, New York: State University of New York Press.

Griffin, D. R. (1981). *The Question of Animal Awareness*, New York: Rockefeller University Press.

Hook, S. (ed.) (1960). *Dimensions of Mind*, New York: Collier Books.

Jones, W. T. (1965). *The Sciences and the Humanities*, Berkeley, Calif.: University of California Press.

Keil, F. C. (1991). 'On Being More than the Sum of the Parts: The Conceptual Coherence of Cognitive Science', *Psychological Science* 2: pp. 283, 287–93.

Kendler, H. H. (1990). 'Looking Backward to See Ahead', *Psychological Science* 1: pp. 107–12.

Koch, S. (1963). *Psychology: A Study of a Science*, New York: McGraw-Hill.

Lamal, P. A. (1990). 'The Continuing Mischaracterization of Radical Behaviorism', *American Psychologist* 45: p. 71.

Laszlo. E. (1972). *The Systems View of the World: The Natural Philosophy of the New Developments in the Sciences*, New York: Braziller.

Libet, B. (1992). 'The Neural Time-Factor in Perception, Volition and Free Will', *Revue de Metaphysique et de Morale* 2: pp. 255–72.

Manicas, P. T. and Secord, P. F. (1983). 'Implications for Psychology of the New Philosophy of Science', *American Psychologist* 38: pp. 399–413.

Matson, F. W. (1971). 'Humanistic Theory: The Third Revolution in Psychology', *The Humanist* 31(2): pp. 7–11.

Nagel, T. (1971). 'Brain Bisection and the Unity of Consciousness', *Synthese* 22: pp. 396–413.

Natsoulas, T. (1987). 'Roger Sperry's Monist Interactionism', *The Journal of Mind & Behavior* 8: pp. 1–21.

—— (1991). 'Ontological Subjectivity', *The Journal of Mind & Behavior* 12: pp. 175–200.

Palermo, D. S. (1971). 'Is a Scientific Revolution Taking Place in Psychology?', *Science Studies* 1: pp. 135–55.

Peterson, R. F. (1990). 'On Sperry's Model', *American Psychologist* 45: pp. 70–1.

Piaget, J. (1970). *Structuralism*, New York: Basic Books.

Pirolli, P. and Goel, V. (1990). 'You Can't Get There from Here: Comments on R. W. Sperry's Resolution of Science and Ethics', *American Psychologist* 45: pp. 71–3.

Popper, K. R. (1972). 'Of Clouds and Clocks', Second Arthur Holly Compton Memorial Lecture, presented in April 1965, pp 206–55 in K. Popper (ed.), *Objective Knowledge*, Oxford: Clarendon Press.

—— (1975). 'The Rationality of Scientific Revolutions', pp. 72–101 in R. Harre (ed.), *Problems of Scientific Revolution*, Oxford: Clarendon Press.

—— and Eccles, J. C. (1977). *The Self and Its Brain*, New York: Springer International.

Prigogine, I. and Stengers, I. (1984). *Order out of Chaos: Men's New Dialogue with Nature*, New York: Bantam.

Pugh, G. E. (1977). *The Biological Origin of Human Values*, New York: Basic Books.

Pylyshyn, Z. W. (1973). 'What the Mind's Eye Tells the Mind's Brain: A Critique of Mental Imagery', *Psychological Bulletin* 80: pp. 1–24.

Ripley, C. (1984). 'Sperry's Concept of Consciousness', *Inquiry* 27: pp. 399–423.

Rogers, C. R. (1964). 'Freedom and Commitment', *The Humanist* 29(2): pp. 37–40.

Rottschaefer, W. A. (1987). 'Roger Sperry's Science of Values', *The Journal of Mind & Behavior* 8: pp. 23–5.

Segal, E. M. and Lachman, R. (1972). 'Complex Behavior or Higher Mental Process? Is there a Paradigm Shift?', *American Psychologist* 27: pp. 46–55.

Simon, H. A. (1962). 'The Architecture of Complexity', *Proceedings of the American Philosophical Society* 106: pp. 467–82.

—— (1991). 'What is an "Explanation" of Behavior?', *APS Observer* 2(1): p. 6.

Skinner, B. F. (1964). 'Behaviorism at 50', pp. 79–108 in T. Wann (ed.), *Behaviorism and Phenomenology*, Chicago, Ill.: University of Chicago Press.

Smith, M. B. (1983). 'The Shaping of American Social Psychology: A Personal Perspective from the Periphery', *Personality and Social Psychology Bulletin* 9: pp. 165–80.

Smythies, J. R. (ed.) (1965). *Brain and Mind: Modern Concepts of the Nature of Mind*, London: Routledge & Kegan Paul.

Snow, C. P. (1959). *The Two Cultures and the Scientific Revolution*, New York: Cambridge University Press.

Sperry, R. W. (1964). 'Problems Outstanding in the Evolution of Brain Function', James Arthur Lecture Series on the Evolution of the Human Brain, New York: American Museum of Natural History.

—— (1965). 'Mind, Brain and Humanist Values', pp. 71–2 in J. R. Platt (ed.), *New Views of the Nature of Man*, Chicago, Ill.: University of Chicago Press; abridged in *Bulletin of the Atomic Scientists* 22(7; 1966): pp. 2–6.

—— (1970). 'An Objective Approach to Subjective Experience: Further Explanation of a Hypothesis', *Psychological Review* 77: pp. 585–90.

—— (1972). 'Science and the Problem of Values', *Perspectives in Biology & Medicine* 16: pp. 115–30.

—— (1980). 'Mind–Brain Interaction: Mentalism, yes; Dualism, no', *Neuroscience* 5: pp. 195–206.

—— (1991*a*). 'Search for Beliefs to Live by Consistent with Science', *Zygon* 26: pp. 237–258.

—— (1991*b*). 'In Defense of Mentalism and Emergent Interaction', *The Journal of Mind & Behavior* 12: pp. 221–45.

—— (1992). 'Turnabout on Consciousness: A Mentalist View', *The Journal of Mind & Behavior* 13: pp. 259–280.

Stapp, H. P. (1982). 'Mind, Matter, and Quantum Mechanics', *Foundations of Physics* 12: pp. 363–99.

Toulmin, S. (1982). *The Return to Cosmology*, Berkeley, Calif.: University of California Press.

Wann, T. W. (ed.) (1964). *Behaviorism and Phenomenology: Contrasting Bases for Modern Psychology*, Chicago, Ill.: University of Chicago Press.

Wasow, T. (1989). 'Grammatical Theory', pp. 161–202 in M. I. Posner (ed.), *Foundations of Cognitive Science*, Cambridge, Mass.: MIT Press.

3 Futures Studies and Sustainable Community Development

JIM DATOR

3.1 Futures Studies and Modern Academia and Decision-Making

I have been a university professor of political science for more than thirty years, including six years when I was an assistant professor in the College of Law and Politics of Rikkyo University in Ikebukuro, Tokyo. For more than twenty of those years, the primary focus of my teaching has been the future. Indeed, I first became interested in—you might say I co-invented—futures studies while I was teaching and researching in Japan in the early 1960s. Then, when I returned to the USA (with much regret, I might add), I created what is often thought to be the first regularly accredited university course on the future, at Virginia Poly-technic Institute and State University, in 1967. At the present time, I teach introductory and advanced undergraduate and graduate future-oriented courses through the Department of Political Science of the University of Hawaii. In-terested students may also combine these courses with others offered elsewhere in the university to obtain a personally tailored BA degree in futures studies through the university's Liberal Studies Program. (One of the most outstanding graduates of this BA course in futures studies is Tom Mandel, currently, and for more than twenty years now, the chief futurist for the well-known consulting firm SRI International, of Menlo Park, California.)

I am also head of the Alternative Futures Option within the Political Science Department of the University of Hawaii. The option provides a way by which people seriously interested in using futures research in their professions may acquire the necessary theories and methods to do so. Many of our graduates now work as futurists for various governmental and private organisations around the world. Others teach future-oriented courses at schools and universities world-wide.

In addition, I am Director of the Hawaii Research Center for Futures Studies, which was established by the Hawaii State Legislature in 1971 and placed in the University of Hawaii to do futures research primarily for the state and the Pacific Island region. We have also done a great deal of futures research for governmental, educational and business organisations all over the USA and throughout the Asia–Pacific region.

Finally, I was for seven years Secretary General, and until August 1993 I am

President, of the World Futures Studies Federation. The WFSF originated in Oslo, Norway, in 1967. It had its second world conference in Kyoto (not far from here) in 1970. I believe Dr Fujii and perhaps Professor Tomita were there— I know I was—and perhaps there are others here today who attended the Kyoto conference. The WFSF is now a network of people and institutions profession- ally involved in futures studies from more than eighty nations in all parts of the world—including Japan. Our next world conference, in just one week, will be in Turku, Finland. Our world conference two years hence is expected to be in Nairobi, Kenya, and thereafter probably in Australia. I invite you to attend each of these conferences and to become acquainted with the growing worldwide community of futurists.

Despite of all these facts, as I will explain a little later, at the present time futures studies is to modern academia and societal decision-making—and, hence, to sustainable global community development—what science was to academia and societal decision-making in the late Middle Ages. Because of this, I am no more likely to be successful in getting most academics, politicians and business- people to take futures studies seriously (and thus to help them and their organ- isations to think and act more helpfully about the future) than Copernicus was in getting the powers-that-were in his time to recognise that the earth isn't the centre of the universe. Since futures studies is not like other, established fields in academia, it is constantly being misunderstood and misused.

The traditional academic world in the West, as revealed by the organisation of its major universities (especially those of the USA) knows of only five kinds of academic pursuit.

First and foremost are the so-called 'natural' sciences: such disciplines as physics, astronomy, chemistry and biology with their necessary handmaiden, mathematics; more recently also earth, atmospheric and marine sciences, and their newer handmaiden, computer and information science. These are the 'real' sciences, based (by and large) on positivist, reductionist methods and assump- tions. They set the standard for everything else. Second are the humanities, always struggling to return to their medieval place of pride before 'science' marginalised them as the *raison d'être* for the 'liberal (i.e. liberating) arts'–or at least struggling to preserve their rank as number two: history, philosophy, religion, Sanskrit, Chinese, Greek, Latin and Arabic, and perhaps the literature of and/or in contemporary foreign languages as well as one's own language. These are proudly and defiantly non-, indeed anti-, positivist disciplines. What is wrong with the world, they might say, is the loss of tradition, discourse, criti- cism, gentility and mystery to the mad dominance of reductionist and utilitarian rationalism.

Third (though often considered part of the humanities) are the performing arts: music, drama, painting, sculpture, perhaps now sometimes including film or video as *beaux-arts* (not as a professional career). Here the emphasis is on aesthetics, self-awareness, idiosyncratic self-expression and performance. As a poster my daughter, Tasha, put up in my office long ago says, 'Dance is the only art wherein we ourselves are the stuff of which it's made.' (I am tempted to add that I have not been able to convince my daughter that I am a dancer by her definition, but I do consider my public lectures, such as this one, to be an aesthetic expression of my inner self, and I do write and perform my own material. So, how do you like my pirouette?)

Fourth, and quite far behind, are the social sciences: sociology, economics, psychology, perhaps anthropology, geography, perhaps even political science. Note that these, too, are 'sciences'. That is what makes them so suspect and yet legitimate. They strive to be scientific (positivist, reductionist), but, alas, they cannot quite pull it off and thus are dubbed derisively as 'soft' in contrast to the true 'hard' sciences.

And finally, and even farther behind (though in some places, perhaps, the real number one), are the various 'applied sciences' and professional schools and disciplines: agriculture, engineering, medicine, architecture, perhaps education, law, urban-planning, social work, perhaps even business and all of its subsidiary concerns. These are strictly instrumental, barely scientific, and certainly not critical. But they are very practical, hard-nosed and successful. To many observers, they appear to be the wave of the future of higher education.

Needless to say, there are many cross-disciplinary combinations of these and the other traditional courses, and even more questionable 'new' courses, though usually they are offered in the mode of one of the five groups above.

The 'Index of Programs' in the fourteenth *Annual Directory of Graduate Programs*, published by the Graduate Record Examination Board and the Council of Graduate Schools in the United States, 1991, is nineteen double-column pages long (pp. 425–44). None of the terms 'futures studies', 'futures research', 'future-oriented studies', nor any other similar set or combination of words, appears in the index—even though there are graduate programmes in futures studies offered by a few US universities.

Similarly, the two-volume encyclopedia *International Higher Education* (Altbach 1991), which contains authoritative discussions of higher education for virtually every country in the world, does not show that futures studies, or future-oriented studies, is offered by any university anywhere on the planet. And yet I know it is.

Given the history and curriculum of contemporary higher education, it is not surprising that most people find it difficult to understand what futures studies is, and what it is not. They quite naturally compare it with one of the five conventional streams of academia. Is it a positivist science that presumes to predict the future? Is it merely some part of the humanities that is interested in utopias and speculative dreaming? Is it a kind of science fiction fit for novels, movies or television shows? Or is it a profession? Can one learn to become a consulting futurist? More to the point: Can one make money as a futurist?

The answer is not clearly yes or no to any of these questions. The answer is 'Well, it has some of those features, but that really is not the best way to conceive of futures studies. It is indeed something else.'

At the same time, I feel that it is wrong to compare futures studies with inter-disciplinary studies, policy studies, environmental studies, women's studies, feminist studies, ethnic studies, peace studies, global studies, even sustainability studies, and all the other ' . . . studies' that are growing and thriving in the halls of academia these days. These, despite what they may claim, are all trying in varying ways to save the old world by reforming it more or less radically. They are all the legitimate sons and daughters of modernity; of Newton and Minerva, you might say.

But futures studies is something else.

3.2. So, What is Futures Studies?

That which we call 'the future'—the present at a later time—is not predictable. If any person says to you, 'I know the future. Here it is! Do this!', then run from that person as quickly as possible. The future is not predictable. No one knows with anywhere near sufficient certainty what the future *will be*. None the less, the fundamental unpredictability of the future does not mean that we should, therefore, not concern ourselves about the future and merely trust in luck, god or fate, or else just prepare ourselves to muddle through when new crises suddenly arise. Rather, it means that we need to take a more appropriate stance towards the future than either a search for predictive certainty, leaving it up to fate or trying only to muddle through. But what might that more appropriate stance be?

First of all, 'the future' may be considered as emerging from the interaction of four components: events, trends, images and actions.

Events

Events are the things that make many people doubt the efficacy of thinking about the future at all. Things just seem to happen. What is going to happen next seems to be utterly unknowable. Who knows when the next war, assassination, earthquake or decision by your boss is going to toss society or you into a completely different direction? For example, for more than forty years the world was locked in a Cold War that consumed trillions of dollars and gigantic amounts of human resources. Suddenly, and for no clear reason, it was over. The Wall fell. It became time to worry about how to spend the Peace Dividend. War was declared obsolete as an instrument of national policy. Only economics was said to matter any more.

Then suddenly some previously unnoticed madman, a new Hitler, was said to have emerged in the body of a former staunch ally, Iraq, and the Persian Gulf was suddenly aflame. Within forty-five days, the USA declared victory and US troops returned home in Yellow Ribboned-triumph, virtually untouched. The 'Vietnam Syndrome' was said to be over, and with it the American public's concern about military overspending on $1,600 screwdrivers vanished as well.

Similarly, for many years the world eagerly, or fearfully, anticipated the emergence of 'Europe 1992' and eventually a United States of Europe. But as the Wall fell, so also did the dream of a peacefully united, economically integrated

Europe. Instead militant tribalism of the most disgusting sort has re-emerged from nowhere. Yugoslavia has vanished in flames. Neo-Nazis murder Turks in Germany. The former mighty Soviet Union limps towards divided chaos.

What's next? Who knows? The future has become completely unforeseeable once again. So why even bother? The best we can hope to do is to muddle through, given some preparedness on our part, and much luck.

Trends and Emerging Issues

On the other hand, many planners believe that it is possible to discern the major contours of the future, and to plan effectively for it. They would have us focus on trends in order to anticipate and prepare for the future. But there seem to be at least three types of trends, each requiring different methods of comprehension.

(1) There are trends that are a continuation of the present and the past. In order to understand these trends, we need to understand what is happening now, and what has happened before. Some of that understanding comes from contemplating our own life experiences. Some of it comes from understanding what the natural and social sciences tell us. Some of it may be revealed in historical, philosophical or religious teachings and traditions. These are the kinds of trends found in most strategic plans.

(2) Other trends are more or less cyclical. Thus, they are not part of our own personal experience, but they were part of some aspect of the more distant past. Here, the successes or failures of our own lives may mislead us in anticipating the future since we never personally have experienced these trends as we will in the future, or as others experienced them before us. But, again, they may be recorded in historical, philosophical or religious documents or traditions and thus be available to us indirectly through them. Other such trends may require some mathematical technique to discover and understand. Still, because we have not personally experienced their impact, we will find it very difficult fully to know what to expect from them.

(3) But there may be things in the future that are completely new; that have never before been humanly experienced. These trends might better be called 'emerging issues' because, though potentially looming in the future, they are barely visible in the present, and were non-existent in the past. Many futurists argue that the most important trends of the future are these utterly new emerging issues, and that they are themselves largely the direct or indirect consequence of new technologies, which permit humans to do things they could not do before (or, conversely, make it difficult for humans to do things that were easy for them to do before) and which also often change the physical environment within which humans live. Methods for determining emerging issues are quite different from the way we can measure and forecast most trends and cycles.

Now, to the extent that our own personal experiences, and the focus of most of the formal educational system, are only on the first and second types of trend (and they overwhelmingly are), most of us may find it very difficult to anticipate the future helpfully if the futurists are correct who contend—as I certainly do—that the third, 'emerging issue' kind of trend is by far the most important for understanding the next thirty years and beyond. As the Pakistani futurist Sohail Inayatullah says, 'The thing that makes the future interesting is that none of us remember it.'

Images and Actions

Now, the third and fourth major factors influencing the future are the images of the future that people hold and the actions they take on the basis of those images. Some of these actions are taken specifically with the intention of influencing the future. Others are not. But all *do* influence it—though seldom ever as intended!

Thus, one of the things futures studies tries to do is to help people examine and clarify their images of the future—their ideas, fears, hopes, beliefs and concerns about the future—so that they might improve the quality of their decisions which impact upon it.

Another thing futures studies tries to do is to help people move their images and actions beyond an attempt passively to forecast the future and then to develop plans of action on the basis of the forecasts. That is only the first step in foresight. The next step is to generate positive visions of the future—to create preferred futures—and to base planning and decisions on them. The future-envisioning workshops of the Austrian futurist Robert Jungk, and of Elise Boulding and many others subsequently, should be mentioned here. Learning to vision, and revision, the future, and then to plan and act in accordance are at the heart of futures studies and futures research as applied to planning and decision-making.

3.3. Futures Studies, Determinism, Incoherence

This is, I believe, what futures studies and foresight is. And because it is not something that most of us have experienced in our formal education, we assume either that futures studies is impossible (and that those who advocate it are frauds or flakes) or else that it is like some academic orientation we *do* understand, such as science, or history, or art or mathematics. But this also misleads us, because futures studies is as different from each of these as science is from art, or history is from mathematics. Although futures studies does overlap with each of these traditional academic disciplines, it is not the same as any of them.

For example, as I said earlier, foresight is not 'prediction'. Neither society nor nature is some deterministic machine that can be predicted if we just understand it correctly and collect and analyse the data properly. Rather, we live in a profoundly—and probably increasingly—incoherent society and environment. We need techniques of foresight, planning and decision-making that acknowledge this. And we need a public (and decision-makers) who understand this, and who permit, indeed demand, the use of techniques that do not assume a deterministic universe. At the present time the public, the electorate, our clients, our boss all generally seem to want predictive certainty about the future, or else they want to hear no information about the future whatsoever. This understandable desire for false assurance is dangerous for the future of democratic society and certainly dangerous for anyone interested in the future of education and sustainable community development. Don Michael (1989) has recently written a very eloquent, if despairing, expression on this human tragedy.

What can and should be done, in contrast, is to place foresight, planning and decision-making within an ongoing, multiple, 'alternative futures' context. This contrasts with the common practice of 'planning' for what is assumed to be the single 'most likely' future, or several of its minor variations. To many planners and decision-makers, the 'most likely' future seems to be the one that might emerge from the continuation of existing trends. But I have already suggested that events as well as cycles and emerging issues make such an extrapolated, linear future highly unlikely indeed.

Thus plans made on the assumption that 'the present will continue' fairly soon result in a variety of planning and policy disasters, which in turn often discredit the entire attempt at planning and foresight. These failures then encourage people to ignore the future entirely and to hope that we can just muddle through somehow, ignorant of things to come.

Likewise, policy made in the name of foresight after a 'one-shot' glance at certain trends, even if the trends are produced by sophisticated computer models and with great mathematical precision, is similarly inadequate and potentially dangerous. Foresight must become a routine, continuing process, not a one-time affair. If you are not going to anticipate the future regularly and routinely, I suggest you don't bother to consider it at all. It is a waste of everybody's time— and probably just a whitewash of somebody else's decisions about the future— to make it a one-shot affair.

And finally, foresight that is undertaken as only a technical, scientific and professional exercise is incomplete. Foresight must also and necessarily be a political, ethical, aesthetic and very broadly participative project. It must take the form of what Alvin Toffler and Clem Bezold have called 'Anticipatory Democracy'. It is absolutely essential that all people who have a stake in a future be involved in determining it. Obviously that means that young people—even the youngest of people—should be deeply involved in ways that make sense to them. It also means that not only the elite but also all marginalised persons should participate fairly, fully and frequently. And that is why future-oriented studies must become the heart and soul of all academic endeavours. You can't learn to do useful foresight overnight, any more than you can learn to do anything else new instantly and effortlessly. Learning to exercise foresight takes lots of time and practice, and involves many mistakes and changes of direction.

Most of the organisations I know to have engaged in future-oriented projects report that a very significant benefit of such activities is that they give them-selves, and their constituents, a broad and common sense of what their purpose and mission is, perhaps for the first time. For example, while at one level 'everyone' knows what the purpose of education is, future-visioning processes help everyone reconsider, clarify and unify that purpose. A secondary benefit groups discover is that, after engaging in a future-visioning process, people may find they then have the political and popular support to undertake necessary reforms, and are thus able to allocate resources more efficiently and effectively once a common mission has been widely sought and jointly identified. And then, to the extent that envisioning and scanning the future become a normal part of the organisation's activities, these benefits too become more routine and more widespread—the community becomes truly 'sustainable'. To the extent that a true cross-section of the relevant public participates genuinely in these futures activities and the subsequent reforms, this public's sense of efficacy and support of sustainable community development grows.

And, if futures activities are found to be beneficial for one community, other communities, presently unfamiliar with or suspicious of foresight, may be inspired to become more future-oriented themselves, and the future of society as a whole may become more secure and sustainable, and less chaotic and drifting.

3.4 Attributes of a Futurist

I was recently asked to describe the attributes of a futurist, or what I thought was necessary if one wanted to become a good student and practitioner of futures studies. This was my response.

To be a good futurist, you need the widest possible knowledge of the history and present condition of as many cultures and civilisations as possible; you must know more than one culture, and thus more than one language, intimately; the widest possible knowledge of all aspects of all the social sciences; the widest possible knowledge of current and emerging developments in the natural sciences, and their emerging subdisciplines and transdisciplines, for example, evolutionary systems theory, chaos theory and brain science; the widest possible familiarity with developments in engineering (especially electronics and genetics), architecture and space sciences; the widest possible familiarity with philosophy, ethics, morals and religions, and certainly the ethical discourse of as many different traditions as possible; the widest possible familiarity with law and planning; an active awareness of aesthetics and the aesthetic element in all aspects of life; a continuing experience of aesthetic expression in some, or preferably many, modes; creativity, imagination and the willingness to think new thoughts, to make unmade connections, to be ridiculed, laughed at and to laugh at yourself; the ability to synthesise, combine, invent and create; the willingness to be politically active and to test out new ideas on yourself first and then while actually trying to create a better world, or improve some portion of it; the ability to try to anticipate the consequences of actions before you act, but also the willingness to risk failure and to learn from mistakes and criticism—indeed to seek out and provoke criticism—and to keep trying to do better, and constantly to relearn what 'better' might be; insatiable curiosity, unbounded compassion, incurable optimism and an unquenchable sense of humour and delight in the absurd. All of this can be described in one word—'aiglatson', which is 'nostalgia' spelled backwards: the yearning for things to come; remembering the future; without being disrespectful to the past (remembering that once it was all that was humanly possible), preferring the dreams of the future to the experiences of the past; always desiring to try something new, to go where no one has ever gone before in all areas of human—and non-human and, soon, post-human—experience.

Is it possible for anyone to do that? Is it possible for anyone, given our current systems of education?

3.5 The Future of Higher Education

So far I have said nothing about the future of education, and hence of the structure or process within which I envision futures studies will be embedded, or 'delivered', in the future. Let me just say that while I would be delighted to see the current campus-based higher education system continue forever, I do not expect it to survive even the 1990s, and certainly not much beyond. I agree that the future of education is a network, and not a place. Also I (regrettably) do not expect to see the continuation, much less expansion, of the unified, publicly financed educational system into the future. Education will no longer be the single-worldview-producing machine it was, and was intended to be, in the nineteenth and twentieth centuries. Instead, there will be many competing, conflicting networks; many claiming monopoly on Truth but none having it.

I believe that Kaoru Yamaguchi and all those who share with him the vision of the 'Network University of the Green World' understand the future of higher education in these terms. Indeed, the fact that they call their university a 'network' makes that completely clear.

Two final points:

Futures Studies Should Be Useful

The development of futures studies as I understand it was very strongly influenced by attempts to apply it in real, practical grassroots situations. In my case that specifically means the old Hawaii 2000 experience of the 1960s and 1970s, and everything that flowed from it, including the establishment by the Hawaii State Legislature, in 1971, of the Hawaii Research Center for Futures Studies. Also, one of the reasons the Alternative Futures Option was created in the mid-1970s by the Department of Political Science of the University of Hawaii, with a strong intern component, was to satisfy a demand for people able to 'do' futures research for various governmental, commercial, civic, non-profit and other groups and individuals.

Similarly, my involvement in the creation and subsequent work of the Institute for Alternative Futures in Washington, D. C., and the need thus to provide useful information about the future to its political, commercial, civic, non-profit and other clients, greatly influenced the shape and content of my understanding of futures studies. Futures studies has never been a strictly educational or theoretical enterprise to me. It has always been driven by the need to be useful both to ordinary people and to elite decision-makers, without giving in to their desire to have The Wondrous Things To Come Foretold by Ye Olde Mystic Soothsayer. Thus, my understanding of futures studies has been strongly influenced (and leavened) by my experiences of the needs and ideas of these people. I suspect the same is true of many other people in the field and thus of the field itself.

I hope that the Network University of the Green World will, therefore, try usefully to serve first the people and leaders of Awaji-jima. The presence here today of the Mayor of Goshiki-cho, and of other local people, also clearly shows that the founders of the Network University also understand this. I am sure that everyone will learn much from such a practical, local interchange of visions, fears, plans, hopes and actions.

Futures Studies is Local and Global

At the same time, my involvement in futures studies has, from the very beginning, been not only at a local academic and community level, nor even only at a national level. Rather, through my early and continuing involvement in the World Futures Studies Federation, futures studies has also been for me, and for many others, a global and globalising exercise. This, too, I think, makes futures studies quite different from most past and present academic orientations, and itself a harbinger of the global future common to all humankind.

I hope that futures studies is given the opportunity to grow and thrive in the nurturing embrace of the citizens of Awaji-jima and all who come here from around the world, and that this first world futures-creating seminar may indeed be the first of many, which lead us soon to the creation of a truly sustainable, peaceful, equitable and firmly future-oriented global village.

That is my hope and challenge to you today and throughout the remainder of this seminar and beyond.

References and Further Reading

Altbach, Philip (ed.) (1991). *International Higher Education*, New York and London: Garland Publishing.

Bell, Wendell (1996). *Foundations of Futures Studies*, vol. 1: *History, Purposes and Knowledge*; vol. 2: *Values, Objectivity and the Good Society*, Rutgers, N.J.: Transaction Publishers.

Bezold, Clem (ed.) (1978). *Anticipatory Democracy*, New York: Random House.

Chaplin, George and Paige, Glenn (eds.) (1973). *Hawaii 2000: Continuing Experiments in Anticipatory Democracy*, Honolulu: University Press of Hawaii, 1973.

Dahle, Kjell (1981). *On Alternative Ways of Studying the Future*, Oslo: Alternative Future Project.

Dator, James A. and Rodgers, Sharon (1991). *Alternative Futures for the State Courts of 2020*, Chicago, Ill.: American Judicature Society.

Godet, Michel (1987). *Scenarios and Strategic Management*, London: Butterworths.

—— (1991). *From Anticipation to Action: A Handbook of Strategic Prospective*, Paris: UNESCO Future-Oriented Studies.

Jungk, Robert and Mullert, Norbert (1987). *Futures Workshops: How to Create Desirable Futures*, London: Institute for Social Inventions.

Kim, Tae-Chang and Dator, Jim (1995). *Creating a New History for Future Generations*, Kyoto: Institute for the Integrated Study of Future Generations.

Kurian, George and Molitor, Graham (eds.) (1996). *Encyclopedia of the Future*, 2 vols., New York: Macmillan.

Marien, Michael and Jennings, Lane (eds.) (1987). *What I Have Learned: Thinking About the Future Then and Now*, New York: Greenwood.

Masini, Eleonora Barbieri (1993). *Why Futures Studies?*, London: Gray Seal.

Michael, Donald (1989). 'Forecasting and Planning in an Incoherent Context', *Technological Forecasting and Social Change* pp. 79–87.

Schwartz, Peter (1991). *The Art of the Long View*, New York: Doubleday.

Slaughter, Richard (1992a). 'Futures Studies and Higher Education', *Futures Research Quarterly* Winter, with articles by Martha Rogers, Christopher Jones, Allyson Holbrook, Wendy Schultz, Richard Slaughter and Kjell Dahle.

—— (ed.) (1992b). *Teaching About the Future*, proceedings of a seminar organised jointly by UNESCO and the Canadian Commission for UNESCO, Vancouver, Canada, 21–23 June, with essays by Howard Didsbury, Wendy Schultz, Martha Rogers, Richard Slaughter, Allen Tough, Kaoru Yamaguchi, Tony Stevenson and Pierre Weiss.

—— (ed.) (1996a). *The Knowledge Base of Futures Studies*, 3 vols., Melbourne: DDM Media Group.

—— (ed.) (1996b). *New Thinking for a New Millennium*, London: Routledge.

World Futures Studies Federation *et al.* (eds.) (1986). *Reclaiming the Future: A Manual of Futures Studies for African Planners*, New York: Taylor & Francis.

4 UNESCO and Future-Oriented Studies

ALBERT SASSON

Since its creation, UNESCO has been involved in future-oriented activities. At the global level there are now two independent international commissions with the task of undertaking future-oriented reflection. The first concerns education for the twenty-first century, and its president is Jacques Delors; the second is on culture and development, presided over by Mr Pérez de Cuellar.

4.1 Contribution to the Progress of Future-Oriented Studies

In 1984 UNESCO decided to go beyond the sectoral approach to prospective studies and create a specific programme called 'Reflection on World Problems and Future-Oriented Studies'. This was Major Programme I of UNESCO's Medium-Term Plan for 1984–9. Within this framework regional studies on Africa, Asia, Europe and Latin America were carried out and published. Major Programme I had two objectives, both of which remain valid under the current transverse programme—'Future-Oriented Studies'—initiated by UNESCO in 1990 (within the Medium-Term Plan for 1990–5).

(1) The first objective was to constitute an observatory and a forum that, thanks to studies done by institutions and experts in the future-oriented field, would enable future trends to be identified and their impact assessed, and to transmit this knowledge to the international community. With this in mind a seminar was organised to highlight the economic, social and cultural implications of biotechnologies, and the results were published in 1991 in a book entitled *Biotechnologies in Perspective*, which was followed by another publication in 1993, *Biotechnologies in Developing Countries: Present and Future*, Vol. 1. *Regional and National Survey*. Another example is the work undertaken on *Islands' Cultures and Development*, resulting in a publication which came out in 1991 in the same UNESCO 'Future-Oriented Studies' series.

(2) The second objective was to contribute to the planning of the Organization's activities; hence the placing of the Future-Oriented Studies transverse programme (the successor to Major Programme I) within the Division of Studies and Programming, which is the division responsible for the overall preparation of UNESCO's programmes.

While emphasis is deliberately being put less on activities that aim to promote the progress of knowledge, it should nevertheless be mentioned that a reflection on the 'Futures of Culture', co-ordinated by Eleonora Masini, has been completed and published in book form under the same title. Priority is now being given to the collection and dissemination of the results of future-oriented work undertaken in the fields of competence of the Organization. For this purpose, a clearing-house in the future-oriented field called FUTURESCO was set up.

4.2 The FUTURESCO Project

In 1992 the decision was taken to set up a computerised bibliographical database in the future-oriented areas related to UNESCO's fields of competence. The creation of this database was preceded in 1990–1 by a series of consultations with some of the most representative non-governmental organisations (NGOs), in particular the World Future Society (in the person of Michael Marien, editor of the bibliographical bulletin *Future Survey*), the World Futures Studies Federation (WFSF), the International Library for the Future, Salzburg, and Futuribles International. These four NGOs supply information to the bibliographical database on a regular basis and make up, together with a representative of UNESCO, the editorial committee of the bibliographical bulletin *UNESCO Future Scan*, the first issue of which (on education) came out in the summer of 1992. In this connection, it should be mentioned that in 1991 UNESCO published the *World Education Report* (No. 1), followed in 1993 by the *World Education Report* (No. 2): *Overcoming the Knowledge Gap, Expanding Educational Choice, Searching for Standards*. In 1994 UNESCO published the *World Science Report 1993*.

The combined second and third issues (on environment) of *UNESCO Future Scan*, now renamed *FUTURESCO*, were published in the autumn of 1993. The fourth one (on culture) was published in June 1994.

Editorial work on the fifth issue of the *FUTURESCO* bulletin (on the futures of human rights and democracy) is in its final stages and publication is expected before the end of 1995.

The FUTURESCO Project comprises:

- A computerised database. Once the software had been devised to enable the UNESCO CDS/ISIS documentation software to be adapted to the specific needs of FUTURESCO and a list of descriptors had been drawn up, the material supplied by the partners in the project (which represented close to a thousand bibliographical entries in English) was entered into the database. This bibliographical material will be transferred to CD-ROM in March 1996. It is then expected that the database will be connected to the central UNESCO computer and that external consultation of the data will be available to interested individuals and institutions.
- A bibliographical bulletin, already mentioned above, which, as of the double number (2–3) that appeared in June 1993, was called *FUTURESCO: A UNESCO Bibliographical Bulletin of Future-Oriented Literature*. This bulletin is divided into three sections: a general bibliographical selection covering UNESCO's fields of competence; a central topic (education in issue 1,

environment in issues 2–3, culture in issue 4); documents and a presentation of the activities of one of the members of the founding NGO/UNESCO network of FUTURESCO. With effect from issue 5 (human rights and democracy), the *FUTURESCO* bulletin was designated as *A UNESCO Bulletin of Future-Oriented Literature*. The word 'bibliographical' has been dropped and the format of the bulletin has been changed. The bulletin now consists of two regular sections and an occasional section. The regular sections are review articles on an approved topic, which must be within the fields of competence of UNESCO, and select annotated bibliographies on the same approved topic.

In addition to the process of computerisation, by 1995 the FUTURESCO project will have developed in three directions:

(1) a quest for new partners, the aim being to associate UNESCO National Commissions that have shown a particular interest in future-oriented studies (including Brazil, Canada, France, Germany, India, Japan, Nigeria, the Republic of Korea and Romania), as well as other NGOs;

(2) a wider linguistic review of future-oriented literature. For the moment, FUTURESCO provides a satisfactory review of prospective work in English, German, French and, to a lesser degree, Spanish. Thanks to the WFSF it also benefits from some information on future-oriented literature produced in other languages; this last point will be strengthened (with the help of some of UNESCO's National Commissions);

(3) co-ordination with future-oriented programmes, implemented at the intergovernmental level. Since the Future-Oriented Studies transverse programme has limited human resources, the FUTURESCO project can only work if it is conceived and implemented as a network comprising other elements both within UNESCO (with the help of the programme sectors or field units) and outside the Organization (co-operation with intergovernmental organisations, NGOs, national commissions, research institutions, and so on).

Through this three-pronged approach, FUTURESCO will be able to collect and make known the content of the best future-oriented work carried out in the world. In this way it will contribute to one of UNESCO's major tasks, the transfer and sharing of knowledge.

4.3 Education and Training

Another objective of the Future-Oriented Studies transverse programme is to promote the dissemination of prospective methods and results by means of education and training activities. Thus, UNESCO has given its support to several activities of this type carried out in Africa, Asia, Europe and Latin America. In June 1992 a seminar on future-oriented studies for countries around the Pacific rim was organised in Vancouver with the idea of setting up a network covering Canada, the USA and the countries of the Pacific area. Hopefully this network will start functioning effectively in 1994–5, its financing being ensured by, *inter alia*, UNESCO's Participation Programme. UNESCO also provides financial assistance to the yearly Asia–Pacific Futures Course and is also co-operating in the setting up of a Network of Teachers of Futures Studies in the Asia and Pacific Basin Region. These courses and the network are expected to assist in the development and consolidation of UNESCO's FUTURESCO database and bulletin.

Handbooks will also be published as a natural complement to these activities. In 1993 UNESCO undertook the publication of two such works, *Why Futures Studies?* by Eleonora Masini and *From Anticipation to Action: A Handbook of Strategic Prospective* by Michel Godet. In spring 1994 it published *The Futures of Cultures*.

Part II

New Framework of Community Economy

5 Sustainability and a MuRatopian Economy

KAORU YAMAGUCHI

5.1 Sustainability

Physical, Social and Ecological Reproducibility

Since the 1992 UN Conference on Environment and Development (UNCED), widely known as the 'Earth Summit', in Rio de Janeiro, Brazil, 'sustainable development' has become a fashionable term in our daily conversations. This might be an indication that our awareness of such environmental crises as global warming, acid rain, depletion of the ozone layer, tropical deforestation, desertification and endangered species has deepened. What, then, is a state of sustainable development, and how is it defined? Here are two definitions that have been proposed:

Sustainable development is development that meets the needs of the present without compromising the ability of future generations to meet their own needs.   (World Commission on Environment and Development 1987: 43)

The simplest definition is: A sustainable society is one that can persist over generations, one that is far-seeing enough, flexible enough, and wise enough not to undermine either its *physical* or its *social* systems of supports.   (Meadows *et al.* 1992: 209; *my emphasis*)

These definitions were phrased to be understood even by children. However, from an economist's point of view, they lack an interrelated view of production, consumption, society and environment. Sustainability is comprehensively defined when all activities in the economy, society and nature are interpreted as reproduction processes, that is, in terms of physical, social and ecological reproducibility. This is how sustainability is defined in this chapter. One merit of this approach is that same economic structure as in the general equilibrium framework is used so that the interrelationship between economic activities and environment is understood holistically (Yamaguchi 1988).

Physical reproducibility. One of the basic activities in any society is production, in which inputs are transformed into outputs for consumption and continued reproduction in the next period. This reproduction process is formalised as:

$$(A, L : \Delta E_s) \Longrightarrow (B : \Delta E_p),$$

where A is the physical input vector whose elements consist of (non-renewable) raw materials, physical means of production such as machines and factories, and goods-in-process; L is the labour input vector whose elements consist of all different types of labour service; B is the output vector whose elements consist of all types of final goods and services, one-period older means of production, and goods-in-progress; ΔE_s is the reduction of non-renewable natural resources (which constitute parts of A); and ΔE_p is industrial wastes discharged as a result of production activities.

For this physical reproduction process to continue in any economy, at least the same amount of inputs, A, has to be replaced out of the outputs, B; that is:

$$B \geq A.$$

This physical reproducibility further presupposes the availability of non-renewable natural resources.

Non-renewable resource availability. Non-renewable natural resources are available only when the earth's limited sources of those deposits, E_s, have not been used up before the present period, t; that is:

$$\sum_{i=-\infty}^{t} \Delta E_{s,i} < \Delta E_s.$$

This condition may also be met if substitutes for these non-renewable resources are discovered or newly invented through technological breakthroughs.

Social reproducibility. For any society to survive, labour forces and the whole population have to be reproduced by daily consumption activities. For this to be so, at least a minimum amount of consumption C_{min} has to be reproduced. It needs to be more than a subsistence level in order 'to maintain the minimum standards of *wholesome and cultured living*' (Constitution of Japan, article 25). Hence, consumption activities can be regarded as a social reproduction process that takes place in a global environment, E.

$$(C_{min} : E) \Longrightarrow (L, \Delta E_c),$$

where ΔE_c is consumer waste discharged as a result of consumption activities. For this social reproduction process to continue, the minimum amount of consumption must always be secured out of net outputs; that is,

$$C_{min} \leq B - A.$$

Note that when this social reproducibility condition is met, physical reproducibility also holds.

Ecological reproducibility. The production and consumption activities formalised above also produce as by-products industrial wastes, ΔE_p, and consumer garbage, ΔE_c, which are, in turn, dumped into the earth and atmosphere in environmental sinks. This dumping process together with the process of extracting non-renewable resources forms a new global environment, E, which consists of the earth's sources E_s and the earth's supportable sinks E_{ss}. Hence, this for-

Table 5.1. The stationary-state reproduction process

$t-1$	t	$t+1$
$\left\{\begin{array}{l} A \\ \\ L \end{array}\right. \Rightarrow B$	$\left\{\begin{array}{l} A \\ \\ C_{min} \Rightarrow L \end{array}\right. \Rightarrow B$	
$\uparrow\quad\downarrow$	$\uparrow\quad\downarrow\qquad\downarrow$	
$\Delta E_s\quad \Delta E_p$	$\Delta E_s\quad \Delta E_c\quad \Delta E_p$	

mation of the global environment is considered as an ecological reproduction process, or anti-physical-reproduction process:

$$(\Delta E_s \oplus \Delta E_p \oplus \Delta E_c) \Longrightarrow E(= E_s \oplus E_{ss}).$$

As a typical example, we can refer to the process of photosynthesis, through which tropical forests and trees produce oxygen as an output from carbon dioxide as an input.

For the ecological reproduction process to continue, waste and garbage sinks resulting from production and consumption activities up to the present period, t, have to be less than the earth's ecological capacity to absorb and dissolve those sinks; that is:

$$\sum_{i=-\infty}^{t}(\Delta E_{p,i} \oplus \Delta E_{c,i}) < E_{ss}.$$

Fortunately, ecological reproducibility, which recycles those sinks into sources and restores the original shape, has been built in the earth in the form of the self-regulatory Gaia mechanism (Lovelock 1988).

This built-in ecological reproducibility may be written as:

$$(\Delta E_p \oplus \Delta E_c) \Longrightarrow 0.$$

This means that industrial and consumer wastes are taken care of by a natural production process and that the environment thus continues to be restored.

At this point in our argument, sustainability has been comprehensively defined in terms of physical, social and ecological reproducibilities. Table 5.1 illustrates these reproduction processes in a *steady-state* case in which production and consumption levels remain the same in every period, so that ecological reproducibility is also maintained.

Exponential Economic Growth

In many cases, economic growth and development are taken to be the same thing. Where sustainability is concerned, however, these two terms have to be strictly distinguished. Economic growth is physically measured in terms of the growth of net outputs $Y = B - A$ or per capita net outputs Y/L, provided the

Table 5.2. The growing reproduction process

$t-1$	t		$t+1$
$\left\{\begin{array}{l} A \\ L \end{array}\right.$ $\quad\Longrightarrow\quad B \left\{\begin{array}{l} A+\Delta A \\ C_{min}+\Delta C\Rightarrow L+\Delta L \end{array}\right.$		$\Longrightarrow$	$B+\Delta B$
$\uparrow\quad\downarrow$ $\quad\quad\quad$ $\uparrow\quad\quad\downarrow$ $\quad\quad\quad\quad\downarrow$			
$\Delta E_s\quad\Delta E_p$ $\quad\quad\quad \Delta E_s\quad\quad\Delta E_c$ $\quad\quad\quad\quad \Delta E_p$			

calculations make sense (i.e. Y is a vector and L is a scalar).[1] On the other hand, sustainable development is defined as a form of economic growth that satisfies the three reproducibilities discussed above.

When the net production level is high enough, that is, $Y > C_{min}$, it becomes possible to have positive increments of physical inputs and consumption $(\Delta A, \Delta C) > 0$ such that:

$$Y = C_{min} + \Delta C + \Delta A.$$

In this state of higher production, economic growth becomes possible in the following fashion:

$$(C_{min} + \Delta C : E) \Longrightarrow (L + \Delta L, \Delta E_c),$$

$$(A + \Delta A, L + \Delta L : \Delta E_s) \Longrightarrow (B + \Delta B, \Delta E_p).$$

See Table 5.2.

Suppose that the economy can grow at a constant annual growth rate of $100g$ per cent so that, for the period t, $\Delta Y(t) = gY(t)$ for a discrete case, or $dY(t)/dt = gY(t)$ for a continuous case. Then, this type of growth path, called exponential growth, can be described as follows:

$$Y(t) = Y(0)(1 + g)^t : \text{discrete growth,}$$

$$Y(t) = Y(0)e^{gt} \quad\quad : \text{continuous growth,}$$

where e is approximately 2.71828. From this formula, the number of years it takes for the economy to double its current size can be calculated. Letting $Y(0) = 1$ and $Y(t) = 2$, we have:

$$t_d = \ln(2)/\ln(1 + g) : \text{discrete growth,}$$

$$t_c = \ln(2)/g \quad\quad : \text{continuous growth.}$$

Table 5.3 summarises these calculations for a various growth rates between 0.1 and 10.0 per cent. It shows that continuous growth doubles a little faster than discrete growth, but that the difference is almost negligible as long as the annual growth rate is small. Thus, we can double production levels and GNP and de-

---

[1] If the calculations do not make sense, then redefine Y as GNP (Gross National Product) such that $Y = p(B - A)$ for a semi-positive price vector $p \geq 0$, and redefine L as a total population.

Table 5.3. Doubling times and economic growth

Growth rate (%)	Doubling years (td)	Doubling years (tc)	Growth rate (%)	Doubling years (td)	Doubling years (tc)
0.1	693.49	693.15	1.0	69.66	69.31
0.2	346.92	346.57	2.0	35.00	34.66
0.3	231.40	231.05	3.0	23.45	23.10
0.4	173.63	173.29	4.0	17.67	17.33
0.5	138.98	138.63	5.0	14.21	13.86
0.6	115.87	115.52	6.0	11.90	11.55
0.7	99.37	99.02	7.0	10.24	9.90
0.8	86.99	86.64	8.0	9.01	8.66
0.9	77.36	77.02	9.0	8.04	7.70
1.0	69.66	69.31	10.0	7.27	6.93

pletion levels of non-renewable resources as well as the levels of sinks in 10 years if our economy grows at a constant 7 per cent. Similarly, in many developing countries population will double in 35 years at its current growth rate of about 2 per cent.

The first two columns of data in Table 5.4 illustrate economic growth changes between 1970 and 1990. The last two columns calculate average annual growth rates between those two years.[2]

Combining Tables 5.3 and 5.4, we can easily predict the future levels of each activity or product if the growth rates of these twenty years are simply extrapolated. For instance, it will take only about 35 years for the present population to double and exceed 10 billion, and twice as many registered cars will flood on to the streets in 17 years.

Limits to Reproducibility

This exponential economic growth will have to be restricted, ultimately, by physical, social and ecological reproducibilities.

Limit 1: A limit to resource availability and physical reproducibility. As material expansion and economic growth continue, non-renewable natural resources will eventually be exhausted, unless substitutes are invented; that is:

$$\sum_{i=-\infty}^{t} \Delta E_{s,i} \geq \Delta E_{s}.$$

When this occurs, physical reproducibility will also be interrupted.

---

2 These growth rates were obtained using the following formula:

$$g_d = \exp\{[\ln(Y(t)/Y(0))]/t\} - 1 : \text{discrete growth,}$$
$$g_c = [\ln(Y(t)/Y(0))]/t \qquad : \text{continuous growth.}$$

Table 5.4. Average annual growth rates in selected human activities and products, 1970–1990

	1970	1990	$100g_d$ (%)	$100g_c$ (%)
Human population (bn.)	3.6	5.3	1.95	1.93
Registered cars (mn.)	250	560	4.11	4.03
Kilometres driven (bn./year, OECD countries only)				
by passenger cars	2,584	4,489	2.80	2.76
by trucks	666	1,536	4.27	4.18
Oil consumption (bn. barrels/year)	17	24	1.74	1.72
Natural gas consumption (trillion cubic feet/year)	31	70	4.16	4.07
Coal consumption (bn. tons/year)	2.3	5.2	4.16	4.08
Electric generating capacity (bn. kW/year)	1.1	2.6	4.39	4.30
Electricity generation by nuclear power plants (terawatt-hours/year)	79	1,884	17.19	15.86
Soft drink consumption (mn. barrels/year, USA only)	150	364	4.53	4.43
Beer consumption (mn. barrels/year, USA only)	125	187	2.03	2.01
Aluminium used for beer and soft drinks containers (kilotonnes/year, USA only)	72.7	1,251.9	15.29	14.23
Municipal waste generated (mn. tonnes/year)	302	420	1.66	1.65

Source: cols. 1 and 2 are taken from Meadows *et al*. 1992: 7.

Limit 2: A limit to social reproducibility. As population increases exponentially, the minimum amount of consumption will also expand exponentially if we are to maintain a 'wholesome and cultured living standard' for each person: C_{min} = per capita living standard × L. Otherwise, the standard of living will deteriorate. Eventually, social reproducibility conditions will be violated unless net outputs also grow exponentially, and thus a portion of the population will starve to death:

$$C_{min} \geq B - A.$$

Limit 3: A limit to ecological reproducibility. As production and consumption activities expand exponentially, environmental sinks, such as industrial and consumer waste, also increase exponentially. The earth's naturally built-in ecological reproducibility, Gaia, will eventually fail to regenerate all of those sinks, leaving a portion of them unprocessed. Thus waste will gradually accumulate:

$$(\Delta E_p, \Delta E_c) \Longrightarrow (\alpha \Delta E_p, \beta \Delta E_c), \quad 0 < (\alpha, \beta) < 1.$$

Even so, sustainable development might be possible for a while provided the accumulated sinks of industrial and consumer waste that the ecological reproduction process failed to disintegrate did not reach environmental capacities. However, if that accumulation continued, eventually an environmental catastrophe would occur that left the earth uninhabitable for many living species, including humans:

$$\sum_{i=-\infty}^{t} (\alpha \Delta E_{p,i} \oplus \beta \Delta E_{c,i}) \geq E_{ss}.$$

Therefore, continued economic growth is not compatible with sustainable development. It has to be stopped at some point, and an alternative path—a sustainable development path—must be sought.

Sustainable Development

It is now apparent that for sustainable development all obstacles to physical, social and ecological reproducibility have to be removed from the path of economic growth.

Limit 1. To stay within the limits of resource availability and physical reproducibility, first of all, we must make efficient use of non-renewable natural resources. For this, the introduction of long-term management of resources will be necessary. Second, the development of substitutes for non-renewable resources has to be encouraged. New technology R&D has to be oriented towards such directions as clean and solar energies and new materials.

Limit 2. To stay within the limits of social reproducibility, population explosion has to be radically curbed. At the same time, our lifestyles also have to be changed to reduce minimum physical consumption levels in favour of an increase in non-physical consumption, such as cultural and service activities.

Limit 3. To stay within the limits of ecological reproducibility, first of all, the total amount of environmental sinks has to be directly regulated so that it falls within the environmental capacity for regeneration. Second, the development of new recycling-oriented products has to be encouraged so that the number of environmental sinks is reduced at every cycle of reproduction and consumption.

It is shocking to realise that our society has already gone beyond the limits of ecological reproducibility:

This book is about overshoot on a much larger scale, namely the scale at which the human population and economy extract resources from the earth and emit pollution and wastes to the environment. Many of these rates of extraction and emission have grown to be unsupportable. The environment cannot sustain them. *Human society has overshot its limits*, for the same reasons that other overshoots occur. Changes are too fast. Signals are late. Responses are slow. (Meadows *et al.* 1992: 2; *my emphasis*)

One main reason why 'responses are slow' is related to the market economic system in which these changes take place. I now turn to this area.

5.2 The Market Economy

Sustainability under the Market Economy

After the sudden collapse of the Soviet Union and Eastern European countries in the early 1990s, it is widely believed that a market economy is the only suitable system for the proper functioning of basic production and consumption processes. The market economy is an institution in which each private economic agent behaves according to his or her own self-interest, irrespective of the welfare of others and without sustainability in mind. Specifically, producers primarily want to maximise their profits, while consumers are mainly interested in maximising their own utilities through massive consumption of goods and services. Such a market system, as advocated by neoclassical economists, is, however, capable of attaining an equilibrium and an efficient allocation of resources: 'Pareto optimality' in their terminology. In this sense the welfare of all economic agents is realised as a result of their self-motivated behaviour for their own economic interests in the market economy.[3] What about sustainability, then? Can such an economic institution actually maintain sustainability as defined above? If it can, what mechanism is built in to enable it to do so?

Resource availability. When non-renewable natural resources become less available, their supply in markets is also reduced. As a result, the laws of demand and supply push up their prices, causing their demand and hence also their use to be reduced. Moreover, the higher costs of non-renewable resources make the use of substitutes relatively less expensive and encourage the development of substitute products, further reducing the use of non-renewable resources. In this way the market economy has a built-in mechanism to regulate the usage of non-renewable resources.

Physical and social reproducibility. For a market economy to reproduce itself the first requirement is that producers have to be able to realise non-negative profits for a semi-positive price vector, $p \geq 0$, and a positive wage vector, $w > 0$:

$$\Pi \equiv p(B - A) - wL \geq 0.$$

Second, total income, consisting of wages and profits, has to be large enough to enable the purchase of a minimum consumption bundle in markets:

$$pC_{min} \leq wL + \Pi.$$

---

[3] I disagree with neoclassical economists on this point. See 'Pareto Optimality versus Marx Fairness', ch. 7 in Yamaguchi 1988.

From these two survival conditions, we have:

$$pC_{min} \leq p(B - A),$$

which implies $B \geq A + C_{min}$. Hence, physical and social reproducibility can be realised in a market economy.

Now suppose that total income is large enough to allow extra consumption, ΔC, and savings, S (defined in terms of monetary value); that is:

$$p(C_{min} + \Delta C) + S = wL + \Pi.$$

Producers may use these savings for their physical investment, ΔA, such that:

$$p\Delta A = S.$$

Hence, we have $B = A + \Delta A + C_{min} + \Delta C$. In this way the market economy enables economic growth.

Specifically, in a capitalist market economy profits can be a source of investment, so that:

$$p\Delta A = \Pi.$$

Hence, producers (and capitalists) try to maximise profits for further investment and expansion, which in turn increases profits. In this drive for profits, wages must be just high enough for workers to survive:

$$pC_{min} = wL.$$

This in turn allows maximum profits, and hence maximum investment and economic growth. In this way a capitalist market economy has a built-in drive for maximum exponential economic growth, driven by the motivation to maximise profits.

Ecological reproducibility. The market economy, however, lacks any built-in mechanism to maintain ecological reproducibility and hence sustainable development. No mechanism exists in a market economy for encouraging investment to prevent industrial waste. Such environmental investment is regarded as an additional cost to producers and capitalists, best avoided in order to maximise profits. Meanwhile, consumers are also allowed to discharge waste free of charge. In other words, markets cannot require the payment of dumping costs. These are typical examples of so-called 'market failures'.

Market Failures

There are many aspects of our better life and sustainable development on which we cannot put a price. The market economy fails to appreciate those values fairly, because it is a system in which only exclusive *ownership* of labour products is exchanged. Accordingly, those priceless quantities, which are not claimed for 'ownership', are destined to be missing in the market economy. Let me consider these missing 'values'.

Labour values. Office and factory labour services that produce goods and services are valued as wages only when their products are successfully exchanged in the market. Management labour services are similarly valued as salaries. However, family labour services at home cannot be given a market value, no matter how valuable they are to society and future generations. Accordingly, women and the elderly are often treated as second class because their services cannot add value in the market. Likewise, labour services protecting against environmental deterioration, often offered by volunteer environmentalists, have seldom been valued in monetary terms, no matter how valuable they are to future generations. On the other hand, ownership of the means of production, such as factories, land and monetary capital, is valued highly, even though it is nothing but a legal right and it cannot contribute to production in the same way as do labour services. Hence, owners are paid profits as capitalists, shareholders and landowners. In this way, the market economy becomes a distribution system based on exchangeable labour services and ownership. But non-exchangeable labour services at home and in environmental protection activities are not allowed to form part of such a distribution system. This distorted distribution system of labour values has to be amended. For instance, a family labour-sharing system could be considered in which a husband is only allowed to work for half of his current working hours and does family work at home for the remainder, while his wife does the same alternately, so that their total income remains the same.

Information values. In the information age, information *per se* becomes another main product alongside goods and services. One of the features of information is that it can be shared without changing ownership. Its reproduction cost is almost negligible; equal to its duplication cost. In other words, its average cost diminishes and its marginal cost is almost zero. In this sense, it is very different from goods and services. Owing to its nature, information is apparently not compatible with a market economy based on an exclusive exchange of ownership. This is why intellectual property rights had to be forcibly introduced into the market economy in order to make information another market product—an extremely inefficient, upside-down use of information. Information can be more efficiently used, and thus more highly valued, when shared. In this sense, the market economy has a fatal deficiency, in principle, as an economic system in the information age.

Ecological values. The earth produces valuable products for us, such as oxygen, but its products can seldom be fairly valued in the market. They are, instead, considered 'free goods' in economics. For example, tropical forests, though they produce a large amount of the oxygen we need, are regarded as free goods for their private owners and public owners, that is, governments. If oxygen was fairly valued in the market, tropical forests, as its production factories, would also be fairly valued. The destruction of tropical forests would then be regarded as a production process with negative value. Thus, if that negative value exceeded the market values of the forests as lumber, the destruction of the forests would automatically be avoided according to a built-in market valuation mechanism. In other words, if a system to value oxygen is built into the market, it will be valued more highly as carbon dioxide increases and the supply of oxygen is relatively reduced. Owners of tropical forests will receive more income as managers of the production of oxygen than for selling their forests as lumber. Hence, ecological sustainability might be better preserved in the market economy. Unfortunately, there is no way in principle that such an ecological value can be claimed in the market economy. This is an inevitable consequence in the industrial age, in which an exchange market between man and nature has not been created.

It is now apparent that the capitalist market economy is a fatally distorted system in the sense that it cannot appreciate the most important values for a better life and sustainable development, such as labour value, information value and ecological value.

5.3 A MuRatopian Economy

The flawed market economy will be or has to be ultimately replaced with a new economic system as the information age proceeds. I have called this new economic system a 'MuRatopian'[4] economy and analysed its main features and functionings in several places (Yamaguchi 1988, 1990; Yamaguchi and Niwa 1994). Let me briefly describe the economy.

Mechatronic Technology

The industrial age has been constructed on mechanistic technology, which is best conceived of as an extension of clock-making technology. The essence of this technology is that it mass-produces goods and pollutant by-products. Mechanistic technology is now being replaced by mechatronic technology, a combination of mechanistic and electronic technology. Mechatronic technology is best symbolised by robots, which consist of mechanistic arms and an electronic nervous system. This new technology enables the customised production of info-goods, info-services and knowledge. Thus, in the information age information is

---

[4] The Japanese word 'mura' literally means 'village'. The mind of the information age is envisioned in the spirit and practice of a traditional Japanese village where villagers live in a self-sufficient community, help each other co-operatively at the busiest time, the harvest, and respect nature's order. The one character word 'mura' may also be regarded as consisting of two different characters: 'Mu' and 'Ra'. 'Mu' implies 'nothingness' or 'emptiness'—the most fundamental concept of Zen Buddhism—and hence concisely reflects the new-thinking philosophy that the world is holistically interrelated and interdependent. The word 'Ra' means 'being naked' or 'having no possessions'. Accordingly, the implications of 'Mu' (nothingness) and 'Ra' (dispossession) are associated with 'mura' (village). 'Topia' is from the Greek 'topos', which means 'place'. Hence the word 'MuRatopia' was coined to signify a new way of thinking that reflects the information age.

pervasive in all types of product. Computers and communication technology are nothing but symbolic indicators of the information age.

One feature of information is that it can be shared; that is, its original owner can still use it after it is given to other users. Moreover, its reproduction cost is a mere copying cost that is socially negligible. In the face of the rising production costs of original information, shared (or joint) use of information becomes the most efficient practice. Hence, *sharing* constitutes a crucial feature of the information age.

The information age is also regarded as a post-industrial age, where the service (tertiary) sector dominates. To emphasise this feature, the post-industrial economy is sometimes called a 'service' economy (which we prefer to call an 'info-service' economy). In this economy, info-service and service-labour productivity are most effectively attained when workers are self-motivated to work for themselves in self-managed organisations. Hence, *self-management* becomes crucial to enhancing competitiveness and efficiency in the information age. To sum up, sharing and self-management are inherent features of the information age.

Possession as an Ecological Niche

In the industrial age mass-produced goods have to be exclusively owned, accumulated and exchanged. To facilitate the exclusive usage of products, private ownership has to be institutionalised as a legal system. At the same time, as a corollary of private ownership, collective and public ownership are institutionalised.

What type of legal system, then, has to be imposed in the information age in place of ownership? It has to be one that is able to facilitate the workings of the main features of the information age, sharing and self-management. We contend that it is a system of *possession as an ecological niche*.[5] Under such a new legal system, those who join a production unit can automatically possess it jointly and participate in its management as co-workers. Moreover, they can no longer be forced out of their workplaces, as used to be the case under private ownership. Accordingly, such a system of possession makes it possible to provide every co-worker with his or her *ecological niche*.

As the industrial age is transformed into the information age, a transition from ownership to possession will be more apparent. Let us point out some examples. In the USA, 'the ESOP (Employee Stock Ownership Plan) is fast becoming a way of life at many of the nation's best-known companies. An estimated 200 public companies have set up ESOPs during the past two years alone. Overnight, employees typically become their company's single biggest shareholder bloc' (*Business Week* 15 May 1989: 116–17). Although this plan allows such anticapitalistic features as worker participation and profit-sharing, its rationale is to 'move toward the most important goal of all: boosting productivity enough to

---

5 For a more detailed discussion of the concept of possession see ch. 8 of Yamaguchi 1988.

make U.S. companies more competitive in world markets' (ibid.: 116). In short, in order to suit the information age, the capitalist market economy has no choice but to adopt *self-destructive* plans such as ESOP. No one seems to be able to stop this trend as the information revolution progresses.

A second example of a transition from ownership to possession is the Community Land Trust (CLT), which is part of the US Green movement (White 1982).[6] A non-profit corporation acquires land through purchase or donation and then uses the land according to the following principles: 'Neither the CLT nor the leaseholder holds the land itself as a commodity' (p. 19); 'The CLT typically offers use rights only to those who will use the land themselves' (p. 23); 'Leaseholders will never be forced from their homes, or from the land they use' (p. 20); 'The CLT provides the assurance that not only the leaseholders' property (the buildings and improvements which they own) but also the leasehold itself (the right to continue the use of the land) may be passed on to their heirs' (p. 21).

This type of land-management by CLT is consistent with the system of possession that is applied to a piece of privately possessed land. In socialist China, farmers were recently allowed to obtain long-term land leases. This new system of land management in China is also consistent with the system of possession.

As a third example of possession, we can point out a recent trend in UNIX culture in which computer software is shared; that is, it is distributed under the terms of the General Public License provided by the Free Software Foundation.[7] The General Public License is briefly explained as follows:

In essence, the General Public License states that anyone who receives GNU Emacs has the right to give copies of Emacs to others; that anyone who receives Emacs may not place further restrictions on its distribution; and if you distribute any improvements to Emacs, they must be distributed under the same terms as the original program itself. You are allowed to charge for distributing Emacs, so 'free software' isn't necessarily cheap in that sense. However, you cannot restrict anyone's (including your customers') ability to use the program or to give it away. The license was crafted to make sure that GNU Emacs and other programs would remain free . . . It prevents a practice that's unfortunately common in the industry: a vendor finds a good piece of public domain software, improves it in some way, and then makes the improved program proprietary. (Cameron and Rosenblatt 1991: 355–6)

The General Public License thus summarised represents an application of a new legal system of possession to the area of computer software. It is indeed unfortunate that, with an introduction of intellectual property rights, most computer software is commercialised so that it is exchanged in the currently prevailing markets and exclusively used by the buyers, like other goods. In other words, information-age software products are forced to fit into the worn-out

---

6 See Chapter 6 below for a discussion of the Community Land Trust, and Chapter 8 for the US green movement.
7 The best-known software provided by the Free Software Foundation is GNU Emacs, a powerful editor widely used among UNIX community (see Cameron and Rosenblatt 1991). In fact, this book has been edited with GNU Emacs. Another such public domain software package is T$_E$X, a powerful piece of typesetting and text-formatting software, with which this book has been formatted. Hence this book has been produced mostly by free software—an information-age work!

industrial-age framework of the capitalist market system. Without intellectual property rights, pieces of software could be freely distributed and utilised to make someone else better off without sacrificing the well-being of their owners. Thus, a market economy fails to attain Pareto efficiency or Pareto optimality in the case of software transactions. By contrast, distribution of software under the General Public License aims to attain Pareto efficiency. Just as land under the CLT can no longer be the target of investment but is part of our life, so software under the General Public License can be part of our intellectual life in the information age.

On the basis of the legal system of ownership, nation-states have been created with artificial borders, borders that ignore natural ecological boundaries. Through the transformation of ownership to possession as an ecological niche, such artificial borders will gradually disappear and be replaced with ecological boundaries based on nature's vegetation, habitats and biosphere cycles. That is, nation-states will ultimately be replaced by new ecological regions that share not only ecologically knit habitats and vegetation but also traditions and culture. We call such a region an 'eco-share' region.

The Economy

The industrial age, which is founded on mechanistic technology and private ownership, produced five separations to facilitate mass production of goods and services: consumers from producers, employees from employers, savers from investors, landowners from tenants, and man from nature. Four of these separations, in turn, generated corresponding markets in which goods, services, capital and land are exchanged: the commodity market, the labour market, the financial capital market, and the housing and real-estate market. Unfortunately, the separation of man from nature failed to create a market.

As to the workings of a market economy in the industrial age, three mutually antagonistic economic schools have emerged: the Walrasian (neoclassical), the Keynesian and the Marxian. The Walrasian school believes in a self-adjusting market mechanism and Pareto-efficient allocation of resources at the market equilibrium. Thus it plays a role as a conservative proponent of the capitalist market economy. The Keynesian school disproves the notion of a fully functioning market mechanism, but believes that the imperfect market mechanism can be supplemented by purposive government policies. Hence, it supports a liberal reformist vision of mixed welfare economy. In contrast, the Marxian school argues that the capitalist economy is an anarchic system that is cyclically hit by economic crises, and that it is also a system for the exploitation of workers by capitalists. Thus it advocates socialism as the best system to solve the problems caused by a capitalist economic system.[8]

---

[8] Following the sudden collapse of USSR in summer 1991, most Marxian economists, losing their faith in Marxian theory, no longer advocate socialism openly. However, its critical analysis of the capitalist economy as a system of exploitation still holds theoretically.

In the information age, mass-production of goods is replaced with customised production of info-goods, info-services and knowledge. It is apparent that the traditional market system can no longer handle these information-age products efficiently. Therefore, the role of the market as a mere place of exchange under uncertainty has to be altered to meet the new requirement of these information-related types of products and technology. What economic system, then, should be created in place of the traditional market? The tired framework of traditional economics, whether it be Walrasian, Keynesian, or Marxian, cannot answer the question properly.

When the system of possession is institutionalised in the information age, the five separations of the industrial age will tend towards reunification. And five new actors will eventually emerge on the main stage of the information age. They are prosumer, co-worker, self-financer, inhabitant and villager. They will begin to act in a networking theatre rather than in a traditional market. Their activities will be beyond the market. The interplays of these five new actors—with the benefits of others in mind—will ultimately create a new MuRatopian economy with the following three features:

Information-sharing networks. As telecommunication networking systems expand on a global scale, prosumers (producers + consumers) and co-workers will begin to communicate with one another for their mutual benefit through network communication systems. A Strategic Information System (SIS) will directly unify producers and consumers through computer and communication networks by circumventing traditional market mechanisms. For instance, organic farmers will be directly networked with consumers so that they can ship their safe farm products straight to them. In this way we will be able to appropriate networking media for the direct exchange and distribution of our products without indirect consultation with specialists through the marketplace, just as villagers once used to exchange their products with each other and consult with one another, irrespective of their professional backgrounds. In this way, producers, consumers, scientists and specialists—in short, people as a whole—will be able to *know each other* globally and locally, as if they were living in a global village.

Self-management and participatory democracy. Co-workers and self-financers will be self-motivated to start managing their own production unit and its financial activities as traditional corporate organisations based around a top-down hierarchy gradually lose their competitiveness owing to their inefficiencies in the information age. Self-management and participatory democracy in corporations will also be adopted in communities as the most efficient way of decision-making, just as villagers used to gather to make decisions directly on their big projects. Decision-making powers will be regained by people and they will once again be in a position to *help each other*.

Sustainable development. Under the new legal system of possession, new global

Table 5.5. A new-thinking paradigm in economics

	Industrial age	Information age
Technology	*Mechanistic technology*: mass production of goods and services; pollutants as by-products	*Mechatronic technology*: customised and recycling-oriented production of info-goods, info-services and information (knowledge)
Institution	*Ownership*: private, public and collective → nation-states	*Possession*: as an ecological niche → eco-share regions
Mode of production	*Markets by separations*: consumer from producer employee from employer saver from investor land-owner from tenant man from nature	*Beyond markets—reunification*: prosumer co-worker self-manager inhabitant villager
Economy	capitalist market economy welfare mixed economy socialist planned economy	*MuRatopian economy*: information-sharing network self-management and participatory democracy sustainable development

Source: Yamaguchi and Niwa 1994: 84.

villagers and community inhabitants will come to view their living area as essential property for their own life and become more aware of the sustainability of their community environment, simply because they are no longer faced with the possibility of being forced out of their living niche, which is a threat under private and collective ownership. In this way, new global villagers in big cities, towns and communities will make efforts to *live sustainably with nature*, as traditional villagers used to do.

Will the MuRatopian economy work, then? The MuRatopian economy in the information age can be shown to be able to overcome many problems of the capitalist market economy, including unemployment, economic disequilibria and unfair income distribution. Hence, the MuRatopian economy is a system superior to the capitalist market economy.[9] Moreover, economic incentives and efficiency are also attained in self-managing and information-sharing Mu-Ratopian organisations. Obviously, freedom and participatory democracy are guaranteed to everybody as a fundamental requirement for the economy to work. Thus the MuRatopian economy can also be claimed to be superior to a

---

[9] See Yamaguchi 1988 for a detailed analysis.

socialist planned economy. In short, we propose it to be the most suitable economic system for the information age.

5.4 MuRatopia as Self-Similar Global Villages

In a few words, the MuRatopian economy is a global village economy in the information age. Why must an information-age economy be a global village economy? Many people may have negative images of villages as poor, isolated and less developed. It is true that most villages in the pre-industrial age were destined to exist under such miserable situations, mainly because villagers could not at that time attain and apply scientific knowledge for a better life. Without knowledge, however, they had attained wonderful wisdom that enabled them to live in severe surroundings. That is to say, village people had to (1) know each other, (2) help each other with big projects, such as the rice harvest and the construction of houses, and (3) live sustainably with nature. These are three fundamental kinds of wisdom with which villagers were born to live. It is understandable that most influential religions were created during these village-life days. The pre-industrial age is often called the 'agricultural' age. However, in this context it would be more appropriate to call it the 'wisdom' age.

The industrial age, which began to emerge with the Industrial Revolution in the middle of the eighteenth century, has been the one to apply scientific knowledge for a better life. In this sense, it may be called the 'knowledge' age. It is unfortunate that, contrary to high expectations, this has also been the age that destroyed the wisdom that villagers had attained in the wisdom age. As industrialisation has advanced in the knowledge age, the following tendencies have become dominant.

- Specialists have become highly respected and have begun to form their own professional associations and live more comfortably within their own small worlds. Accordingly, the opportunity to know others outside these associations has been reduced and less encouraged. Moreover, it is believed that a society consisting entirely of specialists works more efficiently because those specialists are able to identify problems relevant to their professions and thus solve them better than the experienced and older people in villages. For instance, nuclear technology and its applications have been put almost entirely under the control of nuclear scientists in industrial-age administrative institutions.
- Since the publication of *The Wealth of Nations* by Adam Smith in 1776, each individual has been encouraged to pursue his or her own self-interest in the marketplace without helping others, and it is believed that a market economy full of these pursuers of self-interest brings about a harmony, that is, an equilibrium, thanks to God's *invisible hand*, and the optimum allocation of resources. Accordingly, the traditional co-operation in big projects is not required, except for such national projects as wars. For instance,

co-operation for rice-harvesting in villages has been replaced by profit-
motivated corporate business.

* Nature is no longer a place in which we live in harmony. Instead it is
  regarded primarily as a supplier of free natural resources to meet our endless
  greedy desires and free sinks for industrial and consumer waste. Moreover,
  time-consuming organic farming has been replaced with easier, modern
  farming techniques that depend heavily on the use of chemical fertilisers and
  hazardous pesticides. Under such myopic profit motivation, the wisdom of
  sustainability, cultivated for centuries in the wisdom age, is easily forgotten
  or discarded. At this price, urban dwellers now live an affluent life
  materially, but in a mentally poorer state in fear of the total ecological
  catastrophes they and future generations might have to face.

In this way the industrial age can be said to be the age of scientific knowledge
that failed to retain the wisdom that villagers had cultivated for centuries. The
information age could be the age to unify wisdom and knowledge. Fortunately,
they are no longer regarded as separate entities, a development which is due in
part to the so-called consciousness–cognitive revolution in the 1960s.[10] For instance, through this revolution, the integration of religion and science within a
single consistent worldview has been successfully attempted (Sperry 1991: 237).
We have to restore the lost wisdom of villagers and at the same time apply
advanced scientific knowledge for a better life in a harmonious and co-operative
way. Hence, in this context, the information age may be called the 'synthesis
age'.

I have proposed above that the MuRatopian economy is the most appropriate
system to replace the market economy in the information age. Let me now show
how the MuRatopian economy is indeed the system to advance the synthesis of
wisdom and knowledge. The MuRatopian economy can be summarised as
having three features: information-sharing networks, self-management and
participatory democracy, and sustainable development. As the MuRatopian
economy advances in the information age, these three features will become
dominant. Close examination reveals that these three features correspond to the
three kinds of wisdom of villagers mentioned above: to know each other, to help
each other, and to live sustainably with nature.

In this way, these three kinds of wisdom will be wholly integrated into the
MuRatopian—global village—economy. Any group of people can be global
villagers or MuRatopians by constructing their own village economy that
respects these three precepts anywhere—in a country, in a metropolitan area, in
a town or in a small community. MuRatopia thus formed in the information age
becomes an *inseparable* global village consisting of self-similar country villages,
metro villages, town villages and communal villages. In other words, whatever
region we look closely at we can always find a self-similar global village. A whole
MuRatopian economy consisting of its self-similar MuRatopian economies

---

10 See the excellent analysis of this revolution by Roger Sperry in Chapter 2 of this book.

would be highly sustainable and stable. This economy is what advanced information technology offers us as the most suitable economic system in the information age of the twenty-first century. In conclusion, we need no longer look for sustainable development in a market economy, but in the construction of a MuRatopian and global village economy for the next century.

References and Further Reading

Business Week (15 May 1989). 'ESOPs: Are They Good for You?', pp. 116–23.

Cameron, Debra and Rosenblatt, Bill (1991). *Learning GNU Emacs*, Sebastopol, Calif.: O'Reilly and Associates.

Lovelock, J. E. (1988). *The Ages of Gaia: A Biography of Our Living Earth*, New York: Bantam Books.

Meadows, Donella H., Meadows, Dennis L. and Randers, Jorgen (1992). *Beyond the Limits*, Post Mills, Vt.: Chelsea Green Publishing.

Sperry, Roger W. (1991). 'Search for Beliefs to Live by Consistent with Science', *Zygon* 26(2): pp. 237–58.

White, Kirby (ed.) (1982). *The Community Land Trust Handbook, by the Institute for Community Economics*, Emmaus, Pa.: Rodale Press.

World Commission on Environment and Development (1987). *Our Common Future*, Oxford: Oxford University Press.

Yamaguchi, Kaoru (1988). *Beyond Walras, Keynes and Marx: Synthesis in Economic Theory toward a New Social Design*, New York: Peter Lang.

——(1990). 'Fundamentals of a New Economic Paradigm in the Information Age', *FUTURES* 22(10): pp. 1023–36.

——(1991). 'New Thinking on the Economic Development of Islands in the Information Age', pp. 201–13 (chapter 10) in *Islands' Culture and Development*, Paris: UNESCO, Division of Studies and Programming (BPE/BP).

——and Niwa, Hiroyuki (1994). 'New Thinking on Japanese Community Development in the Information Age', *Technological Forecasting and Social Change* 45(1–XX): pp. 79–92.

6   The Community Land Trust Model

CHUCK MATTHEI AND MICHAEL LAFONTAINE

6.1 Structure and Method

Confronted with the combined problems of growing needs and limited public and charitable resources, conventional housing programmes are inadequate to meet the challenge in the USA. Publicly owned housing, while important, only provides limited opportunities to residents, and meets considerable social and political 'resistance' in many communities; but public subsidy of private rented housing perpetuates the patterns of absentee ownership and capital drain from low-income communities. Even subsidised homeownership ultimately results in a loss of affordability and a loss of subsidies, when the home is resold on the open market.

Many community development practitioners in the USA have recognised the need for another approach. The Community Land Trust (CLT) model was designed to be this *third path*, balancing the legitimate interests of individuals with the interests of the community as a whole. Neither *public* nor *private* in the traditional sense, the CLT is a combination of the best features of both.

The CLT model was conceived in 1967, drawing on experiences in India, Israel, Sweden and other countries, as well as the USA, and on the practices of Native Americans and other traditional peoples. Over the next decade, around twenty CLT experiments were undertaken across the country, initially in rural areas and later in urban communities also. However, the housing crisis of the 1980s brought dramatic growth in the CLT movement: there are now 113 CLTs in thirty-one states, with expanding production and widening community participation and institutional support. Total housing units within CLTs exceed 3,500. CLTs are widely distributed: approximately a third are in urban areas, two-fifths in towns and small cities and a quarter in rural areas.

A Community Land Trust is a democratically structured, community-based, non-profit corporation. Membership is typically open to anyone in the community who shares the CLT's philosophy and purposes. The board of directors is usually structured so that one-third of the directors are chosen by the general membership; one-third are chosen by the residents of CLT properties; and one-third are chosen because of the particular skills, experiences and broader perspectives they bring to the organisation. (Several CLTs are composed of neighbourhood associations and NGOs,[1] with individuals participating through

---

[1] Non-governmental organisations. The term is commonly used in the international context as 'non-profit organisations' is used in the USA.

their affiliation with a member organisation. These boards still include residents of CLT properties and public-interest representatives, along with the representatives of member organisations.)

CLTs acquire land, to be held in perpetuity and removed from the speculative market. After a planning process to determine the most appropriate use, land is made available to individual households, co-operatives and other organisations through long-term (usually lifetime) leases that can be transferred to the lessees' heirs. Lessees pay a lease fee, and they must use the land themselves; they cannot become absentee landlords.

CLTs typically separate the ownership of land and buildings. Although lessees do not own the land they use, they may own their buildings, as individuals or members of co-operative associations. However, the CLT retains the option to purchase the improvement (should the owner decide to sell), for the amount of the owner's investment of capital and labour, adjusted for inflation and depreciation.

In this way, CLTs recognise both individual and community interests, establishing a public–private partnership that is both economic and social in character. For individuals, CLTs provide the essential benefits of homeownership:

- lifetime security of tenure;
- fair equity for their investment, and an incentive to improve the property; and
- a legacy for their descendants.

At the same time, the parallel rights and responsibilities of the community are acknowledged:

- equal opportunity, with access fairly available to as many community members as possible;
- community participation in planning, with democratic control over those long-term development decisions that affect the entire community as it evolves over time; and
- an economic base for public benefit, established by preserving the *social appreciation* in property value.

CLTs distinguish between that portion of property value that is created by individual owners and that portion created by community efforts, public investment in infrastructure and services, and larger economic forces. Homeowners are guaranteed a fair equity for their personal investment, and buyers can purchase the home for a fair price (free of the effects of speculation). The community itself gains economic strength through lease fees and the appreciation in land value.

The CLT is a very flexible model. It can be applied in large cities, small towns or rural areas. It can acquire land for residences, commercial facilities, agriculture, social services or any other appropriate use, and the properties need not be contiguous. It can provide any combination of housing opportunities: single-family ownership, co-operatives, condominiums, and even rented housing where it is most appropriate to individual needs (with the CLT owning and managing the buildings, or leasing land to a non-profit rented-housing organisation).

The CLT can work in partnership with other community development organisations. Indeed, many CLTs have been established by such NGOs to serve as the *common ground* linking the various social and economic units in the community.

6.2 Support from Public and Private Sectors

The CLT's ability to reduce community dependence on outside financial assistance makes it an especially effective and efficient vehicle for both public and private investment, whether grants or loans. In contrast to conventional programmes, funds directed to CLTs are retained and reinvested within the community, for repeated use by multiple generations of residents.

Early CLTs originated with NGOs in low-income communities, without government support. In recent years, however, a growing number of city and state governments have been attracted by the model's unique combination of features. In some cases, CLTs have been able to transcend common political stereotypes and mobilise a broad spectrum of supporters. For conservatives, CLTs represent cost-effectiveness, individual homeownership and private sector initiative; for liberals, CLTs strike at the roots of poverty by acting to prevent absentee ownership, monopolisation and speculation.

There are now significant examples of support for CLTs at all levels of government:

- Burlington, Vermont, was the first city government to directly encourage and facilitate CLT development. The Burlington CLT received a $200,000 seed grant for initial operations and land acquisition, a $1 million investment from the public employees' pension fund, and land donations from a private development through the city's *linkage* programme (in which the city grants permits to private developers in exchange for a set-aside of low-income units, or a contribution of land or money to an NGO).
- After a four-year community organising and planning effort by the Dudley Street Neighborhood Initiative, the City of Boston agreed that it would transfer all publicly held (tax-default) properties in the Central Roxbury area to a CLT. Moreover, the city agreed to delegate its powers of eminent domain, to allow the CLT to acquire all vacant privately-owned lots.
- Responding to a proposal put forward by a coalition of community development, social service, agricultural and conservation groups, the State of Vermont established the Vermont Housing and Conservation Trust Fund. Capitalised with more than $30 million in legislative appropriations, and revenue from a statewide property transfer tax, the fund makes loans and grants to CLTs for the development of permanently affordable housing, and to conservation trusts for preservation of family farms and natural areas.

- The Covenant CLT, in rural Maine, is guiding the formation of new CLTs throughout the state. Together, these CLTs lobbied for a $4.5 million CLT development fund, which was approved by voters in a statewide referendum. Covenant CLT is affiliated with HOME Coop, a multifaceted organisation of low-income people, engaged in craft production and marketing, daycare and adult education, emergency shelter and refugee aid, and other activities. HOME's sawmill and shingle mill produce low-cost building materials from timber collected on CLT land, and jobs for local people.
- During the UN International Year of Shelter, the federal Department of Housing and Urban Development selected two CLTs—the Burlington CLT and Common Ground Community Economic Development Corporation of Dallas, Texas—for special recognition. More recently, the federal Farmers Home Administration has agreed to open its housing loan programmes to CLTs.

From the outset, contributions—of facilities, labour and money—have come from local churches and charitable institutions. They wanted to respond practically to their communities' needs, and felt a philosophical affinity with CLTs. As the CLT movement has grown, so has this support, and it has been formalised in new policies and programmes:

- The Community Land Coop of Cincinnati, a CLT in southern Ohio, was organised by neighbourhood churches of many denominations. Most of the CLT's acquisition and development financing has come through loans from religious organisations.
- On New York's Lower East Side, Catholic parishes organised low-income people into co-operatives. They began the rehabilitation of nearly 200 units of vacant city-owned housing, and eventually negotiated transfer of title. The homesteaders were concerned that future residents might convert these limited-equity units to market-rate ones for personal gain to the loss of affordable housing stock in the community. They formed the RAIN CLT to hold the land under all of their buildings, adding another layer of protection by requiring in the leases that the co-operatives remain limited equity.
- The Catholic religious orders in the northeast region of the USA have established a pooled investment programme for low-income housing, and designated CLTs as the preferred model of development. The national Episcopal Church (Anglican) and some dioceses have established Ministries of Economic Justice and Community Investment; they, too, have made CLTs a priority for investment.

Most of the financing for early CLT projects came from socially concerned investors, directly and through Community Loan Funds (organised by community development practitioners and investors, working together). Charitable foundations and individuals have also been important lenders and donors, along with some business corporations.

At first, conventional financial institutions were wary of lending because they were unfamiliar with homeownership on leased land and in many cases reluctant to lend in low-income communities. Over time, however, many banks and housing-finance agencies have made loans to CLTs, and to homeowners with CLT leases. Some lenders have acted alone; others have formed consortia with other banks, jointly participating in large loan packages. Increasingly, banks have come to see the CLT's role as counsellor and service-provider to individual families—and its commitment to retaining land and affordable housing for the community—as providing additional security to their loans.

6.3 Prospects for the CLT Movement

The CLT movement in the USA is still relatively young and small. But although the model has not yet been proven by the test of time, the CLT movement is dynamic and fast growing.

As the CLTs begin to mature, new challenges arise. Many of them are common to all community development organisations. There is the need to acquire more professional skills, without becoming overly *professionalised* and losing touch with the community; the need to meet growing organisational and project budgets, without becoming unduly dependent or allowing the sources of financing to alter the character of the organisation; and the challenge of balancing the demands of management and development with equally (if not more) important public education, community organising, human services and membership participation.

More important than the CLT model itself are the principles and practices inherent in it. Thanks to the examples of CLTs and the efforts of practitioners, these principles are now being incorporated into community development strategies and public policies in many different ways, and in many different places. 'Permanent affordability', a concept rarely articulated even a decade ago, is now one of the central themes of housing debate and policy formulation across the USA.

Despite the challenges already faced and those that still lie ahead, CLTs today are providing significant benefits to their communities, and serving as credible models for policy advocates. CLTs have an important role to play in the USA—and perhaps elsewhere—because of their unique ability to fulfil the three principal requirements for an effective housing programme in these times:

(1) access: to meet *immediate* needs for decent, affordable housing, and offer a range of appropriate housing options;

(2) retention: to meet *future* needs, by preserving the value of public investment and charitable subsidies and ensuring a supply of permanently affordable housing; and

(3) an economic base: to provide an economic foundation for the advancement of individuals and the security and self-determination of communities.

Further Reading

White, Kirby (ed.) (1982). *The Community Land Trust Handbook, by The Institute For Community Economics*, Emmaus, Pa.: Rodale Press.

7   Cultural Paradigm Shift Towards Sustainability

KAZUO MIZUTA

I would like to open my discussion with observations on the situations human-kind has to face and tackle.

7.1 Trends: Politicoeconomic Changes

The Open Moment

Democracy is the prize won by the people in Eastern European countries. In Hungary, the quest to get more decision-making power into the hands of the people started in the 1940s, with the creation of socialist structures. The Hungarian uprising of 23 October 1956 may have been a more significant event. Changing situations resulted in the realisation of democratic elections in March 1989. Yet the search for new orders continues. As soon as the people got the power to decide things for themselves, new struggles for better decisions emerged. The planned economy had to be replaced with free-market economy—but, how and how free, when and where? Technology, finance, regulations—all these elements of the old infrastructure hindered the new planners. It was easy to change the name of the university from Karl Marx University to Budapest University and throw Marxist books out of the windows. To prepare the people for the new historical situation, however, adult education has become very important. Various seminars are being offered at *private* institutions like *Kulturinnov* (the Enterprise for Cultural Innovation and Manager Training) in Budapest.

The unification of West and East Germany on 3 October 1990 highlighted the overwhelming surge towards freedom. Within six months, critics were voicing their anxiety for the future of the unification. Professor John Meersheimer of the University of Chicago expressed concern over the optimism that had spread in the world. The Cold War is over, finally promising lasting peace in Europe; but as soon as the old order was overthrown more turbulence ensued because of the imbalance of power, and the spread of nuclear power and ethnic conflict.

China's Open Policies

China is pursuing open policies on a limited scale. This a good example of the Beijing government trying to participate in the world economy. It gave top priority to importing new advanced technology, which includes three major automobile plants—at Shanghai (Volkswagen), Zhangchun (Audi) and Wuhan

(Citroen)—and three smaller plants—at Beijing (Jeep Coop), Guangzhou (Peugeot) and Tianjin (Small Beagle Daihatsu).

Is China a large market for cars? Small cars have a good chance but, at the present level of income, it takes about ten years to save up the 28,000 yuan needed to buy a small car (*Yomiurishinbun*, 17 April 1991).

What are the people of the advanced countries supposed to make of the changes that are taking place in Eastern Europe, the former Soviet Union and China? The changes are asking us to find the best answer for privatisation, deregulation, adult education, the restructuring of market shares, production and distribution, and more new technologies.

Carbon Emissions

'The major sources of CO_2 are the cars, factories and power plants of the industrial countries and the burning of tropical forests in the less developed world' (*Time*, 2 January 1989). How can a Western (or Oriental) environmentalist convince Hungarians who drive a Travant (an old East German car) to stop because it is polluting the air? The air in downtown Budapest is almost suffocating for visitors, but how can outsiders to that culture say anything to those who have acquired their car after an unimaginable effort? Or should we think, why not tell them anyway—it may work or it may not? The answer can be political, in the sense that politicians can campaign to clean the air; it can be economic, in the sense that financial agents can offer better financial measures. It also requires new technology to develop new vehicles, a clean mass-transportation system, such as street cars or monorail, and electric or natural-gas cars.

Clean-Air Measures

To save fossil fuels and keep the earth from turning into an overheated greenhouse requires more new technologies. At the beginning of the 1990s, Nissan (1991) identified the following development programmes:

- a better engine, to reduce CO_2 and thus prevent the greenhouse effect on the Earth
- a ceramic gas-turbine engine
- methanol as an alternative energy source
- measures to protect the ozone layer
- the reduction of chlorofluorocarbon gases[1]

---

[1] Automobile exhaust gases include such chemical compounds as Carbon Monoxide, CH, NO_x and Pb compounds. Among these chemical compounds, NO_x has been targeted for the reduction. But over the period 1985–91 the air pollution caused by NO_x in such major European cities as Dunkirk, Amsterdam and London has actually worsened, proving that the preventive measures are showing no effect (Ministry of the Environment 1995: 282–3).

Chlorofluorocarbons (CFCs for short) are regarded as the cause of the greenhouse effect. CFCs were believed to be harmless to human beings, but 'there is only one problem. When they escape into the atmosphere, most CFCs are murder on the environment. Each CFC molecule is 20,000 times as

- projects to clean exhaust gas
- recycling
- preventive measures against acid rain
- devices to minimise the emission of sulphur

Natural-gas cars are now receiving more attention. The Tokyo Gas Company is going to organise a project team to begin work on natural-gas cars. According to the Japan Gas Association, the number of natural-gas cars in use in May 1991 was 270,000 in Italy, 30,000 in the USA, 20,000 in the former Soviet Union, with a total of around 600,000 throughout the world. In Japan, less than 30 natural-gas cars were in use. The Tokyo Gas Company used about 20 cars, which the company planned to increase to 200 by 1995. The Ministry of Industry and the Ministry of Transportation are to look into legal preparation for operating natural-gas cars.

The movement towards gas cars was initiated by environmental issues and the new clean-atmosphere law enacted by the USA. According to the new law, auto-manufactures in the state of California had to produce a certain number of clean-emission cars from 1996 onwards. These include electric cars, methanol cars and natural-gas cars. In May 1991 there were 850 electric cars in use and 140 methanol cars (*Yomiurishinbun*, 19 May 1991).

Acid Rain

Acid rain results from carbon emissions (see Table 7.1). It has destroyed great areas of forest in the advanced countries of Europe. In the Netherlands, for example, 55 per cent of forested areas were damaged by acid rain, pollution and other causes in 1986 (*Time*, 2 January 1989). What about the tropical rain forests? Every autumn, vast areas of rainforest in the Amazon are slashed and burned for crops and livestock. According to *Time* (18 September 1989) an estimated 12,350 sq.mi. of Brazilian rain forest—an area larger than Belgium—were reduced to ashes in 1980. Clearing land for crops and livestock may sound harmless, but damage to the forests comes from the levelling of trees by loggers,

---

efficient at trapping heat as is a molecule of CO_2. So CFCs increase the greenhouse effect far out of proportion to their concentration in the air. A more immediate concern is that the chlorine released when CFC molecules break up destroys ozone molecules. The ozone layer, located in the stratosphere, between 10 and 30 miles up, is vital to the well being of plants and animals. Ozone molecules, which consist of three oxygen atoms, absorb most of the ultraviolet radiation that comes from the sun. And ultraviolet is extremely dangerous to life on earth' (*Time*, 2 January 1989).

CFCs are cheap to manufacture and they come in many different products. They have been used as coolants in refrigerators and air-conditioners, as cleaning gases and desiccants for precision machinery and electronic parts, in polyurethane foam material, as propellant gases for sprays and aerosol products, and so on. These products have become an integral part of our lifestyles. Are we now willing to keep piling up plastic foam containers in the kitchen wastebasket?

In view of the fact that chlorofluorocarbons are connected with air pollution, the Helsinki Protocol of May 1989 planned for zero production of CFCs by the end of this century. In April 1992, Nissan declared that it was ceasing the use of CFC11 for foaming and CFC113 for cleaning. But when many car dealers scrap cars they find it too expensive to keep CFCs contained and let them go into the air.

Table 7.1. Net carbon emissions from tropical deforestation, 1980 (mn. tons)

Brazil	336	Laos	95	Ecuador	40
Indonesia	192	Nigeria	60	Vietnam	36
Columbia	123	Philippines	57	Zaire	35
Ivory Coast	101	Burma	51	Mexico	33
Thailand	95	Peru	45	India	33
				Total	1,659

Source: *Time*, 2 January 1989.

flooding caused by dams and poisoning caused by gold-miners, the article declared.

To Brazilians, the cries to protect the Amazon sound like the threats of advanced industrial countries towards developing countries. Conflicts within the nation involve settlers, developers, politicians, conservation groups, Indian tribes and rubber-trappers. The forests are the source of food for the local people. Nevertheless, they offer more than foodstuff; they represent a great stock of evolutionary achievement and their destruction may cause significant climatic disorder.

Deadly Meltdown

No one would deny that we enjoy countless benefits brought to us by science and technology. But it is important to realise that technologies are value-free, too. Giant scientific works can kill us. The Three Mile Island and Chernobyl nuclear power plants exploded, leaving more distrust in advanced technologies and a worsened environment not only for the local people but also for the wider population. There are about 375 commercial nuclear power plants in operation world-wide according to a special report in *Time* magazine. The first plant, at Obninsk in the former Soviet Union, went on-line in 1954. Japan has thirty-two reactors operating and ten on order but not yet operating; France has forty-four reactors operating and seventeen on order; and Germany has twenty reactors operating and five on order.

'In Japan, which draws 26% of its electric power from atomic reactors and has virtually no natural energy sources, the future of nuclear use seems secure,' reported *Time* (12 May 1986). But the people who suffered from the devastating power of the Hiroshima and Nagasaki atomic bombs never stop doubting the security of the atomic power plants. And right after the Chernobyl disaster, the government of Yasuhiro Nakasone emphasised the safety of Japanese plants. Although each successive government has reiterated the safety of Japanese generators, there are very strong feelings against nuclear power plants among the people. For one thing, no one can deny the fact that nuclear generators can go wrong and cause serious damage to the people and environment. These are the reported nuclear mishaps:

- 12 December 1952, Chalk River, Canada
- 7 October 1957, Liverpool, England
- 3 January 1961, Idaho Falls, USA
- 22 March 1975, Decatur, Alaska, USA
- 28 March 1979, Three Mile Island, USA
- 8 March 1981, Tsuruga, Japan
- 28 April 1986, Chernobyl, former Soviet Union
- 4 January 1989, Kerr-McGee Corp., Gore, Oklahoma, USA

Another reason why people are dubious of nuclear power plants is that the public, especially the residents of the area where a new plant will be built, know that they are the last to be asked for their consent to the plan.

The lack of natural resources in Japan, however, forces the decision-makers to come up with practical measures to supply energy—of which, more below.

To the Moon and back

On 20 July 1969, the impact of man walking on the moon made it easier than ever for even an ordinary person to realise that the Earth is really a planet that revolves around the Sun. The Earth floated in the sea of darkness, shining blue, while astronaut Russell L. Schweickart (Apollo 9, 3 March 1969) said, 'It was unbelievably beautiful . . . I flew around the Earth about 4000km/hour and I realised that I was enjoying the beautiful moments as the representative of mankind.' To his eyes, it was just a beautiful star where there were no language barriers, no conflicts whatsoever. It was a moment of truth to sense that it was his Mother Earth. The excitement of opening up the new frontier for humankind was shattered when the Challenger shuttle burst into flames after 73 seconds in flight on 28 January 1986.

What do such high-technology accidents suggest? Don't they caution us to be very, very careful?

More Mouths to Feed

According to the UN *World Population Report 1991*, the world population in 1989 was 5.2 billion, and increasing at a rate of 90 million a year. By the year 2025, it will have reached 8.5 billion. And the report estimates that it will be 10 billion by the year 2050 (see Tables 7.2 and 7.3).

At the moment, 60 per cent of the world's population is concentrated in Asia. China alone holds a staggering 1.1 billion. In Africa, a birth rate of 5 to 6 children per woman will continue. More children are dying not from starvation, but from undernourishment. In underdeveloped or developing countries 46,000 children a day, or 14 million a year, were dying from common colds or diarrhoea caused

Table 7.2. The natural increase of population

	Year	Birth rate	Death rate	Natural increase
Japan	1988	10.8	6.6	4.3
USA	1988	15.9	8.8	7.1
USSR	1987	19.8	9.9	9.9
China*a*	1985–90	20.5	6.7	13.8
India*a*	1987	32.0	10.8	21.2

a UN estimate

Sources: UN *Population and Vital Statistics Report*; for Japan, the *Population Report* of the Ministry of Health and Welfare.

Table 7.3. Changes in world population

	1950	1960	1970	1980	1989
Population (mn.)					
Asia	1,366	1,666	2,095	2,591	3,052
Africa	222	278	357	476	628
Europe	392	425	459	484	497
America	331	415	510	614	713
North and Central	220	269	320	374	422
South	111	147	191	240	291
Oceania	13	16	19	23	26
Soviet	180	214	242	265	286
Total	2,504	3,014	3,683	4,453	5,201
Percentage of total population					
Asia	(54.5)	(55.3)	(56.9)	(58.1)	(58.6)
Africa	(8.9)	(9.2)	(9.7)	(10.7)	(12.1)
Europe	(15.7)	(14.1)	(12.5)	(10.9)	(9.6)
America	(13.2)	(13.8)	(13.8)	(13.8)	(13.7)
North and Central	(8.8)	(8.9)	(8.6)	(8.4)	(8.1)
South	(4.4)	(4.9)	(5.2)	(5.4)	(5.6)
Oceania	(0.5)	(0.5)	(0.5)	(0.5)	(0.5)
Soviet	(7.2)	(7.1)	(6.6)	(6.0)	(5.5)

by chronic undernourishment. Those at UNICEF involved in saving these children call the situation a 'quiet emergency'.

In view of these facts, it is not difficult to evaluate the Chinese policy of one child per family, although whether a married woman wants to have children or not may be a personal matter.

7.2 Some Prospects

A Rosy Scenario for the Year 2010?

The Japanese Ministry of Natural Resources and Energy recently published its report on energy and its consumption (see the Editorial in *Yomiurishinbun*, 27 October 1989). The report estimates that mean GNP growth up to the year 2000 will be 4 per cent; after that it will gradually decline to 3 per cent. The price of a barrel of oil will be at the US$30 level until the year 2000, and rise to US$45 in the year 2010. The demand for energy in 2010, however, will be 1.4 times more than in 1989. How should Japan cope with this?

The report assumes four rather radical situations. One of the most interesting cases is that in which no nuclear power plants are built. In this case, the Japanese economy will depend more on oil and natural gas. Carbon dioxide will increase sharply, by about 1.4 times, which Japan should try to avoid by all means. Today, Japan uses oil and coal to supply three-quarters of its energy. Planners realise they cannot depend on fossil fuel. On the other hand, if Japan uses only nuclear power plants to meet its energy needs and to try to keep to the present level of carbon dioxide emissions, it will need to build seventy more nuclear power plants. Now, it is impossible to do so; there is not enough space or locations for them. The best choice, then, is to supply the necessary energy from mixed re-sources, including oil, coal, natural gas and nuclear power, if Japan wants to maintain economic growth and avoid a worsening environment.

An Insight: Norman Macrae's Prediction

There is a growing awareness among learned men that the centre of world inter-est is shifting from the Atlantic basin to the Pacific basin, and that within two generations a new Pacific community will emerge. Telecommunications and mass air-transportation systems have made the world smaller and smaller; the remarkable economic development that has taken place in Western Europe, the USA and Japan over the past several generations is now happening in Pacific basin countries such as Korea, Taiwan and Singapore. Big business and millions of travellers are seeing what appears to be a borderless world. Some decades ago East and West met face to face in the Pacific basin countries, with the result that diverse forms of nations and cultures now coexist. This complex political, economic and cultural mixture will be the start of a new Pacific culture and community.

Among the opinion leaders who have expressed a view on the so-called Pacific Century, Norman Macrae (deputy editor of *The Economist*) published an article called 'The Pacific Century, 1975–2075' in the 4 January 1975 issue of the maga-zine. Summarising his observations on socioeconomic trends in Japan and the rest of the world, he prophesied that we were entering the Pacific Century. As he described it, the British led the first glorious century of 1775–1875, bequeathing to the rest of the world dreams of wealth through modernisation and exploitation. The dream was inherited in the following century, 1875–1975, by the go-getters of the USA. Now, the heritage of the century that began in 1975 rests in the hands of the 'embarrassed heir' of the Far East.

Referring to the hundred-year period from 1975 to 2075 as the Pacific Era, Macrae observed with wry humour that 'most Westerners resent these sorts of projections'. The resentment surely comes from jealousy, for Japan and other dynamic Asian economies are doing well while the West is not. Nevertheless, Macrae maintained his double-edged tone in comments such as this one about engineers who were developing a pollution-free electric engine:

Japan . . . beat the world in developing an automobile that uses no petrol at all. When I told Japanese engineers of my conviction that today's absurdly high oil prices will crash to below yesterday's absurdly low ones when electric automotive techniques become economic, this raised a sad, wild hiss.

Similarly, in another statement, concerning community development, he said, 'Japan's lessons in housing, culture, health care, transportation and crime prevention suggest a whole new pattern of community living although based, awkwardly, at the epicentre of earthquakes.'

Despite his humour, what he claimed, 'Eastward, look, the land is bright', brought the message home.

The Pacific Era may be just ahead of us. However, one immediate concern for Japan is its relations with the USA. Japanese–US relations today cannot remain strong without regard to the European Union and the new dynamic Asian economies. (Yet the concern for the welfare of the people in the Pacific area should not be solely economists'. It is the concern of the man of various views and interests.)

Japanese policies that have encouraged exports, especially to the US market, have resulted in a great trade imbalance. To alleviate this, the two governments have put various measures into practice. Limiting the numbers of cars exported to the USA and liberalising the exchange rate have had some effect. Yet the red ink on the US balance sheet has never stopped growing. Any effects that government leaders expect come only very slowly.

As a possible solution, the USA is suggesting that Japan become its partner. US leaders want Japan to shoulder a bigger burden. This means that Japan should assume more political and military responsibility. Japanese leaders are hesitant to share the military burden, for good reasons. Since there is strong public anti-war sentiment, a military build-up would meet great resistance among the populace. The public holds the spirit of article 9 of the Constitution, which renounces wars, to be an icon that no one dares disgrace. Also, Japan's neighbours, China, Korea and the ASEAN countries, feel threatened by the idea of a military build-up. This leaves Japanese and US leaders on both sides of the Pacific at a loss.

One possible solution Japanese leaders have already implemented is to help the nation-building of the developing countries in East Asia and the Pacific through public aid. If Japanese leaders must curtail their burden-sharing in the area of a military build-up, then possible alternatives must be peaceful in intent; they must promote understanding and friendship throughout the world.

Some world leaders are uncomfortable with the huge economic presence the Japanese have in the world. They cannot understand the Japanese people. They cannot figure out what the Japanese have in mind. To counteract this, the Japanese must go all out to promote understanding. Promoting a better understanding of Japanese culture is a good beginning. At the same time, Japan has to take the initiative to secure for itself a better understanding of the multiracial and multireligious backgrounds of Pacific area countries.

Japanese leaders must realise that it is absolutely necessary for the future leaders of the Pacific community to have an understanding of the multicultural situation. This understanding should be cultivated in a give-and-take context. It cannot be carried out through one-sided exploitation, as has been done in the past. It must be an approach no developed Western power has ever taken.

The level of development in the Pacific basin countries varies; while most of the young executives in many countries are interested in promoting science and technology to help them modernise their home countries, other groups are interested in energy problems, pollution and space sciences, and still others want to promote a cultural renaissance—that is, an emotional awareness of shared interests and common identity as human beings, or 'a sense of world citizenship' in the words of Edwin Reischauer.

For the future, the Pacific people will have to rely on the realisation of this development for a co-prosperous existence. The Pacific culture must promote the rebirth of mankind by considering balance and harmony in modernisation and nation-building. To make it come into being one should be encouraged by the hope that its strength will promote a more lasting peace.

Education in this context would not only emphasise advanced technology that would enrich everyday life; according to Walter Anderson, the author of *To Govern Evolution* (1987), it would also cultivate an awareness of global culture.

7.3 Global Culture: The Third-Culture Person

Internal and External Elements of Culture

Culture is a complex concept. Internal culture can best be seen in a conversational partner. The partner shows his or her interests and tastes, the values that encourage (or discourage) him or her, decision-making processes and so on. The partner may carry many cultural traits that one assumes to know about that person's culture, but at the same time, the partner may not carry them as expected. If the partner is from the USA, he or she is stereotypically quick to decide, quick to say yes or no, quick to throw in a couple of jokes, believes in free will and is individualistic, and in any situation likes making a profit. In terms of food, he or she prefers steaks to fish of any kind. And if the partner is a Japanese businessman (few Japanese women have yet assumed this role), he may appear to be very slow to come to a conclusion and to be almost too polite in speech to come to a point; he may be meticulously quality-conscious and may expect his partner to be very serious when they are engaged in business talks. In terms of food, he prefers fish over anything else.

Values both businessmen hold for their work may include efficiency, productivity, concern for quality and delivery on time. But why do the differences in working practices emerge? The differences come from the very basic notion of a single person: in Japanese culture, an individual is understood in terms of relationships to others, while a single person in US culture is understood as a point of reference, a free agent. The samurai-warrior mentality can explain the Japanese businessman's mentality to a certain extent, but the old cliché falls short when it comes to explaining a Japanese businessman working in cross-cultural situations. He is more liberal and democratic than any samurai you can imagine. The Japanese have had much longer traditions of keeping up their society than their samurai.

In the same manner, it may be dangerous to see US business as an expression of the macho man or the cowboy; bluffs or threats may be a reflection of the refusal to understand the partner's situation. Justice can mean more than just fairness as one party sees it. Aren't politicians and businessmen interpreting situations in their own terms without realising it?

Traditionally, culture has, so far, been represented in such academic disciplines as language, religion, customs and manners, psychology, sociology, economics and politics. The information accumulated this way is a part of culture, static and past-oriented. The third-culture concept approaches the present situation from a multidisciplinary point of view. We do not regard studies of the past as a waste of time, but we take an inclusive point of view. Culture in motion is individual, single and separate, but it does represent a past and a pattern one has been programmed with in one's mother culture.

Let me elaborate on how personality is culturally formed. In the process of growing up, a person inevitably first absorbs the information necessary to grow up in the culture from the initial contract agents, who are mainly family members, and, afterwards, from secondary agents, friends, teachers and the media. What one has internalised from these agents substantiates one's personality, and may be shared by many others who have grown up in the same culture.

I am presenting this notion in the hope that my discussion of culture will be helpful for developing new thinking among businessmen and women when they make deals with partners who are from different cultures. By 'new thinking' I mean an awareness of both one's mother culture and the partner's culture, not just new business ideas. Of course, to know products is probably most important, whether one is selling them or buying them. What I want to discuss here is an awareness beyond business interests.

As I mentioned above, the satirical tone of Macrae's essay would not be appreciated by most Japanese. For the automobile engineers, it was a serious matter for them to develop an economic, marketable electric engine; a Japanese knows this and so would never try to joke about a serious matter in a serious situation. This does not mean, however, that the engineers hate to laugh. They have fun in different situations. This is typical of what I call a 'third-culture situation'.

Some may prefer to call it a 'cross-cultural situation'. Either term suggests a situation where at least two people from different cultural backgrounds meet together to do something together. In my terminology, the first culture is one's mother culture and the second culture is the partner's. The third culture occurs when two or more people from different cultures try something together: business negotiation or social gatherings. While the term 'cross-cultural' emphasises the dynamic aspects of such situations, the term 'third culture' may suggest a more static view. Nevertheless, both terms try to get hold of the implications of the same situation. In the case of a negotiation where government representatives meet and discuss, the situation is predominantly abstract. The majority of delegates are incapable of handling the languages of both parties.

Bureaucrats do not necessarily represent their own interests, while congressmen may represent their personal interests when it comes to re-election. Here, preparing documents to be signed or securing one's re-election is the goal, rather than buying or selling or manufacturing. The private sector's psychological dynamism operates in a different sphere from that of bureaucrats or politicians.

Since I have mainly been engaged in comparative research on US and Japanese cultures, I am going to present you with a situation where an American and a Japanese meet. Mr Jones is a 34-year-old American from Illinois. After high school, he joined the army and did three years of domestic duty. In the service, he injured his left hand and almost lost his thumb and forefinger. He went to a college run by the Adventist Church. His father was against it, but he went there anyway. Upon graduation, he started working for a construction company. A few years later, he went to Hokkaido as a missionary. He worked there for three years before going back to Illinois to train to teach English as a foreign language. He then came back to Japan, this time to the Kansai area. He got a job teaching English at an English-language school in Kyoto.

Professor Nakamura met Mr Jones at the language school when Mr Jones had taught there for two years. They started meeting for lunch once a week. Soon, Mr Jones learned that Professor Nakamura had studied at the University of Michigan and his English was good. Mr Jones was ambitious and was hoping to get a job at a college. The fact that both of them were in their mid-thirties helped them to share their experiences. It did not take too long before they became good friends.

One day Professor Nakamura invited Mr Jones for dinner at his home. With his Japanese friends or associates, Professor Nakamura would have gone out, but he knew that Americans expected to be invited to one's home. Mrs Nakamura, remembering things her family had enjoyed back in Michigan, prepared fried chicken, mashed potatoes, green salad with tomato slices, and she bought a Californian wine especially for their guest. She did not go overboard to prepare the dinner, but she almost did. After all, the dinner was an unusual event for the

Nakamuras. Mr Jones, however, was a vegetarian and a fundamentalist. He touched neither the fried chicken nor wine. He just finished his salad and mashed potatoes.

Professor Nakamura and his wife were polite enough not to show their disappointment at the leftover chicken and wine. Professor Nakamura had heard about Mr Jones's belief, but he had not dreamt that his faith was so firm. The conversation that night went from faith to military service, relationships between men and women, families, teaching English as a foreign language (not to mention learning Japanese as a foreign language), drugs and many other subjects.

A few days later, Mr Jones asked Professor Nakamura whether he was interested in developing a new textbook. The textbook would be designed for language schools and possibly for college students who did not major in English. It would also aim at oral/aural comprehension rather than reading. Professor Nakamura had been nursing the idea of writing a textbook that had stories for reading and fun listening materials. The two teachers agreed to work on the project. Professor Nakamura was to find a publisher.

Mr Jones was very worried about finding a publisher. He knew it was common practice in the USA to take a plan or outline for a book to a publishing firm. Professor Nakamura explained to him that the practice in Japan, too, was very similar. He was expecting to see a salesman from a Tokyo publisher soon, so he promised Mr Jones that he would mention their project. Meanwhile they worked on the book. Mr Jones wrote stories while Professor Nakamura suggested to Mr Jones what kind of stories and exercises he should write. He also pointed out that each lesson should be planned for a ninety-minute class, and that they needed thirty lessons for one academic year in Japan.

Meanwhile, Mr Jones continued to worry about finding a publisher. And even if Professor Nakamura was successful in finding a publisher, he was worried about the royalty. Professor Nakamura explained to Mr Jones that the salesman with whom he had negotiated would take the project back to his Tokyo office to discuss whether they would publish it or not. Such a contract does not exist in the USA. The royalty would be paid six months after the book hit the market. No percentage of the expected royalty would be paid upon agreement to publish.

To make the story short, the publisher liked the manuscript and it sold more than they expected. Naturally, Mr Jones's worry about the royalty turned into a pleasant surprise. From then on Mr Jones truly trusted Professor Nakamura.

Now, the situation I have just described is what I call the third-culture situation or a cross-cultural situation. Culture in motion is our concern. Culture in motion is individual, single and separate, but whatever one is going to deal with represents at the same time a cultural pattern: one should be aware of how one has been programmed in one's mother culture. Yet, culture is more complex.

Language and Cultural Personality

Let me proceed to general elements that compose the dynamism of cultural personality. The structure of one's language is among the most important forces in forming a cultural personality. The following discussion attempts to analyse spoken Japanese in everyday situations. The analysis will look at the structure of language in relation to culture, rather than take a linguistic approach. Four major areas will be covered. The first factor is how the physical environment generates certain expressions. The second factor concerns the natural environment. The third factor considers phonological and syntactical forces. The fourth factor is sociopsychological.

The physical factor. This factor is connected with how our bodies receive sounds. Japanese people perceive vowels and consonants in the left sphere of brain while Caucasians recognise vowels and white noise in the right sphere of the brain. This has been confirmed in experiments by Dr Tunoda Tadanobu (1978).

In other words, Caucasians recognise vowels and white noise in the intellectual part of the brain. In more general terms, a Japanese person perceives the noise of insects in the same part of the brain that recognises language and does intellectual analysis. So, for the average Japanese, intellectual and emotional elements come together when it comes to theorising. The combination of the intellectual and emotional aspects of situations has value in the Japanese way of thinking. By contrast, Caucasians can separate the intellectual and emotional aspects of situations, so they reach a clear-cut, black-and-white, yes-or-no analysis or conclusion much more easily than the Japanese.

These observations by brain researchers sound especially appealing to those who claim the uniqueness of the Japanese. But there is another possible way of looking at the matter. (Remember, some members of the US Congress put a lot of emotion into their judgements on trade issues.) The Japanese-American in the USA can observe and analyse like the Americans around him. The cultural matrix of everyday situations seems to determine the mental blueprints of both. Nevertheless, it is important to recognise that emotional elements play a significant role in judgements.

The natural environment. The natural environment here includes climate (temperature, rainfall and humidity), fauna and flora. Our discussion will explore how environmental elements become part of personality and generate certain words and expressions. One of the most striking characteristics of the Japanese climate is the rainy season, which begins in the middle of June and lasts until the middle of July. In Kyoto, the rainfall in the months of June, July, and August amounts to close to 40 per cent of the total annual rainfall. The average annual rainfall in the period 1941–74 was 1,638 mm. And during these months, the mercury soars to about 95–100 degrees Fahrenheit. A typical rainy day in the month of July can almost suffocate one, with humidity close to 90 per cent at about 100 degrees Fahrenheit. The Discomfort Index goes up to the point of a 'mental meltdown'. In areas where there is no rainy season, such as the western USA, the combination of humidity and heat almost never presents a situation that is unbearable. The freezing wind and temperature in the Japanese winter can be seen as a counter to the rainy season. 'Windy city' is one expression for the physical environment. In monsoon areas, living is adjusted to climate: houses with palm leaves, very light clothes and so on.

The importance of the rainy season in the context of a discussion on culture is that it is related to rice-planting; the weather necessitates certain goods like fans, cool noodles and beer served in halls on top of anti-earthquake buildings.

In regard to rice-planting, farmers usually begin planting rice in this rainy period. A series of ceremonies, from offering grains to local shrines to receiving young rice plants, accompany the planting. Meanwhile, farming people wish for a good crop in the fall. There are naturally a number of related expressions, and an expression such as '*tauematsuri*' (rice-planting ceremony) is an active word in daily life. What one observes today, however, is that many farmers' sons and daughters have come to work in automobile plants or computer assembly lines. Yet these young people may still take a weekend off to attend rice-planting ceremonies. In certain communities, these rituals are taken up by local business-men. The farmers' co-op handles everything from planting to harvesting.

Fauna also present us with peculiar cultural expressions, simply because people in a particular country are familiar with certain insects, birds or other animals. On insects and fish, the noted translator of *The Tales of Genji,* Edward Seidensticker, explained some of the problems of translation. Referring to the various insects Japanese are fond of, he mentioned that there are no insect dealers in the West, whereas children in Japan can buy 'bell crickets' or beetles at a department store. As for the 'bell crickets', the name itself is the translator's neologism.

Ayu is a favourite fresh-water fish with a rainbow-coloured body that reaches about 5 inches when it is fully grown. When the fishing season opens in early summer, hundreds of thousands of people go fishing for this small but beautiful fish, which adds a very seasonal taste to the dinner table during the rainy weeks of June and July. Seidensticker preferred to use the original 'ayu' with a foot-note, simply because there is no English equivalent (see Mizuta 1993: 6–8, 1994).

Phonology and syntax. The third factor has to do with the structure of the language itself. The accent pattern of the Tokyo dialect is, at present, considered to be the standard accent. It is a little different from other major dialects, such as the Osaka or Kyoto or Tohoku accents. Unlike the Kyoto dialect, which once differentiated classes, as a result of extensive compulsory education, today's Tokyo accent does not separate people into different classes. Nevertheless, it is prestigious. A country boy or girl from an area outside Tokyo finds his or her local accent disadvantageous. The young person has to go through vigorous training, like Eliza in *My Fair Lady*.

Sociopsychological factors. Besides the above-mentioned forces for generating certain expressions, there is a still more complicated concept for an alien to grasp: sociopsychological patterns. If consideration for another person is an important psycholinguistic element of using honorifics (including humble expressions), both Japanese- and English-speakers share equal concern. Japanese, however, has developed a complicated system of honorifics, basically to show respect to listeners and humble oneself. One cannot use straight and frank language at the beginning of an association. Mr or Ms Average cannot call his or her associates by their first names from the start. 'Call me Ron' cannot easily be translated into Japanese. But both are trying to be polite in their own way.

7.4 Are We the Only Life on the Earth?

It is believed that life appeared on this planet some three billion five hundred million years ago. To figure out when humans came into being, we usually imagine a line indicating the flow of time. Let's say 1 mm represents 1,000 years. Since *Homo sapiens* appeared some 30,000 years ago, it will be marked just about 3 cm to the left of the present day. Beijing man is believed to have existed some one million years ago, so it will be marked about 1 m away from the present day. The first life to appear on the earth will be placed 3.5 km away from the present day. And in the 3.5 km history of life on earth, the history of the present instance of humankind will be 2 mm long on the scale. Aren't humans too young to do anything with the rest of life on Earth?

Another important consideration is the food chain. To maintain its organic activities, each organism functions so as to support itself. Symbiosis starts with the sun; one construction of the food chain would be: photosynthesis $\Rightarrow$ vegetable plankton $\Rightarrow$ small animal plankton $\Rightarrow$ larger animal plankton $\Rightarrow$ small fish $\Rightarrow$ human beings. An awareness of the food chain turns our attention to any atmospheric disorder, such as the holes in the ozone layer. As we now know, these holes allow through excess ultraviolet rays, which kill the phytoplankton (or 'krill') on which the life of whales and penguins depends.

Why should we toy with an idea like this? What's the point of trying to locate man in the history of this planet? Because in this way, we can realise that human beings are just one form of life. We are then forced to understand the mechanisms and interrelationships of molecular organisms.

This is a world of elements, a microcosmos. The key terms are DNA, RNA, carbonised compounds and so on. The process of multiplying oneself includes the flow and expression of information. The transformation takes place in the world of darkness at the level of micron and nano quanta. According to Dr Fujio Egami, a biochemist, to search for the leap from chemistry to life one must understand life as a set of mutual relationships between molecules. Out of ten basic elements (H, O, C, N, Ca, P, S, Na, K, Cl), nine elements are commonly found in both the human body and sea water.

What I see in these trends and events is rather obvious. The surprisingly fast development of production technologies since the Industrial Revolution, together with the spread of highly developed capitalism from Western Europe to the USA and Japan, has enabled humans to bring about a tremendous abundance of products. This bounty, however, was accompanied by neglect of the natural order. Mass production and mass consumption have caused all kinds of pollution. As a result, we are just about to strangle Mother Earth to death.

7.5 The New Paradigms, Who Are They for?

As we have seen so far, the global situation definitely calls for new rules and new thinking. There is a new awareness of the need to reduce population growth, pollution and consumption of natural resources, and for measures to increase food production, to create more jobs and to innovate more new *clean* technologies.

A much more important thing is the measure to prepare young people to think this way. New thinking has to be tackled within new education systems and curricula. We must cultivate our young people to be ready to participate in decision-making processes, to believe in free enterprise, to be innovative, to conserve, to be sensitive to environmental effects and to be conscious of political processes.

To achieve these goals, politicians and financiers must work together to shift the flow of capital and change the way government aid is applied to developing countries. Researchers and academics should be able to provide adequate information and know-how. It may be impossible in our time, but it may not be too late to start thinking about a clean and healthy Earth, with the hope that the next generations will not suffer as a result of the mistakes we have made.

The goal is far away from us. People have their own interests. Who will be the best agent to promote new thinking: politicians, financiers, environmentalists? Education must be a clue. The new paradigms are indicators for new behaviours. The paradigm shift requires a lot more effort than we expect.

Now, let me suggest that Goshiki-cho should plan to build a Village Human Centre that can serve as an information centre and at the same time as symbol of the hometown. The centre must be able to provide something that is emotionally satisfactory for the residents while offering new information as knowledge. The Village Human Center as a human space is going to be a sizeable greenhouse that functions by solar energy and the energy that can be drawn from burning the waste of the community. At a 1986 seminar in Tokyo, Paolo Soleri said that utopia exists in the process of making it. We can take the first step here in Goshiki-cho by way of keeping up an ecological economic order.

Community culture must change as we change. The physical aspects of the hometown change, although the image of the hometown may often remain unchanged and serve as an anchor for a floating consciousness. It holds a sweet spot in one's heart. With this sweet spot in our heart, new awarenesses are still capable of preparing us for new phases of history, with new information and new approaches. In other words, holding to the sweet image of our hometown, we can still adapt ourselves to become citizens of the new world.

To conclude this brief presentation, let me say that our concern with the global situation may have given to the participants a sense of something very remote. It is not remote for people with new awareness. To talk about global culture we must begin within ourselves, each one of us, and then transfer the awareness to others so that it is linked in a greater network. The goal is to save ourselves and our planet. 'The world is too much with Us,' as Wordsworth said. To unbind oneself from the ties of one's mother culture is the beginning of a paradigm shift. We must offer the kind of education that cultivates and promotes the awareness of the third culture and a sense of world citizenship, and teaches young people to answer the question 'Where are you from?' with 'I'm from a village called Earth'.

References and Further Reading

Anderson, Walter (1987). *To Govern Evolution*, New York: Harcourt Brace, Jovanovich.

Egami, Fujio (1980). *In Search of Life*. Tokyo: Iwanami Shoten.

Ministry of the Environment (1995). White Paper on the Environment.

Mizuta, Kazuo (1993). *The Structures of Everyday Life in Japan in the Last Decade of the Twentieth Century*, Lewiston, N.Y.: Edwin Mellen Press

—— (1994). 'The Futures of Japanese Cultures' in *The Futures of Cultures*, UNESCO.

Nissan (1991). *Thanks*, a Nissan quality car life magazine, 1 January.

Tadanobu, Tsunoda (1978). *The Brain of the Japanese*. Tokyo: Taishukan.

Teramoto, Ei *et al.* (1985). *Lifescience: City Seminar*, Tokyo: Baifukan.

Part III

Building Sustainable Communities Globally

8 The Green Alternative: Towards a Future of Sustainable Communities in the USA

BRIAN TOKAR

8.1 New Movements for Change

The USA today leads the world as an example of the unsustainable use of the earth's resources. We are less than 5 per cent of the world's population yet, according to some estimates, may be liable for up to half the world's total consumption. Our country is directly responsible for a quarter of the world's consumption of energy, having used more in 1989 than the entire continent of Asia, and more than ten times as much as Africa. The USA is by far the largest generator of waste—Japan, with half as many people, comes in a distant second —and US industries and cars emit one-fifth of the world's output of climate-altering carbon dioxide. Our continent's last remaining undisturbed forest eco-systems are being destroyed at a pace that would have been unimaginable just a decade or two ago.[1]

Yet the vast majority of US citizens receive little benefit from all this excess consumption. The richest 1 per cent of families in the USA now own more than 40 per cent of all the wealth, while one out of every four children is born into poverty (Nasar 1992; Sklar 1992). Cancer rates are still rising, and the incidence of birth defects is doubling every ten years. Recent studies have shown a very strong correlation between poverty, racism and pollution, with the most toxic industries and waste facilities consistently located in the poorest and most racially diverse communities (United Church of Christ 1992). Our government still supports vast arsenals of nuclear and so-called 'conventional' weapons, de-signed to defend us against an 'enemy' that no longer exists. Prison-construction is the fastest growing public expense, while schools, hospitals, child-care centres and our inner cities are suffering from the most demoralising and disheartening kinds of abandonment and neglect.

We live in discouraging times, economically, socially and also politically, since the ability of most people to influence the important decisions that affect their daily lives falls far short of the American ideal of democracy. Even many of the people and organisations once known as defenders of the poor and downtrodden,

[1] Statistics from the UN Statistics Office and the World Bank, compiled by the World Resources Institute (1992–3; in collaboration with UNEP and UNDP).

champions of endangered ecosystems and tireless campaigners for peace are so demoralised by the present political and social climate that they have become used to compromising their moral principles just to maintain the possibility of personal access to government agencies and other centres of power (Tokar 1990; Foreman 1985). The environmental movement, which since the early 1970s has been looked upon as a source of vision and inspiration for a different kind of future, has in recent years narrowed its focus towards short-term policy objectives attainable within the limits of existing political and economic institutions. By limiting their vision to proposals confined by such an unsustainable, limited view some of the leading US environmental organisations are compromising away the tremendous visionary potential of ecological thought (Tokar 1992*a*; Stavins 1992). This has helped set the stage for the most concerted political assault against environmental protection in decades.

In local communities all across the USA, however, a very different kind of environmental consciousness has taken root. In some of the most unexpected places, out of view of the international news media, ordinary-seeming people are asserting their basic democratic rights and working to create a more ecologically sound future for their communities. This is not a new phenomenon. It has roots in the social movements of the 1960s, in the grassroots anti-nuclear movement of the 1970s and in the various popular campaigns against industrial pollution that began to sweep the world in the 1980s. What is new is that these various small, local efforts are helping people learn from each other's experiences, develop a more holistic, international perspective, and create a more conscious, unified movement for ecological renewal, community empowerment and a greener vision of the future. I will address four key manifestations of this emerging consciousness: the environmental justice movement, radical wilderness activism, bioregionalism and Green politics. I will explore the contributions of these social movements to a new vision of ecologically sustainable communities.

Probably the most widespread of these new developments is the growing movement for environmental justice. This dynamic new movement began nearly fifteen years ago in the aftermath of the Love Canal incident when Lois Gibbs, and others who had successfully pressured the federal government to evacuate homes in the vicinity of a major chemical waste dump, began to forge alliances with people in similar predicaments all across the country. Most of these people lived in communities that depended upon highly polluting industries for their economic survival. But when people began to discover that their jobs were making them sick and destroying the health of their children, they found the courage to say no. In urban neighbourhoods and small towns alike, people organised to halt the construction of new landfills and incinerators and to pressure toxic industries to begin cleaning up their act (Gibbs 1982).[2]

In the late 1980s and early 1990s, the anti-toxics movement evolved into a fully fledged nationwide movement for environmental justice. As people began to

---

[2] For continuing coverage of these campaigns, see *Everyone's Backyard*, journal of the Citizens Clearinghouse for Hazardous Wastes (P.O.Box 6806, Falls Church, Va 22040, USA).

discover that the most toxic industries and waste dumps are invariably located near the homes of poor people and people of colour, they realised that issues of public health and environmental protection could not be separated from issues of economic justice and racial equality. In recent years, the environmental justice (or 'Green Justice') movement has brought together migrant farmworkers from Mexico who are threatened by toxic pesticides in the fields, Native Americans struggling to prevent the siting of toxic chemical and nuclear waste dumps on their reservations, and black and white Americans, from Southern towns that were once consumed by racial hatred, who are joining together for the first time to protect their health and their children's future. In doing so, the movement has evolved from relatively isolated local campaigns to a more global ecological consciousness (see e.g. Bullard 1993; Hamilton 1993).

The past decade has also seen a tremendous resurgence of grassroots activism around issues of wilderness preservation and biodiversity. In the early 1980s, wilderness advocates across the USA came to realise that, despite the rise of environmental awareness across the land, the native ecosystems of our continent were disappearing faster than ever before. In the Pacific Northwest, home of ancient redwood and mixed conifer forests that support unique populations of wildlife, sustain the health of diverse mountain watersheds, and inspire people throughout the world with their grandeur, the rate of timber-cutting increased by two or three times in some areas during the 1980s as a result of changes in government policies and an epidemic of corporate takeovers. People began to realise that traditional environmental advocacy was completely unable to slow this unprecedented assault on our forests.

Whether under the banner of 'Earth First!'—a loose international alliance of no-compromise environmentalists—or any of the dozens of local forest-protection groups that have emerged across the country, people began putting their bodies on the line to protect endangered ecosystems (Scarce 1990: 57). People have blockaded logging roads to protect ecologically important stands of ancient trees. They have hoisted themselves up on small platforms and lived high in the trees, sometimes for weeks at a time. Some of these groups have also come up with detailed plans for the restoration of degraded wilderness areas, and are now working towards a continent-wide proposal for a network of ecological reserves that would be linked up by living corridors and buffer zones to allow the free migration of wildlife throughout North America. Under the auspices of the international Native Forest Network, activists have been forging links to keep abreast of current developments in forested regions, strengthen ties with indigenous peoples that depend on the forests for their survival and mount a co-ordinated response to the still-growing threat to the integrity of the whole world's forests (Noss 1992; Tokar 1994).

Forest-preservation has become an incredibly polarised issue in the USA in recent years, with loggers and mill-workers in economically depressed parts of the country often blaming environmentalists for the loss of their jobs. In the redwoods of northern California, activists are working to change this situation by forging new alliances between loggers and environmentalists (Bari 1994).

Much of the loss of jobs in the Northwest in recent years has been the result not of environmental protection, but of shortsighted policies that increase corporate profits at the expense of local communities. Large milling operations have been moved to Mexico to take advantage of cheaper labour costs, and shiploads of whole logs from giant old-growth trees are often sent overseas at bargain prices. In Oregon, for example, logging increased nearly 20 per cent statewide during the 1980s, while employment in the timber industry dropped by 20 per cent (Donnelly 1993; Van Dalen 1993). People who have worked in the woods all their lives are slowly beginning to realise that, at present rates of logging, there will simply be nothing left in a decade or two, and that they are unjustly being treated, much like the forests, as expendable commodities.

In one Californian community that succeeded in saving its own last grove of intact redwood forest, Earth First! activists are working with unemployed loggers to form a woodworking co-operative. They plan to cut younger redwoods in already damaged and recovering areas in a very selective, ecologically sustainable manner, and hope to sell their lumber to people who are willing to pay a little bit extra to know that their purchases are helping to restore rather than destroy the forests. This model of sustainable forestry is spreading from the Pacific Northwest all across North America, offering hope that people can work together to save the forests and also the economies of communities that have long been dependent on logging. The sustainable forestry movement offers an important practical model of a co-operative, locally based economy that can sustain forests and forest-based communities far into the future (Katelman 1994).

8.2 Bioregional Visions

A somewhat different kind of movement, the bioregional movement, has emerged over the past two decades as part of a visionary search for a deeper sense of identification between people and the place where they live. A bioregion is a part of the earth defined not by political boundaries like cities, states and countries, but by the natural features that shape the real biological identity of a place. Bioregions are identified by their mountain ranges and rivers, their vegetation, weather patterns and soil types. Unique ecosystems also sustain unique cultures of people. Instead of the rigid, straight-line borders we see on our contemporary maps, bioregions have fluid, rather permeable boundaries that encourage the migration of birds, the replenishment of waters and the open exchange of ideas and future visions among people, within an overall framework of co-operation and community-based self-reliance (Andruss *et al.* 1990; Berg 1978; Aberley 1993).

On the bioregional scale, people and communities are discovering more ecologically sound and sustainable ways to live in their particular place on the earth. They are creating new co-operative models of community that complement, instead of destroying, the flows and cycles of nature, often with the aid and inspiration of the native people whose ancestors lived sustainably in their particular region long before the arrival of the first European settlers. For people who live in cities, a bioregional awareness is helping them see how they can live in a spirit of harmony and sharing with the surrounding countryside, instead of the parasitic relationship that characterises most US cities, with their seemingly endless suburban sprawl. Bioregional activists have helped create a Green Cities movement that encourages new, ecological ways to design buildings and entire neighbourhoods that complement the natural patterns of the land, recycle wastes and water resources, reduce energy-use and gradually bring the diversity of the natural world back into the city (Berg *et al*. 1989; Canfield 1990).

People inspired by bioregional ideas are engaged in a wide range of activities that are prefigurative of a future ecological society. Bioregionalists are involved in detailed mapping of their communities and regions, seeking better to understand the relationship between human settlement patterns and ecological realities, and bringing this understanding into the curriculum of local schools. Sometimes, efforts to map out a watershed fully inspire community efforts to restore the biological integrity of their region, such as in the Mattole river valley of northern California, where bioregional activists have been working for ten years to restore the native salmon runs that were once almost suffocated by the residues from excessive logging. Many bioregionalists are active in the appropriate technology movement, working to design new technologies to heat homes, pump water and carry out other necessary activities without further depleting the earth's non-renewable resources. These technologies often bring together natural design concepts from traditional pre-industrial societies with some of the most sophisticated new electronic control systems, variable speed motors and high-efficiency materials.

In many areas of North America, bioregionalists are involved in sustainable agriculture, seeking to grow and distribute healthy, organically grown food that is well suited to the climate and soils of their region. They are developing regionally appropriate ways of growing food that replenish the soil rather than degrade and deplete it over time, as occurs with large-scale, chemical-intensive, monocultural methods. People are also seeking ways to meet the basic needs of their communities using more craft-oriented methods of production, as an alternative to the mass-industrial techniques that have led to the severe degradation of the earth. There is also a great range of efforts to create alternative modes of economic organisation at the community level, combining new ideas and institutions, such as Community Land Trusts, Community-Supported Agriculture, local community currencies and computerised local trading networks, with tried and tested approaches based on barter, community 'barn-raisings' and the like.

Finally, people inspired by a bioregional outlook gather every year or so in their home regions—from the Pacific Northwest to the Ozarks of the Southeast —to celebrate what is unique about their place, develop political strategies to heal the land and waterways, and share their visions of an ecological way of life. Semiannual Turtle Island Bioregional Gatherings (from the name that the northeastern Iroquois people first gave to the continent we now call North

America) bring together activists, artists and visionaries from all over the USA, Canada and Mexico to further the bioregional vision on a continent-wide basis. The bioregional movement has inspired some of the most dedicated activism in defence of people's home places and some of the most inspired poetry, music, stories and rituals to express the special closeness people feel to the portion of the earth they, their families and their communities know best (Zuckerman 1989; Dolcini *et al.* 1991).

8.3 The Greens

The fourth of these new ecological movements, the Green politics movement, has tried to provide a more unified public voice for ecological ideas and for the values articulated by a wide spectrum of new movements for change. Greens are seeking to uncover the social and political roots of ecological issues, while at the same time working to expose the origins of many of our economic and social problems in the unhealthy separation from the natural world that our modern civilisation has imposed upon all of us. This holistic Green view has important resonances with Eastern philosophical insights about ways to realise more harmonious relationships between people and the natural world from which we have emerged. The Greens, in particular, offer a model of political organising based on co-operation and consensus, and a holistic view of the many interrelationships among ecological, social and political issues (Tokar 1987).

In some places, the Green political strategy includes running candidates for public office. Greens have been elected to a wide variety of local offices in the USA, from school boards, water boards and planning commissions, to city and county councils and to the position of mayor of the city of Cordova, Alaska, which is right on the shores of Prince William Sound, where an Exxon oil tanker ran aground and spilled some 11 million gallons of crude oil into the sea just a few years ago. In other places, Greens are working at the local level to apply a holistic, ecological understanding to a wide variety of immediate problems, from toxic pollution, nuclear waste and offshore oil-drilling, to transforming the inner cities, the political empowerment of women and the development of co-operatives and other locally based models of economic renewal.

Greens in the USA are united around the same four philosophical pillars that inspired the formation of Green movements and political parties across Europe and around the world: ecology, social justice, grassroots democracy and non-violence. To these, Greens in the USA have added some additional principles that are closely related to these four pillars, but help us address the unique challenges of contemporary political life in the USA. These include an explicit focus on decentralisation—returning both political and economic decisions to the local level, where people can meet face-to-face and decide the course of their own future. Community-based economics is seen as the basis for a human-scale alternative to the global marketplace of transnational capital.

Greens embrace the values of feminism, which seeks equality and full liberation for women and all people, and also teaches us that the personal is political—that even the most private and intimate aspects of our lives are shaped by wider social realities. The earth-centred philosophy of ecofeminism has helped us understand the historic parallel between the subjugation of women and the widespread myth that humans, particularly men, can control nature. For Green feminists and social ecologists, this means that an ecological future requires moving beyond all forms of human relationships that are based on domination instead of co-operation (Diamond and Orenstein 1990; Shiva and Mies 1993).

Embracing racial and cultural diversity in our society is another important aspect of this. The Green value of respect for diversity teaches that the diversity of relationships among people in a multicultural society such as ours can be an important source of strength and stability in every community, much as the complex web of relationships among living species is essential to sustain diverse natural ecosystems. Finally, our Green values also include personal and global responsibility, and a clear commitment to a future focus based on ecological and social sustainability. Many of these are familiar concepts to students of futures studies, and Greens in the USA and around the world offer a holistic approach to putting these values into practice.

These Ten Key Values of the Greens have inspired the formation of literally hundreds of Green political groups, both large and small, all across the USA. Greens have offered their organising experience and holistic worldview to struggles for environmental justice, efforts to rebuild decaying inner cities and the efforts of several Native American nations to protect their land and water from mining and the storage of nuclear waste. Greens have sought controls on excessive urban development, protection to keep our food supply safe from the excesses of biotechnology, sustainable alternatives to the incineration of wastes and expanded use of solar energy and new energy-saving technologies. There are now at least ten statewide Green Parties running campaigns for state and local office based on detailed platforms for ecological and social renewal. All over the country, Green activists are bringing discussions of global issues such as climatic change and ozone depletion, trade policy and nuclear disarmament directly to the local level, and exploring ways that small changes in our daily lives and the lives of our communities contribute to lasting solutions to many of the world's most pressing problems.

It is clear that tremendous obstacles still exist to realising the goals of these movements. The economic and political institutions that have evolved in the industrial era have proven tenacious and surprisingly resilient, even as they race like a train out of control on a course towards ecological collapse and social chaos. Our movements often seem completely inadequate to stem this virtual tidal wave of destruction. Activist groups tend to be relatively small, very local-ised and extremely under-funded. Though we have a great deal of confidence in locally rooted solutions to global problems, we also know that fundamental change will require a high level of exchange and co-operation by like-minded people across the country and around the world. At the same time, there are literally thousands of individuals and small groups working for an ecological future in relative isolation from any larger movement. While this gives us tremendous hope that people can step outside the confines of their daily lives and begin searching for a different way, it sometimes makes it more difficult to translate their actions into a coherent program for significant social change.

Still, the paradigm of social change that has emerged from these various ecological movements has gained widespread support among many sectors of the American public. This is sometimes manifested in indirect and very personal ways, such as changes in eating habits and patterns of consumption, the increased popularity of wilderness-exploration and organic gardening and enthusiastic support for urban recycling programmes, as well as relatively subtle changes in cultural attitudes and aspirations. We see, in the USA, and throughout the so-called 'developed' world, a widespread dissatisfaction with the ways of mass-industrial society and a tremendous longing for a way of life that is more community-oriented and more in tune with the patterns of the natural world. This stands in marked contrast to the culture of unbridled greed and conspicuous consumption that often defines our country's image in the world today.

8.4 Democracy and Harmony

Thus an increasingly coherent alternative vision of the future has emerged from a wide spectrum of ecological movements in the USA. It is a vision of decentralised communities practising local self-reliance and responsibility to their home bioregion, while working together in a spirit of co-operation to solve larger global problems. It embraces efforts to create co-operative economic institutions at the local level that can begin to relieve people's destructive dependencies on a decaying industrial system. Greens seek to enhance democracy and cultural diversity, use recycled materials wherever possible and try to give back to the earth at least as much nourishment as we take for ourselves. Our human creativity and understanding of the earth's cycles and the ecology of our bioregions will guide us towards the goal of living peacefully and harmoniously on the earth.

In North America, the ideal of face-to-face participatory democracy—preserved in the lasting tradition of the New England Town Meeting—and the pioneer traditions of independence and self-reliance offer widely accepted cultural models that resonate in many ways with this model of ecologically sustainable, self-reliant communities. However, democracy, as practised in the USA, is often constrained by the same habits of competitive individualism and narrow self-interest that have sustained the current exploitative relationship between people and the land. Our vision also needs to be informed by the practice of harmonious relationships among people that sustains traditional communities in the East.

This relationship between ecological sustainability and the Eastern ideal of social harmony is best articulated in Kaoru Yamaguchi's concept of MuRatopia (see Chapter 5 above). MuRatopia combines the antimaterialistic values of Zen Buddhism ('Mu' = 'emptiness' and 'Ra' = 'without possessions'), the practice of harmonious relationships and mutual aid that governs life in the traditional Japanese village (or 'mura') and a model of ecological sustainability aided by information-age technologies. New communication technologies, especially where they are implemented in an open and participatory manner instead of simply for profit, have proved to be an essential means for maintaining channels of dialogue and co-operation between communities. Communities in isolation from the rest of the world can be breeding grounds for all manner of provincialism and narrow-mindedness. This is one reason why the Green and bioregional models of sustainable communities encourage widespread voluntary exchanges of ideas, material goods and cultural values, regional and global co-operation among locally based producing co-operatives and the active confederation of communities to achieve common goals and solve common problems in an interdependent world. This requires the wide dissemination of tools to facilitate communication and exchange that minimise the use of non-renewable resources. It is the place where appropriate technology meets the information age.

Confederations of bioregional communities are thus an essential step towards realising the goals of the new ecological movements and a co-operative vision of the future. If this cannot be achieved, we may face a highly managed future in which a few powerful institutions appropriate the language of 'sustainable development' to rationalise the continued exploitation of the earth and its peoples (Tokar 1992*b*; Orton 1994). Such a future would be surrendered to corporations, governments and international agencies like the powerful World Trade Organization established under the 1993 General Agreement on Tariffs and Trade, in exchange for a promise of continued economic growth and ever-expanding levels of consumption. Industrial development and the globalisation of production would continue to be promoted as the keys to a better life, while the system's worst excesses were hidden behind the rhetoric of efficient global resource-management. In this version of the future, all the earth's inhabitants are merely 'resources' to be bought, sold and traded to help maintain the system.

Some in the corporate world genuinely understand that the Earth's ecosystems are in crisis, but they are attempting to use the increasing global awareness of this crisis to increase their own power and influence. This became apparent on an international level at the 1992 United Nations 'Earth Summit' in Brazil, where the World Bank—which for decades has been responsible for many of the world's largest and most destructive so-called 'development' projects—was given control over the largest share of funds for environmental protection (Tickell and Hildyard 1992; Ling 1994). Donations offered by the wealthier countries to help protect the environment are now being used to mitigate some of the environmental consequences of massive developments like huge dams and resource-extraction projects that should have been completely rejected from the beginning on the basis of their severe ecological consequences. The UNCED conference, for all its positive accomplishments, gave new legitimacy to the dangerous and misleading notion that Northern economic models and industrial technologies are the answer to the growing human and environmental problems of the South.

8.5 Rethinking Globalism

As we work to rebuild our communities and institutions along ecologically sustainable lines, we need to be wary of those who would use the images and language of environmentalism to perpetuate an outmoded industrial system. We value our global visions and planetary outlook, but also see that the managerial, pro-development approach to global problems proposed by the World Bank and large transnational corporations is a continuation of the same colonial attitude towards the world's land and peoples that has caused so much destruction in the past and continues to this very day. This situation was described in a stark and perhaps somewhat surprising way by Indian physicist and ecofeminist Vandana Shiva, who is one of the most articulate and insightful spokespeople for a new Green consciousness that is gradually emerging from the so-called 'developing' world. 'The image of planet Earth', she wrote, citing the inspiring satellite photographs that have come to symbolise the emerging global outlook, 'is invoked by the most rapacious and greedy institutions to destroy and kill the cultures which use a planetary consciousness to guide their daily actions' (Shiva 1993: 28). In other words, many aspects of what we in the North see as an inclusive global vision are often viewed by people in the South as merely new rationalisations for privileging the industrial powers' regional economic interests over their own.

This presents a profound challenge for those of us who are trying to give shape to a new Green vision of the future. In our search for sustainable communities and MuRatopia, we also need to step outside the boundaries of the privileged, Northern industrial, consumerist worldview and try to understand how the world looks to people in the so-called 'developing world', especially the surviving members of the world's original earth-centred cultures. From the North American Indians, to the Ainu of Japan, to the indigenous peoples of the tropical rainforests, African village-dwellers and the Aborigines of Australia, indigenous cultures are the guardians of the knowledge that has made it possible for human beings to survive for tens of thousands of years without destroying the earth that gives us all our sustenance. They have witnessed the rise of militarism, industrialism, colonialism and, in our own time, a global capitalist market. Today, these cultures—and the ecosystems upon which they depend—are severely threatened by forces of economic development and global management that have the power and technology to explore and ravage every last corner of the earth. But indigenous peoples also have the insight and wisdom to help us see what is ecologically and humanly sustainable in our own diverse cultures. Instead of telling native people what we think is best for them, we need to work together to consciously evolve a way of life that respects and honours the land and all living creatures, both human and non-human.

We obviously cannot simply copy indigenous ways, nor can we simply go back to a pre-industrial way of life. The world has become very crowded and complex, and most of us are adapted to the ways of a fast-moving, multi-faceted global culture. We also need to develop the tools to clean up all of the toxic horrors created by two hundred years of industrial civilisation, and to sustain the quality of communication that will allow our ecological awareness to blossom into real solutions to global problems. But we can share each other's ecological and spiritual insights, and learn once again how to live within the earth's natural cycles in harmony with all of life. First, we must remember that we are all part of nature. Then, we can join together with the victims of toxic spills, the defenders of natural ecosystems, the bioregional pioneers, and all who share a vision of a greener future. We can reject a way of life that reduces us, like cogs in a machine, to mere producers and consumers, and rejoin the earth community in all its diversity and splendour, as a unified voice for healing, co-operation and a peaceful, harmonious, more compassionate future.

References

Aberley, D. (ed.) (1993). *Boundaries of Home: Mapping for Local Empowerment*, Philadelphia, Pa.: New Society Publishers.

Andruss, V. *et al.* (1990). *Home: A Bioregional Reader*, Philadelphia, Pa.: New Society Publishers.

Bari, J. (1994). *Timber Wars*, Monroe, Me.: Common Courage Press.

Berg, P. (ed.) (1978). *Reinhabiting a Separate Country*, San Francisco, Calif.: Planet Drum Books.

—— *et al.* (1989). *A Green City Program*, San Francisco, Calif.: Planet Drum Books.

Bullard, R. (1993). 'Anatomy of Environmental Racism and the Environmental Justice Movement' in R. D. Bullard (ed.), *Confronting Environmental Racism: Voices from the Grassroots*, Boston, Mass.: South End Press.

Canfield, C. (ed.) (1990). *Report of the First International Ecocity Conference*, Berkeley, Calif.: Urban Ecology.

Diamond, L. and Orenstein, G. (1990). *Reweaving the World: The Emergence of Ecofeminism*, San Francisco, Calif.: Sierra Club Books.

Dolcini, M. *et al.* (eds.) (1991). *Proceedings of the Fourth North American Bioregional Congress*, San Francisco, Calif.: Planet Drum Books.

Donnelly, M. (1993). 'The Great Timber Famine Fallacy', *Wild Forest Review* 1(2; December): p. 22.

Foreman, D. (1985). 'Making the Most of Professionalism', *Whole Earth Review* 45 (March): pp. 34–7.

Gibbs, L. (1982). *My Story*, Albany, N.Y.: State University of New York Press.

Hamilton, C. (1993). 'Coping with Industrial Exploitation' in R. D. Bullard (ed.), *Confronting Environmental Racism: Voices from the Grassroots*, Boston, Mass.: South End Press.

Katelman, T. (1994). 'Sustainable Forestry', Redway, Calif.: Institute for Sustainable Forestry.

Ling, C. Y. (1994). 'A Floundering GEF Erodes Confidence in Green Funding', *Third World Resurgence* 42/43(February): pp. 4–5.

Nasar, S. (1992). 'Fed Report Gives New Data on Gains by Richest in '80s', *New York Times* April 21: p. 1.

Noss, R. E. (1992). 'The Wildlands Project Land Conservation Strategy', in 'The Wildlands Project', special issue of *Wild Earth*: pp. 10–25.

Orton, D. (1994). 'Struggling Against Sustainable Development', *Z Papers*, Winter: pp. 13–19.

Scarce, R. (1990). *Eco-Warriors*, Chicago, Ill.: Noble Press.

Shiva, V. (1993). 'The Greening of the Global Reach', in J. Brecher *et al.* (eds.), *Global Visions: Beyond the New World Order*, Boston, Mass.: South End Press.

—— and Mies, M. (1993). *Ecofeminism*, London: Zed Books.

Sklar, H. (1992). 'Imagine a Country', *Z Magazine* November: pp. 21–4.

Stavins, R. N. (1992). 'Harnessing the Marketplace', *EPA Journal* (US Environmental Protection Agency, Washington, D.C.) 18(2; May): pp. 21–5.

Tickell, O. and Hildyard, N. (1992). 'Green Dollars, Green Menace', *The Ecologist* 22(3; May): p. 82–3.

Tokar, B. (1987). *The Green Alternative: Creating an Ecological Future*, San Pedro, Calif.: R. and E. Miles; rev. edn., Philadelphia, Pa.: New Society Publishers, 1992.

—— (1990). 'Marketing the Environment', *Z Magazine* February: pp. 15–20.

—— (1992*a*). 'Regulatory Sabotage', *Z Magazine* April: pp. 20–5.

—— (1992*b*). 'After the Earth Summit', *Z Magazine* September: pp. 8–14.

—— (1994). 'The New Forest Activism', *Z Magazine* January: pp. 34–9.

United Church of Christ Commission for Racial Justice (1992). *Toxic Wastes and Race in the United States: A National Report on the Racial and Socio-Economic Characteristics of Communities with Hazardous Waste Sites*, New York: United Church of Christ.

Van Dalen, C. (1993). 'Save America's Forests', fact sheet, Washington, D.C.: Save America's Forests.

World Resources Institute (1992–3). *World Resources 1992–93: A Guide to the Global Environment*, New York: Oxford University Press.

Zuckerman, S. (ed.) (1989). *Proceedings of the Third North American Bioregional Congress*, San Francisco, Calif.: Planet Drum Books.

9 Towards Global Sustainable Community: A View from Wisconsin

BELDEN PAULSON

9.1 Dinosaur Mentality

Inasmuch as universities are the prominent and accepted institutions of the knowledge/information infrastructure of modern society and they play such a crucial role in defining the realities upon which we shape our future, it is rather amazing that a number of global thinkers like ourselves should have to assemble here to ponder the creation of a future-oriented university. Every country should already have at least one. Despite the tremendous strengths of our universities, there is a 'dinosaur mentality' that seems to have prevented them from seriously taking on futures studies. Let me simply cite three reasons, among others:

(1) Universities are fragmented. They are classic examples of the Cartesian model of subdividing wholes into small compartments. Academic disciplines and narrow specialisations certainly have their place in understanding the complexities of the world, but today there is a crying need to comprehend larger wholes and how the disparate variables of reality fit together—economic, political, ecological, cultural, psychological, spiritual. One of the achievements of some scientists in the last twenty years has been a healthy humility about how little they really know and a recognition of the need to create more holistic models. Your new university here will need to create processes to transcend not only boundaries of nations and culture, but also the fragmentation of knowledge.

(2) Universities have great difficulty in dealing with values and larger visions. For almost fifty years the Western democratic world focused its most creative energies (and material resources) on containing Communist expansionism. Now we are in need of new visions that will focus and mobilise our creative energies as we move into the new century. It is interesting to note that an international, interdisciplinary, multicultural study now underway, organised by the American Academy of Arts and Sciences, is focusing on 'fundamentalisms' in seven continents. In identifying fourteen different fundamentalist movements, most of which are surging in membership and influence, the study notes that despite their differences, the fundamentalisms share certain strongly held underlying values— for example, fighting back against modern secular society. These values have their ramifications in politics, economics, education, family and sexual relationships and so on. We, too, need to be able to deal with value concerns on the

deepest level, while maintaining an openness to dialogue, as we search for truth and promote the larger common good. The new unifying vision for the years ahead may well be the recognition that we live in an *interdependent global community, where the future consequences of our present actions have taken on great importance*. I assume that this is an essential premiss of the new university under discussion.

(3) Universities lack imagination. The future does not exist; it is an image in our minds. However, it is the limits of the limitlessness of our own imaginations that will determine the possibilities of whichever frame of reference we choose to focus on. In the twentieth century, imaginations have been fertile in certain fields of science and technology, but there has been a compelling dearth of imagination in reshaping institutions, such as education. Our American colleague Michael Marien (1989), who edits *Future Survey*, sees the university as a 'trivia factory', with the academic penchant to think small. 'Academics are locked into a pattern of trivial pursuit, and even rewarded for it.' In the context of seeing the world as a whole, the University of the Future needs to identify trends, visualise and estimate future possibilities, prepare students to be discriminating in identifying preferred futures and give stimulus and energy to 'go for it'.

For years in Wisconsin I have been committed to dealing with these difficulties, as have you in Japan and others of you here at this meeting. In approaching the subject given me—sustainable community development in Wisconsin—I'd like to relate to four themes placed in the broad context of this seminar, 'Renewing Community as Global Sustainable Village':

- the idea of community as the organising principle undergirding the eventual outcome of the global village;
- the establishment of local/regional centres that become the building blocks, the central nervous system, of larger networks that can make their contribution to universities of the future committed to sustainable world community;
- the use of a 'think-tank' mechanism (which in a way is what this seminar really is) dedicated to sustainable community development, and itself a process for working on a significant complex undertaking, such as establishing a future-oriented university committed to sustainable world community;
- the paradigm shift that is required for this kind of work.

9.2 The Idea of Community

I'd like to begin by speaking from personal experience. In 1980 my wife, Lisa, and I co-founded a small intentional community in Wisconsin called 'High Wind' (everyone came to the community with the 'intention' of living a certain way and pursuing a certain philosophical path). Today fourteen people live there, on 148 acres of land in a rural area an hour's drive north of Milwaukee. At various times more than twenty people have lived in the community. High Wind has gone through a fascinating process of evolutionary change, which parallels to a considerable degree the experience of many other communities with which we are familiar around the globe.

High Wind began as a construction project that focused on solar energy. A number of participants in my University of Wisconsin futures classes in the late 1970s, when the world energy crisis was pushing people to think about renewable energy, were anxious to know how they might engage in a 'real-world' project. Lisa and I had a small farm and we agreed to use this property for such a project. The group established a non-profit organisation and a seed-money grant was awarded by the US Department of Energy to build an experimental passive solar structure called a 'bio-shelter'. Soon a group of volunteers materialised who actually built the structure. This building was to be part residence/seminar space and part greenhouse for growing food and farming fish—a non-consuming micro-farm. Over a period of several years more and more residents appeared on the scene to undertake this and other construction projects, engage in organic gardening and, as the public became aware of the project, to sponsor educational programs and tours. Gradually a community evolved, with these kinds of commitments:

- nurturing personal and collective growth with openness and acceptance;
- fostering ecological sensitivity and stewardship of the land and other natural resources;
- developing social, economic and political relationships founded on co-operation and mutual growth, while at the same time efficiently utilising available resources and skills;
- creating increasing economic sustainability, including providing as fully as possible food and fuel from within the 148-acre ecosystem;
- applying ancient and traditional wisdom from our various heritages to encourage balance and peace in our time;
- viewing ourselves as a village within a global context ('High Wind' 1991).

Soon the 'community' aspects of High Wind took on far more importance than the initial physical work of building shelters and food-production. Take, for example, governance issues. People joining High Wind tended to hold a vision about redefining power. Ideas were discussed such as full member involvement in making decisions instead of a small elected elite as in representative government; decision-making based on consensus instead of majority rule, which tends to reduce decisions to their lowest common denominator; and a minimal bureaucracy and hierarchical structure that would mean more informal leadership and organisational effectiveness based on 'consciousness' rather than coercion.

Economic issues, likewise, became significant. In the early years there was little discussion of money, other than to fund completion of the construction or to buy seed or to cover other basics. People lived simply. Lisa and I paid the taxes on the property and funded building renovations and everyone contributed to food and utilities. All work was volunteer, and monies received from seminars and guests were used for general expenses or divided among the people who did the work.

There was a kind of 'pressure cooker' existence—many people crowded into small spaces and doing everything together. The land itself, besides being an economic resource, took on a kind of mystical quality. The ecological ethic had high priority: organic gardening, woodland stewardship, composting garbage, conservation and recycling practices, solar heating and super-insulation and educating others about these issues.

In recent years we have been receiving more and more letters from people around the USA and also from abroad who would like to join the community. But within High Wind itself some other types of pattern developed that had negative consequences. One was the so-called 'founders' malaise': the several of us, with our strong commitment 'to make this experiment work', invested a considerable amount of our own resources and energies in the community, and thus gave the impression that we 'owned the vision' and, further, that if others were to leave the community, Lisa and I and David Lagerman, the other co-founder, would always be there to pick up the pieces. This latter psychology changed somewhat once people began building their own homes. A second negative pattern was the 'efficiency malaise'. The political and economic ideas about consensual decision-making, constant meetings to 'process' conflicts and investing time in 'relating to each other' rather than 'getting things done', brought highs of community cohesion and solidarity when everything worked; but often things didn't work. The result was paralysis and ineffectiveness. A third pattern that developed was the 'expectation malaise'. At times community members felt they really were on to something unique—a new model of living—but at other times, which became increasingly frequent, they felt frustration. Lack of money, interminable meetings, spartan living conditions, personality rifts, ideological conflicts between the early members who were the 'vision-holders' and later arrivals, and differing expectations of each person about what the ideal community should be like raised questions about the whole concept of community (Paulson 1991).

Six years ago High Wind, through its board of directors, agreed on significant changes. The identity or image of intentional community was abandoned in favour of 'ecological village'. On the surface this seemed only a subtle change, but psychologically it was very important. It removed the sense of obligation to process feelings, go to meetings, volunteer endlessly for the 'work of the whole' and behave in a certain manner. The strong commitment to an ecological ethic remained, however, and the educational functions of High Wind continued, but only for those who wanted to participate. There was no obligation.

I discuss these details of High Wind because our extensive contacts with many other communities confirm an amazing degree of similarity of experience. The thirst to create community, both on the local level and in the sense of global village, is very real. There is a romantic image of community, especially among people who have not had the kind of intimate experiences briefly described. Eco-villages, in particular, are taking on increasing importance, as confirmed by a recent study that summarises material on ninety eco-villages in twenty-one countries. The study defines an eco-village broadly as a human-scale full-featured settlement in which human activities are harmlessly integrated into the natural world in a way that is supportive of healthy human development and can be successfully continued into the indefinite future.[1]

'Human-scale' refers to a size in which people know each other, usually a maximum of 500 people. 'Full-featured settlement' means that all the major functions of normal living may be included on-site: residence, work, leisure activities, social life and commerce, in contrast to much of the industrialised world where life is much more specialised and fragmented. (A number of community members, however, may also work outside the community, as is the case at High Wind.)

'Human activities harmlessly integrated into the natural world' relates to the principle of equality and balance between humans and other forms of life, so that humans find their proper place in the natural world rather than dominating as is prevalent in industrial culture. 'Supportive of healthy human development' recognises the importance of both the health of individuals in the community and of the community as a whole. Health means all aspects of life—physical, emotional, mental and spiritual. 'Successfully continuing into the indefinite future' is the sustainability principle, taking care of today's needs without compromising the ability of future generations to fulfil their needs.

Why are people today so interested in community? There are undeniable academic reasons, such as the need to move beyond narrow jurisdictions—be they the local area or the sovereign state—towards world community; the need to create a transnational community where justice prevails through appropriate flows of capital and labour; and the crucial mandate to create global ecological community. Specifically, however, why are people drawn to High Wind and similar communities?

- Today's world is frightening in many ways. Change is so rapid and often so incomprehensible that people have lost their internal anchors. They're looking for a safe refuge, which they believe community will provide.
- The job market is increasingly strained. In the emerging global economy where one's skills and human energy are competing with millions of others who all hunger for the good life, a community may seem to offer security, where one can live in a relatively non-competitive environment.
- Family structures have broken down. In past times families seemed to stick together and take care of their own. In today's fast-moving culture, where almost nothing lasts, including family relationships, community becomes a support system, a kind of substitute family or even substitute parent.
- People are genuinely searching for alternatives. Community projects an image of love and kindness and caring, a new model of living, a sensitivity to the natural world, a microcosm of what society could become—a kind of

[1] Taken from 'Characteristics of Eco-Villages' 1991: 7–9. The material that immediately follows is also taken from this source.

oasis away from materialism and runaway consumption, from the exploitative workplace, from disempowering government, from the spiritual desert
characteristic of much of mainstream culture.

Because our goal in this seminar is to contribute to sustainable communities
on a global level, and to design educational institutions towards this end, what
are some insights we can draw from this kind of intimate experience with community? There are countless definitions of community; here is one:

A healthy community keeps in balance the needs of its individual members and the needs
of the larger whole. In this process of fulfilling both, a dynamic tension and interdependence is created that maximises and highlights the unique richness each person brings as
well as the shared common interests that brought them all together in the first place.

The key point is to create a chemistry that provides a balance between group
agreement and individual autonomy. On the one hand, there is order and unified
action and, on the other hand, non-conformity that enhances personal freedom
and self-actualisation. Group order and unified action could lead to a new kind
of world order for humanity—a sustainable global village if you will—but, if
carried to an extreme, can bring authoritarian control and totalitarianism. Individual freedom and self-actualisation can enhance the ultimate goal of human
self-fulfilment, but, if carried to an extreme, can lead to disorder and chaos. It is
the interplay or creative tension between the two that is important.

The universal principle of the natural world is differentiation; everything and
everyone is unique. But when individuals interrelate with each other in a way
that transcends their separateness, a system of wholeness is created—the ecology
of the natural world, the music of an entire orchestra. This is community.
Referring back to the High Wind experience, people were drawn there above all
because of the separation and alienation of the world they sought to leave. At the
beginning, the sense of 'oneness' of the High Wind community, the commonal-
ities shared, was empowering, but in time this created its own malaise. A new
balance had to emerge that held on to the unifying strength of the community
but gave more space for the nurturing of individual members. In the High Wind
experience, this was the transition from intentional community to ecological
village.

9.3 Plymouth Institute in Wisconsin, Committed to Sustainable Community Development

Instead of offering an inventory of the variety of activities in Wisconsin committed to sustainable development, I will focus on one initiative, Plymouth Institute.
I do this for three reasons: I am knowledgeable about the details because, as a
co-founder, I have direct personal involvement; it is closely linked to a number
of universities, which means there could be potential for relationships to the

initiative being focused on at this seminar; and, finally, because the agenda of Plymouth Institute is future oriented and uses a whole-systems approach, it interweaves with the discussions here.

Before introducing Plymouth Institute, let me comment briefly on the concept of sustainable development. Since this phrase was popularised by the path-breaking document *Our Common Future* in 1987, sponsored by the United Nations Commission on Environment and Development (UNCED), a plethora of literature has emerged. There have been many national and multinational actions, culminating in the Earth Summit held in Rio de Janeiro in June 1992, and policies established by governments since then. The basic conclusion is that there has to be an altogether new kind of economic growth, designed to meet the needs of the present without compromising the ability of future generations to meet their own needs.

Much of the UN and related discussion has centred on economics and natural resources and their relationship to the environment. It has become clear, for example, that a sustainable world requires: (*i*) a population that is stable and in balance with its natural support system; (*ii*) an energy system that does not raise the level of greenhouse gases and disrupt the earth's climate; and (*iii*) a level of human material demand that does not exceed the sustainable yield of forests, grasslands and fisheries or systematically destroy the other species with which we share the planet.

Since the dialogue has increasingly involved both the industrially advanced countries and the less-developed countries (LDCs), the widening gap between richer and poorer people in the world has become a central issue. The urgency to eliminate poverty among the LDCs and the poor in the wealthier countries has taken on an importance equal to mounting environmental concerns. Just as the industrial countries have been urging various countries in the southern hemisphere to stop decimating the world's forests, which are shrinking by more than 17 million hectares per year, or turning productive soils into wastelands through mismanagement, the LDCs are complaining about the unfettered appetites of the industrial countries for pumping carbon into the atmosphere by burning fossil fuels, thus contributing to increased global temperatures, and continuing to use environmentally damaging chemicals, such as CFCs, which threaten the earth's protective ozone layer.

To deal with these myriad concerns, a series of strategic policy actions has begun to emerge, which includes: (*i*) the need for a new accounting system that would add a new set of indicators to the traditional Gross National Product to reflect environment costs; (*ii*) a range of new technologies to increase energy efficiency in transportation, heating and lighting, appliances and industry; (*iii*) the use of incentives to encourage beneficial environmental behaviours (for example, subsidies for conservation practices) and disincentives for harmful practices (for example, taxes on practices that degrade natural systems); (*iv*) new forms of development assistance that help countries economically but also promote sustainability (for example, debt-for-nature swaps); and (*v*) global collaboration for sustainable development, where co-operative efforts and joint economic ventures direct investments into environmentally sound projects (Paulson 1992).

All of these good ideas make sense, but they require a radical transformation in thinking. A new state of mind is the precondition for moving beyond the rhetoric to actual change. Governments will move when the people are ready, and the people will be ready when they become convinced there is no alternative to preparing to live in a sustainable culture.

Unfortunately, there has been little in-depth examination of the question 'What is a sustainable culture?' Even in the massive set of papers that provides the basis for Agenda 21, the action plan on the global environment for the twenty-first century prepared for the 1992 Earth Summit, the explorations are limited. This points up, once again, the need for future-oriented learning institutions committed to these broad sustainability issues—the theme of this seminar.

While the United Nations passes resolutions and governments explore how to promote sustainability, there is a wealth of activity *on the ground* at the local level *doing it*. Plymouth Institute is one such effort, a relatively new endeavour committed to creating models for sustainable living. It is a group of designers/ builders, educators, farmers, businesspeople and entrepreneurs and artists, located in Wisconsin and elsewhere in the midwestern USA, with counterparts around the country and the world. It serves as a regional resource centre for rural and urban communities, and a kind of strategy centre and think-tank for leaders in the sustainability movement.

It is a partnership of representatives of a number of colleges and universities and school districts, working alongside the High Wind community. Its broad agenda is to define, demonstrate and communicate values and practices of sustainability; to promote whole-systems thinking and global perspectives; to advocate ecological stewardship; and to build multicultural, interdependent communities of life-long learners.

Plymouth Institute is an umbrella organisation that draws on the rich history of the High Wind Association, with its solar buildings, small businesses, such as an organic farm now feeding 350 families, flourishing bookstore, educational programs and retreats and learning drawn from years of a small group of people living in community. It also utilises the unique advantage of holding stewardship over 292 acres of a whole valley with ecological diversity of woods and meadows and wildlife, two million gallons of spring water flowing through the property daily, numerous fish ponds, and access to 12,000 acres of adjacent State Forest.

One major project is the creation of SpringLedge Eco-Village. This is a state-of-the-art land condominium with a land-use covenant that combines private individual and community ownership of land, home construction using re-newable energy and non-toxic materials, and a sewerage system using biological systems to process waste into clean water. This project, interrelated with nearby businesses using the pure water and fish resources being developed on the property, provides an arena for an exciting display of technical, economically feasible experiments that demonstrate sustainable use of resources.

A second major Plymouth Institute project is the development of a field-experience campus, which gives students of all ages access to a rich natural environment, introducing them to whole-systems sustainable futures thinking in a practical hands-on setting. Close co-operative arrangements with various educational institutions offer opportunities for creative thinking about new models of learning.

9.4 Towards a Global Think-Tank for Sustainable Community Development

The term 'think-tank' only entered our vocabulary about forty years ago, and it has taken on various meanings. Simply put, we define the term as concentrated intellectual and intuitional energies that focus on practical problems so as to prepare policy options for decision-makers. In the USA there are over 1,200 private non-profit research institutions concerned with public policy, with most located in universities, and at least 150 in Washington, D.C. All are small compared to the vast research operations of government, but they have taken on increasing importance as the problems facing society outrun the solutions, and with the increasing inability of decision-makers to define the problems facing society and to propose well-thought-out solutions. The speed of change, the complexity of problems and the high costs of failure have created a fertile field for this kind of mechanism.

Despite the proliferation of think-tanks for dealing with every possible problem area, there is a glaring deficiency, seen in the perspective of our discussion. There are very few efforts that look at the world in fundamentally different ways to respond to the question 'What is a sustainable culture, and what policies and learning will move people in the direction of a sustainable world economy?' In dealing with these questions, the think-tank mechanism needs a global orientation and participation must include a diversity of viewpoints drawn from different cultural and national backgrounds.

Notwithstanding the valuable work of United Nations agencies, the seminal advances made by the 1992 Earth Summit and subsequent meetings, and the notable contributions by scores of organisations both governmental and non-governmental, we have only begun to fathom the meaning and implications for our lives of sustainable living, which will probably require radical changes we have hardly begun to address. People are beginning to project what a new age would look like based on values and assumptions that transcend those that emerged during the industrial age of the last 200 years. But we are only starting to explore questions related to how we utilise natural resources, how we define and measure *progress*, the meaning of work when high productivity may no longer require the full workforce presently employed, how sustainability issues intersect with the issues of poverty and different stages of economic development, and how to enlist public support when concerns about one's earning a living conflict with those about one's preserving the environment. There are countless other questions.

Plymouth Institute is committed to working with others in such think-tank-type explorations that place its education and R&D activities into a broad conceptual and policy-oriented framework, while at the same time not departing from the specific concrete projects with which it's engaged. Exploratory initiatives, such as this seminar at Awaji Island, a possible University of the Future that might someday emerge, and a number of programmes reported on at this assembly, all contribute to this search for new thinking.

Concluding Comment

In essence, the discussion in this paper, as at this seminar, is about a paradigm shift. Physicist Fritjof Capra (1986) redefined slightly Thomas Kuhn's classic ideas about the meaning of *paradigm*, as follows:

A constellation of concepts, values, perceptions and practices shared by a community, which forms a particular vision of reality that is the basis of the way the community organizes itself.

Two key words: *values* and *community*. I think there is a close affinity between the values of a sustainable culture and those of a healthy community. A key characteristic of both is the dimension of balance between the needs of the individual and of the larger whole. This creates the synergy of interdependence. When we refer to 'whole-systems thinking', in simple terms we're focusing on the system made up of all the parts that constitute the whole. I would include the following whole-systems values as among the most essential to a sustainable culture:

Co-operation: interrelationships where the parts of the whole work together for the common good;

Empowerment: each part gives strength to the others, so that all benefit with a *win–win* result;

Compassion: each part extends open arms to the others, giving without expectation of a particular return, thereby creating an underlying trust in the viability of the overall system, even though some participants may be perceived as contributing more than others;

Long-term perspective: each part places its needs of the moment into a time continuum that far transcends its own existence;

Global outlook: each part sees fulfilment of its own needs in the larger context of the earth and humanity;

Sustainability: a sustainable community keeps in balance the unique needs of its individual members while serving the needs of the whole, fulfilling the needs of today's generation without compromising the needs of future generations.

References

Capra, F. (1986). 'Paradigms and Paradigm Shifts', *Revision* 9(1): p. 11.

'Characteristics of Eco-Villages' (1991). pp. 7–9 in *Eco-Villages and Sustainable Communities*, A Report for Gaia Trust by Context Institute.

'High Wind' (1991). p. 65 in *Eco-Villages and Sustainable Communities*, A Report for Gaia Trust by Context Institute.

Marien, M. (1989). Paper presented at a University of Wisconsin seminar on 'Universities in an Era of Multiple Transformations'.

Paulson, B. (1991). 'Birthing the Village—Evolutionary Steps', *Windwatch*, Journal of the High Wind Association, Summer/Fall: pp.10–12.

—— (1992). 'Whole System Approach to Sustainable Development', *ICIS Forum* 22(4; October): pp. 39–42.

10 Advancing MuRatopian Community Development in Japan

HIROYUKI NIWA

10.1 Postwar Economic Development

Postwar economic development in Japan, which was predominantly influenced by industrial-age thinking, originated from several democratic economic reforms, including the dissolution of the *zaibatsu* and land reforms in 1945. It was accelerated by the windfall demand created by the Korean war in 1950. Since 1955, the time when the postwar reconstruction period is said to have been completed, miraculously rapid economic growth has taken place. One of the national development policies was to develop seaside industrial complexes—a policy aimed at reclaiming a tract from the sea on which petrochemical and other heavy (smokestack) industrial complexes could be built. It was believed to be the most suitable development practice for Japan, which is a geographically small, mountainous country surrounded by the ocean.

The seaside development policy that started in 1950s, however, resulted in an enormous amount of air and other complex pollutions, causing diseases of the respiratory tract and internal organs among the people living around these complexes. Victims began to fight against the pollution by bringing their cases to court. The Yokkaichi asthmatic suit and the Minamata suit against mercury poisoning are typical of those struggles, which drew nationwide attention. In many cases the government and corporations were blamed for the pollution, and the victims won the lawsuits.

As a result of these struggles, Japanese industrial development policies have begun to shift away from a single-minded industrial-age objective: the pursuit of productivity and profits. Gradually, emphasis has been placed on people's health and a clean environment. That is to say, people and corporations have begun to realise that they are in the same boat. Consequently, new development policies were implemented, such as the diffusion of industries throughout the nation with the creation of the New Industrial Cities in 1962, and of the Fourth Comprehensive National Development Plan in 1987. During the 1970s, the Japanese economy was gradually restructured from an industrial-age to a post-industrial-age one.

This paper, which is partly based on Yamaguchi and Niwa 1994, was written in collaboration with Kaoru Yamaguchi, Nagoya University of Commerce, Japan.

Unfortunately, the policies to diffuse integrated industrial complexes failed. Socioeconomic and industrial power, as well as political power, continued to concentrate in the Tokyo metropolitan area. Some local communities and regions were successful in inviting big corporations to their areas. It turned out, however, that relocation of big corporations to the local areas did not bring the economic returns that were initially expected. Socioeconomic infrastructures in the local communities improved and local employment increased, but human development among local people was not promoted and transfer of technological know-how did not take place as was originally planned. Local government and people failed to take the initiative to establish their own identities, resulting in more dependence on the central government and a massive concentration in the Tokyo metropolitan area. In this way, Japanese economic development in the postwar period failed to develop self-reliant communities and local regions.

10.2 Renewing Furusato

As a challenge to the industrial-complex development mentioned above, a former governor of Kanagawa prefecture (which is located to the west of Tokyo), Kazuji Nagasu, proclaimed 'the age of local community' in 1977. This initiated a movement to restore the self-reliance of community as *furusato*[1] and to revive its cultural heritage. At the same time, the central government took steps to strengthen its control over local communities through its financing powers. Accordingly, the gap between cities, towns and villages began to widen, disabling the effort to attain 'the age of local community'. To counter this devastating situation, in 1987 Kawasaki city in Kanagawa prefecture held a symposium that was attended by representatives of many cities, towns and villages, and presented a vision of a new age of local community. The vision comprised the autonomous solution of regional problems through close co-operation between local government and community people, and through the establishment of interregional networking among different communities and residents. The vision materialised in Ohita prefecture as a movement in which each village aims to produce its own specific product, and in Kumamoto prefecture as a movement to restore lost cultural heritages that are worthy of national attention. (Both prefectures are on the southern island of Kyushu.)

This *furusato* vision was aimed at restoring a local picturesque landscape and a local taste, which were lost as the price of industrial and commercial development in the postwar period. During that period local communities tended to be underpopulated, owing to the domestic migration of young people to large cities. It is true that, during the 1960s and 1970s, when industrial development was under way, this domestic migration helped supply a labour force to the industrial

[1] 'Furusato' is a Japanese word that literally means a birthplace or a native place. It actually refers to a village or a town where people grew up, used to live or are currently living. It also refers to a place that people feel dear to their hearts. Hence, for the Japanese, the word 'furusato' implies not only a geographical place but, more importantly, a mental place they revert to spiritually.

complexes and contributed to rapid economic growth in Japan. The result, however, was to widen the gap between large cities and sparsely populated local communities. Only elderly people were left behind in the local communities. Hence, the *furusato* vision was also intended to stop this trend.

As the Japanese economy restructured itself towards the information age in the late 1970s, large cities once again began to attract younger people, this time as a 'brain force'. The information age requires the integration of research and development, value-added production and production of information and software. The integrated information itself produces powerful knowledge. It is possible to transmit such knowledge through network communication. However, spoken information can hardly be networked without the direct face-to-face contact of people themselves. This is why both information and brain power needed to be accumulated in the Tokyo metropolitan area. It is paradoxical that the information age, which was supposed to help decentralise economic and political power, promoted this domestic concentration of brain power. The *furusato* vision could not stop it.

With the intention of reversing this trend towards the concentration of power in the Tokyo metropolitan area, former prime minister Noboru Takeshita introduced a policy called 'Renewing *Furusato*' in 1988 with the catch-phrase 'Renewing *Furusato* of ourselves, by ourselves, for ourselves'. It was a high-profile policy that provided 100 million yen equally and unconditionally to each city, town and village nationwide (about 3,300 in total) as a seed fund to renew *furusato*. Local government recipients were allowed to use the fund at their discretion: building infrastructure, holding festivals, establishing a foundation for continuing education among local people, and so on. The policy was intended to encourage local communities to come up with new ideas and unique projects so that their regions would be rejuvenated. The central government later created the Furusato Foundation in order to further finance such activities free of financial interest. It has already started financing projects.

The policy was heavily criticised for blindly distributing money in order to gain popularity for the Takeshita government and the Liberal Democratic Party, which held the majority in the government. Initial enthusiasm also seems to have faded, despite the efforts of the government to encourage people to get directly involved in the activities. This is because the local offices of cities, towns and villages have to make reports to their prefectural government concerning their fund-related activities and ask its administrative advice in return. In this sense, the fund is a tied-aid.

Even so, some projects were reported to be very successful. Let me give some examples.

- The mayor of Tsuna-cho, a small town on Awaji Island, spent the whole amount of 100 million yen on a gold ingot to show townspeople how valuable the money was, until they came up with a better idea for renewing the town community with that amount of money. Unexpectedly, the gold ingot itself began to attract lots of tourists who wanted to touch the ingot with their own fingers. And the town suddenly became a target of tourism.

- Uji city of Kyoto-fu established the Murasaki Shikibu Literature Awards in 1989, named after the famous eleventh-century writer of *The Tale of Genji*, the oldest romantic tale of Prince Genji (in 44 volumes), and his illegitimate son, Prince Kaoru, (volumes 45–54, known as Uji Jūjō). Among 279 project proposals this was selected by the committee of twelve citizen representatives, mainly because Uji city is known as the location of Price Kaoru's romance in the story and the city wished to support the activities of female writers like Murasaki Shikibu.
- Saga city, Kyushu island, used to be known as a city full of clean rivers and creeks until they began to be severely polluted. In 1980 the city promoted a city-wide movement to clean up the polluted waters. Under these circumstances the Dragonfly Sanctuaries project was selected in 1989 from among 108 applications in the hope that it will change citizens' attitude towards clean waters and natural habitats for dragonflies. Schoolchildren now use their pools as dragonfly hatcheries and release young dragonflies into the rivers every year. Dragonfly Pond was completed in 1993 in the city park. Dragonfly photographic contests were established in 1990, and in 1992 there were 312 entries, a number that is increasing.
- The Nagoya branch of NHK public broadcasting, in central Japan, ran a series of participatory television programmes at lunchtime called 'Renewing *Furusato* Plaza' from 1991 to 1994. Many local people who were skilled in traditional arts and crafts, community products and folk dancing and singing took part in the programme. This series in turn reactivated the movement to conserve cultural heritage and traditions in these areas, which had produced several famous samurai warriors and shoguns in medieval Japan.

10.3 The Second Stage of Renewing Furusato

In 1992, the fifth year of the Renewing *Furusato* project, the Ministry of Home Affairs distributed questionnaires on the *furusato* projects among local government recipients in order to evaluate how effectively the funds had been used so far. Of the recipients, 94 per cent evaluated the programme positively and wished to continue their *furusato* projects. Specifically, they argued that *furusato* projects helped local people to participate in many activities voluntarily, renew community development with creative and original ideas and promote their planning and managerial abilities. Tables 10.1 and 10.2 summarise the *furusato* projects.

At the same time, local government recipients also pointed out negative aspects of the projects. These were that the projects did not increase local incomes and employment, and that they failed to stabilise the flow of population. Moreover, more than half of the recipients complained that they could not accomplish the projects as a result of the budget constraints caused by the economic recession. These negative evaluations discouraged the central government and the Ministry of Home Affairs. However, it is felt that these *furusato* projects have to

Table 10.1. Classification of material *furusato* projects, 1994–5

	Number	(%)
Conservation of historical sites and ruins	146	5.8
Cultural and educational facilities	289	11.5
Sports and recreational facilities	511	20.2
Environmental protection and amenities	848	33.6
Urban infrastructure	489	19.4
Promotion of local industries	31	1.2
Communications and networks facilities	51	2.0
Multi-purpose halls and facilities	92	3.6
Other	68	2.7
Total	2,525	100.0

Source: Koda *et al*. 1995: 39.

Table 10.2. Classification of service *furusato* projects, 1995

	Number	(%)
Support for NGO activities	2,729	7.1
Software and communications networks	792	2.1
Interregional exchange programmes	1,499	3.9
International exchange programmes	2,196	5.7
Recycling and environmental activities	3,743	9.7
Welfare services for the elderly	3,239	8.4
Reinventing local economies	5,044	13.1
Sports and well-being programmes	3,855	10.0
Preservation of cultural heritage	4,515	11.7
Promotion of social and adult education	2,879	7.5
Furusato events and festivals	3,234	8.4
Establishment of foundations and other	4,811	12.5
Total	38,536	100.0

Source: Koda *et al*. 1995: 40.

be continued despite the difficulties, because *furusato* communities are where people grew up, used to live or are currently living, and are dear to their hearts. Without prosperity and the better environment of *furusato* communities, we cannot attain the well-being of people or, consequently, the wealth of nations. Reasoning this way, the central government decided to continue to fund *furusato* projects as a second stage of the Renewing *Furusato* programme for the period 1993–5 with the following objectives in mind:

• continuation of support for the on-going *furusato* projects so that local people continue to feel attached to their home places;

- establishment of local identities and future visions through the development activities aimed at renewing communities;
- construction of affluent local communities through the expansion of local industries and social capital.

Based on these objectives, Renewing *Furusato* grants of between 60 million and 160 million yen, this time depending on the size of the local government recipients, were provided for the three years between 1993 and 1995. Their effects remain to be evaluated in the near future. The third stage of the renewing *Furusato* fund is to follow, starting in 1996.

10.4 Community as an Eco-Share Region

The government-led Renewing *Furusato* programme has so far failed to renew local communities and reverse the trend towards mega-cities in Japan. This is because the programme has been pursued within a worn-out industrial-age framework. However, some projects seemed to be in accordance with the new-thinking paradigm of the information age that is presented in Chapter 5. We can observe three new-thinking features that have emerged out of the *furusato* projects started in 1988. They are ecologically sustainable development, the revival of cultural heritage and tradition, and participatory democracy.

These features have seldom been observed in the postwar period of economic development in Japan. In this sense they can be said to reflect a new-thinking paradigm of community development in the information age. However, this nationwide fad of *furusato* development was, as discussed in section 10.2, originally initiated by a fund apportioning 100 million yen as seed money to each *furusato* project, though the grants have been extended every year since then. Many local communities began to promote projects that just looked like something new without being guided by the new-thinking paradigm of the information age. Accordingly, owing to the lack of a new-thinking vision, most of the *furusato* projects seem to have been lost in the midst of the old framework of the industrial age. To further advance *furusato* projects and community development, therefore, it is absolutely necessary that they are guided by the new-thinking paradigm of the information age. Here we will show how the old paradigm is impeding the further advancement of community development.

The Japanese prefectural system was introduced in 1871, immediately after the Meiji restoration, by eliminating the system of samurai clan districts of the Edo period. In the creation of this prefectural system, the ecosystem was not seriously taken into consideration. As a result, traditional cultural regions along the rivers were separated into artificial prefectures across the rivers. This was unfortunate for community development, because community life had been supported by the rivers, and community activities along the basin of the rivers had been very natural. The history of the rivers has been the history of human beings and communities since the time ancient civilisations originated along the river basins.

Let us take the example of the Nagara river, which was the only major river without a dam in Japan until recently. The upper Nagara runs through Gifu prefecture and the lower Nagara is shared by Aichi and Mie prefectures; these three prefectures are located in central Japan. The central government began constructing a dam at the mouth of the river for better water-management in the region. The dam was completed in April 1995, even though its construction was very controversial and many people objected to it. If the dam is built, grassroots activists complained, it will destroy the ecosystem of the region and endanger animal and plant species. To make matters worse, an agreement had not been reached among the three prefectures on the efficient use of the river, because each has different economic interests in the river basin. Gifu prefecture on the upper Nagara argued that the construction of a dam would obstruct the free traffic of the Japanese sweetfish, *ayu*, while Aichi and Mie prefectures wanted it in order to secure their water resources. If prefectural administrations had been unified along the basin of the river, a holistic environmental assessment would have been made possible, before the construction of the dam, for the benefit of people and all other living things along the river. This is just an example of how community development is hindered by the prefectural system of the industrial age.

There are quite a few examples of this type. For instance, many communities have built, and are still building, gorgeous community halls and multi-purpose facilities (see Table 10.1) without regard to the size of their population and without a plan for their efficient use. And expensive information-processing and network communication systems and audiovisual devices have been installed in most of these facilities. Instead of building their own halls, many communities could have built joint halls, sharing not only construction costs but also communication equipment without additional cost. Community halls are public goods and information facilities can be more efficiently used by sharing. The present prefectural system, however, discourages a sharing of these facilities. What a waste of resources!

It is now apparent that the present prefectural system, based on the nation-state framework of the industrial age, has become irrelevant for the information age. For the further advancement of community development in Japan, this hundred-year-old administrative system has to be totally redesigned to be suitable for a communal system of ecoshare regions. There is an argument in central government and among business leaders that this system of forty-eight prefectures should be restructured into a new administrative system consisting of 10 broad states. We strongly oppose it because these new divisions of Japanese land only consider economic efficiencies and do not reflect the ecological aspects of the communities.

Sustainable community development will be advanced and cultural activities will be reactivated only within ecoshare regions that are separated by ecological boundaries based on nature's vegetation, habitats and biosphere cycles. Moreover, only in the ecoshare regions will a sense of community be cultivated and the unity of man and nature be promoted for the welfare of all. Therefore, we have to create new ecoshare regions out of industrial-age prefectures, based on a holistic perspective on their natural ecosystems and sociocultural traditions. This is a first but very important step towards creating MuRatopia, the framework for which has been laid out in Chapter 5.

10.5 MuRatopian Communities

The ideas behind the three new-thinking traits that have emerged out of the renewing *furusato* projects are not new. What is new is that local government and community people have seriously tried to incorporate these ideas into their community development projects—ideas that had been neglected under the objectives of economic efficiency and profitability in the industrial age. To advance these features, however, they have to be guided by the new-thinking paradigm of the information age.

For ecologically sustainable development, the utilisation of public and private land has to be carefully managed. Specifically, speculation in land values should not be allowed in the area of community development, since it has often caused the inefficient utilisation of land and inequality of income distribution in Japan. These were most typically revealed during the so-called 'bubble' economy in the early 1990s. The Community Land Trust (CLT), which is discussed in Chapter 6, should be more carefully considered as a method of avoiding land speculation, and as a way of establishing community-based ecoshare regions. This is one way that landowners and tenants can be reunified as community inhabitants.

It is also essential for sustainable development to handle the recycling of industrial products efficiently. Products have to be designed with their recycling uses in mind. Products without a recycling attribute should be discouraged as outdated industrial-age products. When communities introduce new projects or invite new investment and industries, they have to set up very strict recycling criteria. If all communities adopt similar criteria, business corporations will have no choice but to be community corporations supporting sustainable development. It will be a challenge, therefore, for all communities to incorporate these two requirements—that is, the efficient use of land and recycling-oriented products—in their community development projects. Only by meeting this challenge, will a reunification of man and nature ultimately be attained and communities become truly MuRatopian.

Participatory democracy is one of the most essential features of the information age—participatory democracy in business management and community administration. Information and communications network technology makes the direct participation of people possible for the first time in history. Any organisation, private or public, that does not allow this information-age democracy will be driven out of market and community through the competitive forces of the market. Every citizen should be allowed to initiate not only renewing *furusato* projects but also community ordinances. Moreover, participatory democracy has to be practised among business corporations in the MuRatopian community. In other words, if they want to operate in the community, they have to accept a system of self-management by co-workers, or at least the Employee Stock Ownership Plan (ESOP), which is discussed in Chapter 5. This is one way that employers and employees can be reunified as co-workers. Eventually, participatory democracy will pervade a whole MuRatopian community.

I have now briefly shown how three new-thinking traits that have emerged out of the *furusato* projects can be further advanced so that an industrial-age community is transformed into a MuRatopian community in the information age. Through this transformation we are led into a new information age. A community that hesitates to transform itself and tries to stay in the old industrial framework will be left behind in this information revolution.

10.6 Conclusion

The information age is characterised by two fundamental features. First, it is *a global networking system*, enabled by satellite and computer communications, such as the Internet (specifically the World-Wide Web), as though they were providing our body with a nervous system. Hence, like our body any *local* incident will inevitably create a *global* impact in the information age. This entails a holistic view of the globe. Second, endowed with complicated communications networks, the information age operates as if it has its own *mind*. Hence, it becomes creative like our brain. Accordingly, the globe itself will be viewed as if it has a mind and self-adjusting body. In this sense, the information age truly becomes the age of Gaia (Lovelock 1988).

In conclusion, as an inseparable part of the global community, each community in Japan has its own human feelings and is able to share feelings of joy and sorrow with other communities. In this way a MuRatopian community becomes considerate of other communities. That is, it becomes a community with a human mind. This is our MuRatopian vision of community development in Japan in the twenty-first century.

References and Further Reading

Koda, Masaharu *et al.* (eds.) (1995). *Strategies for Community Development*, Gyosei.
Lovelock, J. E. (1988). *The Ages of Gaia: A Biography of Our Living Earth*, New York: Bantam Books.
Niwa, Hiroyuki (1991). *Studies on Furusato in Central Japan*, Mainichi Shinbun.
—— and Kogure, Nobuo (1992). *Age of Creating Regional Cultures*, Gyosei.
Yamaguchi, Kaoru and Niwa, Hiroyuki (1994). 'New Thinking on Japanese Community Development in the Information Age', *Technological Forecasting and Social Change* 45(1–XX): pp. 79–92.

11 Sustainable Philosophy for Global Community Development: A Korean Perspective

YOON-JAE CHUNG

11.1 Politics as Leadership

During the past decades, in Western political analysis, politics has usually been regarded as a *power-struggle* and political leaders merely as *power-seekers*. Modern political scientists have tended to neglect the value of governance and the role of leaders in the political processes. They assess politics and democracy more in terms of *input* functions, paying less attention to the *conversion* and *output* functions by which political leaders consider alternatives, make decisions and implement policies. One US political scientist argued that leadership phenomena and aspects of governing in politics have been neglected by modern social scientists because modern social sciences have been predominantly influenced by the European determinisms—evolutionary, psychological, and economic (Paige 1977: 6).

However, in retrospect, we can see that most civil revolutions have been accomplished through the prominent leadership of revolutionary leaders—Oliver Cromwell, Napoleon Bonaparte and George Washington, for example. And Third World modernisation has been successful where resolute presidents or prime ministers have exercised strong leadership in the course of national development: for example, Lee Kwan-Yew in Singapore, Park Chung Hee in South Korea, Chiang Kai-shek in Taiwan and Deng Xiaoping in China. It follows that, for successful and efficient community-building, firm, purposive and legitimate leadership is indispensable.

Meanwhile, when we witness such serious global problems as the threat of nuclear war, famine, ecological crisis, energy depletion and the newly emerging ethno-nationalism, we can no longer regard politics simply as a power-struggle. Instead, we have to redefine politics as *leadership* or the *art of governance* in an attempt to save humankind from these global crises and to prevent the worst catastrophe. Since the crisis is global in its scope and eventual impact, and demands a globally concerted set of actions to bring it under control, concerned leadership must diagnose the situation and devise the course of action for the people. In this regard, one prominent US political scientist, Robert C. Tucker, criticised conventional power-oriented political analysis as being of little use and proposed a leadership approach to contemporary crisis situations, aimed towards safer and more humane community development in the world (Tucker 1981: 1–27, 114–58).

In this context, it is generally suggested that present world leaders, compared with such past leaders as Churchill, Roosevelt, de Gaulle and Nehru, have limited vision and no sight of the elusive new world order as they sway from one opinion poll to another.[1]

It seems that concerned scholars and commentators have begun to view the *developmental dictators* in a more friendly light than before. They admit that people in those developing areas need a strong state and political stability more than a democratic parliament and elections. They now even suggest that it is wiser to encourage efficient leadership in Third World countries than to try to transplant Western democratic institutions (Talbot 1993: 37; Barro 1993).

Based upon these understandings and observations, in this chapter I define politics as leadership or governance and attempt to explore some ideal political-leadership principles that could promote sustainable community development in the global age. For this purpose, I examine the Korean philosophical interpretation of the concepts of *governance, freedom* and *nation* that was provided by An Chae-hong (1891–1965).[2] Concerned scholars and political leaders should find some useful philosophical insights to help their attempts to overcome the contemporary, post-Cold War dilemmas of ideological uncertainties and emerging ethno-nationalisms.

11.2 A Universal Principle of Governance: The Ideal of *Tasari*

Korea has remained divided since 1945, and it has experienced serious ideological conflict throughout the whole process of development. Communist North Korea and Republican South Korea replicated, as it were, the ideological war between the Soviet Union and the USA. Subsequently, Korean intellectuals and political leaders, An Chae-hong among them, have made serious attempts to overcome the ideological and territorial division of the nation. Concerned with national integration through a holistic Korean political idea, An Chae-hong criticised both Marxism–Leninism and bourgeois democracy and proposed his unique concept of Korean democracy, *Tasari*. He argued that bourgeois

---

[1] *Time*, 12 July 1993 and 2 August 1993.

[2] An Chae-hong was one of Korea's prominent political leaders during the postwar transitional period from 1945 to 1948. He studied politics and economics at Waseda University in Japan. He interrupted his career as an writer and historian to enter politics, with the clear purpose of establishing One Korea in the face of Cold War politics. He founded Kungmin-dang (the Nationalist Party) and was Civil Administrator in the US Military Government. During the Korean War, he was kidnapped and taken to the North by the Communists, and he died in 1965 at Pyongyang. On his ideas and political life, see Chung (1988).

democracy had degenerated into plutocracy in the years following the French Revolution. He also attacked the antihumanistic totalitarianism in Communist countries and criticised Karl Marx's theory of economic determinism and pseudo-scientific diagnosis of industrial society.

Tasari is a Korean word that means 'the cosmological principle that governs the universe', and An Chae-hong understood it to be the fundamental principle of politics or governance when it is applied to the management of human affairs on earth. He expounded that *Tasari* ultimately means 'politics itself' or 'democracy' as an ideal form of politics. With this, he attempted to provide a Korean definition of politics in an effort to establish a new political community free from ideological cold wars. According to his unique linguistic interpretations, *Tasari* involves a pair of universal democratic principles indispensable in the development of a healthy human community.

Tasari represents the ideal of *Manmin Ch'ong'on*, *Manmin Konghwa*, *Chinbaek* or *Kaebaek*, which mean that 'every individual is endowed with the basic right to express his or her opinion in a community', or 'all are speaking'. He explained that this is because *Tasari* shares the same linguistic root as the Korean word *Ta Sario*, which means 'by allowing all the people to speak their individual opinions'. *Tasari* also represents the ideal of *Manmin Kongsaeng*, *Taejung Kongsaeng*, *Chinsaeng* or *Kaehwal*, which mean 'all the people should live together in a balanced human condition'. He explained that this is because *Tasari* also has the same linguistic root as the Korean word *Ta Sallinda*, which means 'to let all the people lead their own lives as decent human beings'.

An Chae-hong was one of the Korean political leaders who struggled against the ideological conflicts between Left and Right in postwar Korean politics. He attempted to find an alternative theoretical prescription to heal such cold war situations. Thus, with this linguistic interpretation of Korean political ideas, he emphatically demonstrated that *Tasari* is a holistic political ideology that involves the democratic principle of *Manmin Ch'ong'on* or individual freedom as a practical means of reflecting the people's voice and opinions in the political process, and also the democratic principle of *Manmin Kongsaeng* or social well-being for all as the ultimate goal of politics. He argued that *Tasari* should be adopted as the principle of governance for a future unified Korea and that a parliamentary system should be institutionalised to carry out reforms according to these democratic ideals (Chung 1988: 117–33, 166–71).

Needless to say, in modern political history, liberal democracy and socialism have been the standard theories or political ideologies for ideal community life. But now the world is entering into a crisis situation in terms of political ideology as well as ecology and the threat of nuclear war. Socialism had already lost its ideological rationale with the collapse of the Communist countries, while capitalist liberal democracy is being morally challenged in both advanced Western countries and developing countries. Consequently, we can argue that a new, future-oriented community-building effort need no longer rely upon these antagonistic ideologies. Instead, we may have to develop and practise a holistic system of universal values of *Tasari* in the concrete process of problem-solving.

11.3 An Organic Worldview: Freedom of *Na, Nara, Nuri*

In search of a new concept of freedom or anti-totalitarian principle to counter ideological extremism, An Chae-hong reasoned that every cosmic entity could be free and still maintain an organic harmony with all others. He did so by demonstrating the identical linguistic origin of the three Korean words *Na, Nara* and *Nuri*, which mean 'individual', 'state' and 'the world', respectively. *Na* means 'I' and *Nat'ta*, which has the same linguistic origin as *Na*, means 'to bear'. From this he reasoned that Koreans consider that everything in the world is meaningful or is recognised as an existing entity only when *Na* as an individual is born and assigns a subjective value or meaning to it. From this, it can be inferred that Koreans value the individual as fundamental in projecting the ideal state of human life.

By a similar logic, An Chae-hong argued that *Nara* is meaningful only when *Na* is born and exists, and thus *Nara* is not merely an institutional entity that should disregard the voluntary consent of individuals. Accordingly, it is natural to say that all laws and government institutions should be the consequential reflection of the free will of individuals as constituents of *Nara*. Furthermore, focusing on the harmonious and integrated relationship of *Na, Nara* and *Nuri*, he discussed his ideas of freedom and the ideal relationship among the cosmic entities of individuals, nations and the world.

First, *Na* is the actual subject on the earth, who embodies and practises human ideals. *Nara* is a spiritual co-operative as well as an institution, and should take care of individuals' desires for life and happiness. Accordingly, a *Na* must be free from other *Na* and *Nara*, and a *Nara* must be free from foreign *Nara*.

Second, *Nara* forms, develops and advances, realising the ideals or desires of *Na* as an individual. Thus, it may rightly be said that when all laws and government institutions reflect the will and ideas of each *Na*, individuals can be truly free and happy.

Third, it follows that a mechanistic totalitarianism, which would oppress the freedom of individuals, must infringe upon the universal principle of *Tasari*. For this reason, imperialist states that would invade independent sovereign states and disregard the freedom of individuals must be repelled.

Fourth, *Nara* is not merely an administrative instrument for political rulings; it is a spiritual entity. *Na* is a fundamental basis of *Nara*, while *Nara* is the extension of *Na*. In their ideal form, they are inseparable and united as one. That is why one can say *Na* is *Nara*, and vice versa. The idea of an inseparable relationship between the two entities is rooted in traditional Korean philosophy, which includes the orthodox universal principles that 'One is Many' and 'One is the Great'. Thus any political ideology that devalues the individual as merely a passive agent of the state is unacceptable.

Fifth, *Nuri*, or the world, involves *Na* and *Nara*, and it embodies the Fair Principle of the Universe. Just as an independent *Na* is the basic unit of the *Nara*, so an independent *Nara* is the basic unit of the *Nuri*. Yet *Na, Nara* and *Nuri* contribute together to maintaining the organic order of the universe (Chung 1988: 163–6).

In sum, An Chae-hong attempted to demonstrate the organic relationship among individuals, states and the world as the ideal state of being from a Korean philosophical point of view. He argued against any anti-humanistic ideologies and any form of violent and extremist politics, and advocated individual freedom, national sovereignty and world peace. He also emphasised the principle of 'Cosmic Togetherness'[3] in the search for the ideal state of human existence at every level of community life—local, national, and global.

11.4 Beyond Ethno-Nationalism: *Kyore* as Cultural Community

Although An Chae-hong envisioned the Korea of the future as a unified and independent nation, he also expounded Western and Asian experiences of nationalism alongside his own views on nation and nationalism. He defined nation as 'a cultural community of ethnic homogeneity and common destiny within a definite geographical boundary', and stressed the cultural element as the most important in forming a nation. He maintained that 'each nation in the world has its own culture; its time-honoured cultural tradition needs to be reflected in the formative process of the future national society as well as in the present national life'. In a cultural approach to nationalism, he argued that 'the concept of nation or nationalism is not necessarily the historical product of civil revolutions or capitalist development in the Western countries'. He continued to argue that 'nationalism has raison d'être to be proclaimed anywhere and anytime as long as it sincerely advocates the human ideal of international peace and co-operation'.

But, for An Chae-hong, a nation was 'a living co-operative for the domestic people' and also 'one of many sharers of goodwill in the international society'. Thus, suggesting the idea of 'international nationalism' or 'national internationalism', he once argued that the truly free and healthy internationalisation of a global community could only be achieved through each nation's political and cultural enlightenment. From this point of view, he specifically criticised the extremist nationalisms in Germany and Japan. During the past imperialist period, as a result of their overemphasis on *pure blood* and overestimation of national superiority, both nations had invaded neighbouring nations and consequently broken regional and world peace.

Nation is *Kyore* in Korean. According to his interpretation, it has two different linguistic origins, and thus two meanings. One is *Kyollium*, which means 'inner solidarity' or 'solid organisation within'. The other is *Kyorum*, which means 'to duel, to compete with each other' or 'to resist'. This demonstrates that the word *Kyore* implies a very realistic and universal mechanism within a nation

---

[3] This concept was cited in Lee 1992: 6.

as a human organisation. But it does not hint at an ethnocentric concept of nation, and thus one may infer that ethnicity is not a critical element in the formation of *Kyore* or nation. He also explained that *Kyore* is a pre-*Nara* concept in Korean history because the word *Kyore* had been used by the ancient Koreans even before the Three Kingdoms period when *Nara* or the state had first emerged in Korean history (Chung 1988: 171–4).

In sum, An Chae-hong discussed nationalism in the context of international relations moving towards global peace and co-operation, and opposed imperialist nationalism and ethnocentric discourses of nation. He advocated a concept of nation not as ethnically homogeneous community but as cultural community that would communicate and transact with other communities as one of the sharers of goodwill in an open global society.

11.5 Conclusion

As a conclusion, let us summarise some philosophical or theoretical implications for future political leaderships that are concerned with sustainable community development.

First, seeing the world face the crisis of several global problems, politics needs to be defined as leadership that guides the people to participate in problem-solving processes. Yet, in order to prevent the re-emergence of fascist leaderships, we may have to examine the emerging discussions of the need for the 'good tyrant' or 'philosopher–king'[4] and the theories of 'totalitarian democracy'[5] very carefully in a post-modern approach to the ideal form of politics or democracy.

Second, for successful community-building at any level of politics, political leaders should develop and practise a holistic ideology, such as the Korean democratic ideal of *Tasari*, which regards individual freedom as a means of reflecting the peoples' will and opinions in decision-making processes and takes social well-being for all as its ultimate goal. Of course, it may be idealistic to expect all political leaders to theorise a holistic ideology by themselves. But holistic leadership principles can be represented and practised by new political leaderships that want to try to avoid capitalist immoralities and socialist inefficiencies.[6]

Third, the principle of 'Cosmic Togetherness', which was suggested in the discussion of the Korean concepts of *Na*, *Nara*, *Nuri* and *Kyore*, needs to be emphasised in order to cure ethno-nationalist political diseases and the ecological crisis. And in this regard, national and even local community initiatives should be taken in the global context as a critical part of human efforts to be free from such political and ecological crises. An open mind based upon this principle of

---

[4] This concept appeared in *Time* (13 May 1991) in discussions of Plato's Philosopher–King, Singapore's Confucian dictator Lee Kwang-Yew, and Vaclav Havel as a strong-willed philosopher–king.

[5] The best introduction of this theory is Talmon 1985.

[6] A good example at local level was reported in Whyte and Whyte 1991.

'Cosmic Togetherness' may enhance mutual communications and co-operation in the course of establishing a new world order with global peace, ecological balance and regional neighbourhood.

References

Barro, Robert A. (1993). 'Pushing Democracy is No Key to Prosperity', *Wall Street Journal*, 14 December.

Chung Yoon-Jae (1988).'A Medical Approach to Political Leadership: An Chae-hong and A Healthy Korea', Ph.D. dissertation, University of Hawaii at Manoa.

Lee Myung-Hyun (1992). 'Paradox of Techno-Utopia', a paper presented at the International Philosophy Conference in Seoul, 18–20 August.

Paige, Glenn D. (1977). *The Scientific Study of Political Leadership*, New York: The Free Press.

Talbott, Strobe (1993). 'Why the People Cheer Bad Guys in a Coup', *Time*, 4 May.

Talmon, J. L. (1985). *The Origins of Totalitarian Democracy*, Boulder, Colo. and London: Westview Press.

Tucker, Robert C. (1981). *Politics as Leadership*, Columbia: University of Missouri Press.

Whyte, W. F. and Whyte, K. K. (1991). *Making Modragon: The Growth and Dynamics of the Worker Cooperative Complex*, New York: Cornell University Press.

12 The Development of Rural Communities in China under a Socialist Market Economy

QIN LINZHENG

12.1 Introduction

After fourteen years' practice of reform and openness, and through theoretical discussion for years as well, China has clearly realised that the establishment of a socialist market economic system should be set as the goal of economic reform in order to liberate and develop productive power further, to quicken the steps of socioeconomic development and to enable China to move towards industrialisation and modernisation.[1]

As a developing country, China is known for its agricultural base; most of the people are peasants living in rural areas. By the end of 1991, the number of social labourers in China engaged in agricultural productive labour or agricultural activities reached 438.57 million, more than 75 per cent of the total of 583.65 million. There are only 476 cities (including 289 at county level) in the whole country; there are 1,894 counties (more than four times the number of cities), which consist of rural communities at three different levels: 43,660 townships, 11,882 small towns and 804,153 villages (State Bureau of Statistics 1992: 17).

Owing to the special position occupied by the rural communities in China, this is where many great changes and reforms in the country are initiated. The founding of the socialist market economic system means another significant change in rural China, following on from land reform, the mutual aid and co-operation movement, people's commune and the responsibility system based on the household joint production and contract, which both challenges and provides opportunities for the development of rural communities.

12.2 The Targets of the Socialist Market Economic System

There are similarities and differences between the socialist and capitalist market economic systems. Their common ground lies in their both being market economies, following the law, the mechanism and the rule of market activities. The

---

[1] The selecting of this goal was officially announced by Jiang Zemin in his speech at the Fourteenth National Congress of the Communist Party of China in October 1992. See Communist Party of China 1992.

socialist market economy of China is a particular form of market economy, as are the co-ordinative or co-operative type of Japan and Korea, the social market economy of Germany and the scattered type of market economy of the USA (Li 1992: 27). The difference is one of pattern, the result of the distinct situation of each country. The differences between the socialist and capitalist market economies are determined mainly by their economic base. The former is principally based on public ownership; the latter on private ownership. In addition, they can also be distinguished from each other in terms of their distribution system, macro-regulation and macro-control—the level of regulation and control by the state, including state planning, to adjust the development of the economy.

The Chinese socialist market economy also differs from market socialism (first initiated by the Polish economists), although both emphasise the utilisation of the market mechanism (Ruxin 1988: 834). They diverge primarily in their understanding of a planned economy, but not in terms of public ownership of means of production. Unlike market socialism, which calls for socialism to be built on the foundations of a market economy, the Chinese system believes that a planned economy is not peculiar to socialism, since capitalism also involves planning, and that a market economy is not peculiar to capitalism, since socialism also has a market; market economies and their planned counterparts are both economic means, rather than an essential distinction between socialism and capitalism, as Deng Xiaoping suggested (Communist Party of China 1992: 21). In other words, the Chinese system does not equate a planned economy with socialism and a market with capitalism, whereas market socialism regards a planned economy as being specific to socialism and equates such an economy with socialism.

What is clear by now are China's main targets in building the new economic system:

- to develop the market economy in a socialist way by combining it with the basic system and the nature of socialism. Thus the new economy will become socialist by keeping such characteristics as an ownership structure based principally on public ownership, a system of distribution according to work and a mechanism of macro-regulation and macro-control by the state;
- to liberate and develop productive power further, and combine the market mechanism (price, competition and so on) with macro-regulation and macro-control (including state planning);
- to organise a nationwide and unified market system within which the market economy can develop well and become a greater part of the world economy. The advanced management techniques and administration methods of other countries of the world are being incorporated and used for reference, and foreign capital, resources, qualified personnel and private economy have been introduced;
- to apply economic policies, economic laws and regulation, planning guidance and necessary administration and management in order to ensure the healthy development of the market and overcome its inherent weaknesses and negative side, and combine present with long-term interests.

12.3 The Challenge to Rural Development

The socialist market economy is now challenging decision-makers at different levels in rural China to solve more quickly the remaining obstacles to communities' development in the future. These are the starting points for that challenge:

A widening gap between the rich and poor rural communities and peasant families. Development and change in the rural communities of China are unequal. The general tendency is towards faster development and greater changes in rural communities in the coastal areas and suburbs of big cities, and less development and slow change in rural communities in inland and remote regions. The gap between the rich and the poor is widening. The average income gap between rural communities has increased from 2.9 times in 1978 to 4.5 times in 1990 (Zhu 1992: 73). The gap between the rich and the poor can also be seen in income differentials between peasant families, which have already reached factors of tens, or even more than a hundred. In recent years, these gaps have continued to widen. The first challenge the rural decision-makers face is how to narrow such gaps and create a short-cut to common richness.

The poverty of rural China. Another challenge is how to free the rural communities from the yoke of poverty through the development of the market economy. In the last forty years or more, especially since the reform of the economic system, the state of poverty in rural communities has been alleviated to a great extent. But compared with the per capita incomes of domestic cities and towns, and of other countries, most of the Chinese rural areas are still lands of poverty. According to an investigation in 1991, the average annual per capita income of peasant families was about US$130 (State Bureau of Statistics 1992: 50). In some of the poorest rural communities, the problem of food and clothing has not yet been thoroughly solved, clean water is short, the electricity supply is insufficient and the rate of infant death is higher than elsewhere. Their backwardness in industrialisation and information technology has further broadened the gap between such communities and modernised societies.

Agricultural shrinkage and recession. Owing to the shortage of funds for buying agricultural products since 1989, the state used to buy its main agricultural products cheaply from peasants with 'white notes'.[2] Thus the peasants actually received no payment, and their income was greatly reduced. In 1990, the state selling price of means of production was doubled while the state buying price of agricultural products remained the same. The initiative was dampened, a large number of peasants left their farms and more than 100 million of them thus

---

2 'White notes' are written notes for which a peasant selling products to the state would someday be paid. The 'white note' problem was widely discussed in the mass media, and basically solved through state intervention.

became unemployed.[3] Agricultural shrinkage and recession also resulted from other factors, including the course of rural industrialisation, the real estate craze and the zone for economic development craze.

The heavy burden of over-population. Over-population has been a fundamental factor conditioning the development of the Chinese economy and society, and of rural areas in particular. Needless to say, the policy of birth control has been a great success, but there are signs that the birth rate has begun to rise again in some rural communities in recent years. The continual enlargement of the population in rural areas led to a rapid decrease in the quantity, and the excess consumption, of natural resources per capita, and to the deterioration of productive conditions in rural China (Xie 1992: 52). As a result, the decrease in per capita growth in agricultural products has quickened to the point where rural China will reach a level of zero, or even negative growth.

The deterioration of the quality of the rural environment. As a result of such factors as the increase in population size, continued industrialisation, the loss of water and the erosion of soil, the unceasing expansion of arid and water-logged areas caused by natural disasters, and the drop in soil fertility and quality, the endless deterioration of environmental quality has already become a major threat to the development of Chinese rural communities. About 300 million mus of cultivated land in China have been polluted by big industry, village and town industry and farm chemicals, creating tremendous economic losses (Xie 1992: 52).

The shortage of inputs into agricultural production. Inputs into agricultural production include such factors as labour power, capital, industries for agriculture, and science and technology. The input shortage in Chinese agricultural production combines with the low productivity of peasants, which is associated with the fact that less developed agriculture is labour intensive and of high added value. Since 1985, only about 3 per cent of total investment has been in agriculture, which is even less than in the late 1970s and early 1980s (Shi 1992: 22). Owing to the need to repay foreign debts and develop industry, it will be impossible to increase agricultural investment in the future. The lower standards of culture and education and the backwardness in science and technology in rural areas are also unfavourable to the increase of scientific and technological input.

Heightened social problems. The social problems caused by peasants have tended to become more and more acute. They are the results of the complexity of social relationships, the spread of social contradictions, unemployment, immigration, crimes and so on. The increasing rate of peasant crime, in particular, has become an important cause of social turbulence.

[3] This number is based on Xie Shusen's statistics. There are different sources indicating the size of rural unemployment in China. According to Xiao Lijian, the surplus labour power in rural China was more than 129,652,500 in 1990, reaching nearly one-third of total labour power in rural China. See Xie 1992; Xiao 1992.

As well as all these problems, the extremely low rate of social security coverage,[4] the underdeveloped rural market, the lack of an information economy and educational backwardness are also challenges that the decision-makers, especially those in rural China, cannot avoid. To a great extent, the success of the new economic system will lie in the effective solution of these critical problems.

12.4 New Basic Principles of Rural Renewal

The founding of the socialist market economic system sets new demands on the renewal of Chinese rural communities. According to the new system, the main principles such renewal should follow are:

Persistence in reform and openness. Rural communities must renew themselves continuously, by unceasing reform and openness. The economic reform is only part of their overall reform. Social, educational, cultural and other aspects are also in need of reform and openness. Without comprehensive development, it will be hard for Chinese rural communities to renew themselves as a modernised, sustainable and global village in the information age.

Pursuit of sustainable and co-ordinated development. The development of rural communities should be sustainable and well co-ordinated. The socialist market economy requires the optimisation of resource allocation, co-ordination between present and long-term interests and the common well-being of community members. Accordingly, Chinese rural communities must co-ordinate economic development with the development of society and the improvement of the environment and quality of life. They must make full and harmonious use of all forms of appropriate technology–traditional and high.

Combination of development with macro-regulation and macro-control. In order to ensure sustainable and co-ordinated development, a close combination of the development in rural communities with macro-regulation and macro-control is needed. This will help rural communities to make use of national regulations, including state planning, economic laws and different policies to enhance their management. It will also contribute to keeping the basic socialist line unchanged and society and the polity stable.

12.5 The Future of Rural Development

Reform and openness, the development and change in rural communities, have obviously contributed to defining the goal of China's economic reform: building

---

[4] The rate of social security coverage was 20 per cent in China as a whole, and only 1.6 per cent in rural areas (Research Group of Social Development 1991: 24).

a new system based on the socialist market economy. In turn, the founding of such a system will provide opportunities for the development of rural areas. These opportunities are of economic, social, political and cultural significance to the future of rural China.

Turning rural community into marketplace. The planned economic system of agriculture separates rural area and peasant from market. The market economy mechanism creates an opportunity for rural communities and peasants to enter the market directly. This enables them to make decisions on production and management totally by themselves. The proportion of the price of agricultural products that is determined by the market has been increasingly enlarged, and has already reached 80 per cent (Li 1993: 8). The structure of production can be adjusted according to market demand. There has been a diversification of products, which has resulted in freeing products from the main patterns of *grain–pig* type and *eating–wearing* type; and well-known, high-class and special products with high economic benefit have begun to sell well on the markets.[5] As a result of the initial benefits of the market economy, peasants' productivity has been enhanced, their income increased and their life obviously improved. Along with the gradual development and growth of rural markets, rural communities have become an important part of the large nationwide, unified market.

Setting up more enterprises and increasing the speed of industrialisation in rural communities. Before the responsibility system of joint production and contract was put into practice, the industrial structure in rural areas was extremely irrational. Secondary and the tertiary industries were exceedingly underdeveloped. Along with the setting up of market economy system, primary industry continues to be divided into secondary and tertiary industries, and a large number of village and town enterprises and individual (private) enterprises have arisen. According to a statistics in 1991, there were 19.079 million village and town enterprises, with 96.091 million workers. By the end of 1991, the value of their outputs made up 26.6 per cent of the total output value of society as a whole, and 59.2 per cent of the output value of rural society (State Bureau of Statistics 1992: 67). The development gap between rural communities has already come to be centrally measured by the degree of their development of enterprises and industrialisation. Now the average annual rate of growth of the Chinese village and town enterprises is higher than 30 per cent, and remains in a phase of rapid growth. The opportunity for the rapid development of tertiary industry in rural communities is also provided by the growth of the market economy and the guidance and choice of the state.

Leading rural communities to the world market. Thanks to the founding of the

---

[5] The diversification of agricultural products resulted mainly from the shift in decision-making from the state to peasants, the successful solution from the point of view of the food and clothing problem, market demands and profit considerations.

market economic system and the rapid development of village and town enterprises, it is no longer a dream to expect rural communities to be open to the world and march along the road to internationalisation. Varieties of transnational action have arisen in some of the rural communities, enabling Chinese peasants to begin to go out into the world. Aiming at the large international market, they are no longer satisfied with running such big enterprises as airline companies for domestic transportation. The peasants from Shanghai and provinces like Zhejiang, Shandong and Xinjiang have started transnational companies or conduct other transnational economic activities in Canada, the USA, Western Europe, the former USSR and countries and regions in South-East Asia.[6] The transnational actions of the rural communities that took the lead in becoming rich have not only brought them financial resources, but also quickened the internationalisation of the Chinese economy.

The opportunities provided by the market economy for the development of the Chinese rural communities mentioned above are all within the economic domain. In social terms, the opportunities can also be seen in such aspects as urbanisation, the change in social structure, the outflow of population and the enhancement of peasants' living standards. Among these, the opportunity provided for urbanisation deserves special attention.

Urbanisation through the development of new types of rural community. The development of the market economy and the improvement in peasants' living conditions impel peasants to move and settle down in rural economic centres with transport facilities, a developed economy and the ability to provide better services; thus a new type of community with characteristics of urbanisation is formed: a market town in a rural area. The tendency towards urbanisation is more obvious in China's coastal areas, where there are developed village and town enterprises, and developed economies, like Daqiu village and Huaxi village, the two richest villages in China, famous for their developed economy and industrialisation. The development of market towns not only leads peasants to flow to them, but also attracts many city residents and talented city professionals. As both residential and economic centres, the market towns promote the further development of village and town enterprises, which in turn pushes forward the urbanisation process and enables market towns to develop gradually into new economic, social, political and cultural centres in rural area. As the products of industrialisation and urbanisation processes in rural communities, market towns narrow the gap between cities and villages, between workers and peasants, and lead to the economic development of rural China. Therefore, they are observed with interest and highly regarded by the rest of the world, and by the developing countries in particular.

---

6 Reports on transnational actions taken by Chinese peasants can be seen almost every day in the mass media.

Changing the function of rural governments. Politically speaking, the opportunity provided to rural communities by the socialist market economy is to some extent related to the functional change of local governments. The reform of the political system in rural communities has been in progress for several years. Since the Law of Organising the Village Residential Committee was issued by the state, the leaders of one million villages across the whole country have been directly elected by villagers (Chen and Lu 1993). Putting into practice the self-government of villagers promoted the course of democratisation in rural communities. In terms of range, democratisation is now spreading from village to *Xiang* (a bigger community consisting of many villages) and from *Xiang* to county, forming numerous autonomous villages and counties ruled by villagers themselves. Such a political system allows a beneficial functional shift of government sectors so that they can deal well with villages, operate with better staff and simpler administration, increase efficiency and serve to develop the market economy in rural areas.

Encouraging the pursuit of scientification and informatisation. Opportunity in scientific and cultural areas can be divided into two parts: scientification and informatisation. The trend towards scientification and informatisation is of great importance to the renewal of the Chinese rural communities as global villages in the information age. Pushed on by the development of the market economy and market competition, Chinese rural communities are now actively pursuing scientification and informatisation. There is already a move in the countryside to seek scientific knowledge or technological training. Peasants are studying cultural knowledge and market information, and activities to develop agriculture by learning and using science and technology are flourishing.

The speed with which scientific and technological achievements are transformed and spread has quickened, which enables the productive decision-making, management and administration of agriculture and of village and town enterprises to progress along the road of scientification.

A large number of qualified scientific and technological personnel were introduced, trained or borrowed by village and town enterprises, and groups of scientific and technological professionals from cities were attracted to work in these enterprises. The proportion of scientific and technological personnel in some village and town enterprises is equal to that in some state-run enterprises. These valuable professionals have brought to village and town enterprises very high economic benefits (Yuan and Song 1993).

Now community peasants are beginning to understand the place and role of information for decision-making in production, management and administration. They realise that they should base their decisions on useful information if they want to participate in market competition, which is full of risk. To obtain or to buy information through scientific and technological personnel, mass media or other means marks the first step towards informatisation in rural communities.

Enhancing the level of spiritual civilisation. The socialist market economy will provide rural communities with the potential to become richer at either a faster or slower speed. In those communities that have become richer in past years, peasants are now able to go after spiritual civilisation and enhance the level of such civilisation. This pursuit has already become a fashion. Many communities have set up new schools to develop community education, established reading centres, libraries, cultural centres, cinemas and theatres, or even organised peasant's orchestras. All these would seem unthinkable without the development of the rural economy and the improvement of peasants' living conditions. Such enthusiasm and action are of great significance to the construction of spiritual civilisation that will continue to be an inseparable part of community development in rural China.

Needless to say, the socialist market economy also provides to rural communities such opportunities as changes in social structure, outmigration and the improvement of environmental quality. China as a whole (including its rural areas) is now becoming a huge marketplace where both China and other countries can all attempt something and accomplish something.

References

Chen Yan and Lu Weijiang (1993). 'Five Years' Trial Implementation of the Law of Organising the Village Residential Committee', *People's Daily* (overseas edition), 17 May.

Communist Party of China (1992). *Collection of Documents of the 14th National Congress of the CPC*, Beijing: People's Press.

Li Mu (1992). 'Selections of Main Arguments on the Socialist Market Economy', *The Current Conditions and Overall Strength of China* 6.

Li Peng (1993). 'The Working Report of the Government', in *Collection of Documents of the 8th National People's Congress*, Beijing: People's Press.

Research Group of Social Development and Social Indicators (1991). *Materials for Social Development and Social Indicators* 5.

Ruxin (ed.) (1988). *A New Dictionary of Social Sciences*, Chongging: Chongging Press.

Shi Chenglin (1992). 'Impeding Factors in Agricultural Development and Strategical Orientation of the 8th Five-Year Plan', *The Current Conditions and Overall Strength of China* 6.

State Bureau of Statistics (1992). *A Statistical Survey of China: 1992*, Beijing: Statistical Press of China.

Xiao Lijian (1992). 'Five Inadaptabilities of Population Economy in China', *The Current Conditions and Overall Strength of China* 6.

Xie Shusen (1992). 'The Current Conditions and Problems of the Rural Population in China', *The Current Conditions and Overall Strength of China*, 6.

Yuan Yanghe and Song Chao (1993). 'Increasing Profits by Introducing Professionals', *Xinhua Daily Telegraph*, 24 February.

Zhu Qingfang (1992). 'Four Types of Income Gap: An International Comparison', *The Current Conditions and Overall Strength of China* 6.

13 The Operational Style of the Chinese Market Economy in the 21st Century

ZHANG ZERONG

13.1 Socialist Market Economy

The twentieth century will be over soon, and the twenty-first century is appearing before our eyes. Market economics will be the operational style of the Chinese economy in the twenty-first century. The Chinese market economy is the socialist market economy, and China is in the process of building this economic system.

In the late twentieth century, China has carried out an arduous probe into how to develop its economy, and it has at last chosen the route towards a market economy. China plans to build a preliminary market economic system before 2000. And over the whole thirty-years reform period (1980–2010), the Chinese economy will travel the entire way to a market economy and merge with the dominant current of the global economy.

It was in 1992 that the purpose of the reform was established as being to build the socialist market economic system and develop a socialist market economy. It took fourteen years for China to get to this point.

Before 1978, China always thought that its economy was and could only be a planned economic system. In 1978 China began to reform, and in 1982 people began to think differently. We came to think that the Chinese economy could contain some market-adjustment mechanism, but with the proviso that the planned economy would come first, and market adjustment would be secondary. In 1984 our view underwent a fundamental change. We no longer thought of our economy as a planned economic system; we thought of it as a 'planned commodity economy', and this became the new purpose of China's reform. In 1989, in light of the economic situation in China, we put forward new visions of economic reform and development: to put a planned economy and market adjustment together. Clearly, China had turned its back on the old 1982 view that the planned economy was first, and market adjustment secondary. At this time, 'Leftist' thinking in China returned. Some people regarded the developing market economy as the manifestation of bourgeois liberalisation. In 1992 the views of reform changed once more. We no longer thought that 'plans' and 'market' were connected with the social system, and this cleared the way for building a socialist market economic system and developing a socialist market economy. And, finally, this became the established purpose of reform in China.

At present, China is trying to build its economic system in four ways. First, government and collective enterprises must be free to operate and produce goods under the principles of autonomous management, sole responsibility for one's own profits or losses, self-development and self-restriction. Through fourteen years of this reform, collective enterprises became the first independent commodity producers. But the reform of government enterprises remained very difficult. The most difficult point of the reform is how to reconstruct these enterprises so that they function in accordance with the demands of the developing socialist market economy in China. So we have tried three ways to transform the government enterprises: a stock system, a contracting system, and a lease system. In addition, some other ideas have been suggested, such as the state-owned individual-management system.

Second, in order to build and construct its market economic system and market order, China needs to make legitimate laws. According to the present interpretation, the Chinese economy has become a market economy. Yet, since the laws governing it are not perfect, there remain many points of confusion and questions in running the market economic system: issues of buying authority, counterfeit and inferior commodities, credit, financial order, market supervision and market management, and so on. All of these questions must be solved for the development of the Chinese market economy.

Third, the task of the reform is to build a new macro-adjustment and macro-management system to supersede the macro-management system that existed in the past in the planned economy. We must use laws to standardise and supervise the market and adjust the economy in terms of money, credit and tax. Recent financial reform is one indication that we are trying to do so.

Finally, we must build a new social safeguard system.

13.2 The Economy at Work

It is very difficult to build a socialist market economic system in China. It will take five to ten years, or even longer to do so. We are sure, however, that we will slowly develop the system and firmly go forward, as confirmed by the last fifteen years of China's reform.

The way the market economy is run in socialist China must be the same as in other countries of the world. A market economy is run by the forces of demand and supply. It is run by the law of value and price. Commodities and money are exchanged continually in the market. Enterprises act as commodity-producers and managers in the market. There is a macro-adjustment system and a social safeguard system. All market activities are standardised and supervised by laws and run in order. In this respect, China must carefully study the experiences of other countries, including Japan, the USA, France, Germany and Singapore.

Even so, the Chinese socialist market economy differs from the market economies of other countries: the Chinese pattern of ownership of the means of production is one of public ownership, and the Chinese mode of distribution is one of distribution according to work.

The first feature of the Chinese economy determines how commodities are produced and exchanged between labourers. It includes production and exchange between one labourer collective and another, between labourer collectives and individual labourers, and among labourers. In this way the exchange relationship inherent in the Chinese market economy is very different from that of other countries in the world. As for the second feature, during the past fifteen years of reform, China has developed a new kind of distribution model based on work. That is to say, an enterprise's income is controlled by market, and a worker's income is associated with the enterprise's income and his or her share of labour. This model of distribution is now being further developed and perfected.

In 1992 China first proclaimed that it would develop its economy on the model of the market economy, and the great majority of residents in every province, autonomous region, city, and country enterprise expressed a warm welcome to this reform activity. In the same year, the growth rate of GNP reached 12.8 per cent—a very significant achievement. Ever since then the Chinese economy has maintained a high growth rate of more than 10 per cent p.a.

Many people have recently wondered if the Chinese economy has entered a period of high economic growth—growth at a speed of 10 per cent every year? In spring 1993, China changed the planned rate of economic growth from 6 to 8–9 per cent per annum. The Chinese government has reached the conclusion that the Chinese economy has entered a period of high-speed growth. Many economists share this view. If this is right, I think that this view will be important to economic development in China and the Asia–Pacific region, and even the world.

13.3 Rectification of the Economy

Nowadays, there are many active and 'hot' areas in our economic development, such as housing and land, stocks and capital construction, and so on. During the transitional period from a planned system to a market system, such issues cannot be avoided, and can be solved only through development.

Recently, China has done its best to rectify its financial arrangements, which have been in some confusion since 1992. Many banks set up housing and land co-operations by themselves. They used credit funds to speculate. They casually raised their loan rate without orders from the government. They reaped staggering profits through the interbank money market. These activities hindered normal industrial and commercial activities, and reduced bank deposits so much that China is faced with the prospect of currency inflation again. We must now rectify this confusion to ensure the order of the Chinese market economy. Bank deposits must begin to rise, and rising prices must be controlled.

In order to stop tax evasion and the drain of wealth in fiscal activities, China is examining taxation in great detail. The existing Chinese tax structure and tax administration turned out not to be suitable for the requirements of the Chinese market economy. China must police tax receipts every year, though this is a kind of remedial measure. The more fundamental way is to reform Chinese tax structure and tax administration through legislation. Counterfeit and inferior commodities as a result of loose market supervision and management have now become social and public hazards. China must rectify these public hazards with a 'Quality ten thousand miles walk', so that the whole of society pays attention to the issue.

Government corruption is another important issue that must be studied and solved carefully for Chinese economic development. Many sorts of questionable activity have been highlighted, including the exchange of rights for money, spending public funds freely, eating and drinking public foodstuffs without restraint, buying houses and fast cars with public money, unreasonable apportion and forfeit to enterprises and farmers as well as the offence of bribery, and so on.

The final great issue is that a few people have suddenly become rich. This, too, must be resolved for economic development.

China is able to solve these issues. And through solving these issues it can build a market economic system and make its economy develop healthily. Then it will be able to contribute to the world in the twenty-first century.

13.4 Towards the Twenty-First Century

It is very important for the development of China to know and study its future and to look into the future. The world we live in is undergoing the following big changes.

(1) The structural composition of GNP is altering. In the pre-industrial age the primary industry was agriculture. During industrialisation, its contribution to GNP declined, and it now constitutes less then 7 per cent of GNP in industrialised countries. The contribution of industry to GNP has also been reduced, and now only makes up 30 per cent of GNP, or less, in developed countries. At the same time the contribution of service industry has gone up, making up 60 per cent of GNP and 80 per cent of employment. It is estimated that direct machine workers will constitute only 1 per cent of all workers by the year 2000. This indicates that the industrial age is over and the service age is starting.

(2) A new knowledge industry is developing rapidly. The knowledge industry produces knowledge in the form of databases, news, shows, symbols, cultures and views of value. From the middle of the nineteenth century to the middle of the twentieth century, capital and labour were the two important factors in the economy of developed countries. Now these factors have become less important and knowledge is taking their place as the primary factor. We are going to the age of the knowledge industry. In this age, the most important factor will not be natural resources, capital and labour, but knowledge. In the year 2000 workers in the production and transportation sectors will make up 1 per cent of the workforce, while those in the knowledge and service industries will represent the

two primary strata. In the twenty-first century, the output of the knowledge industry will exceed that of the service industry, and the same will be true in workforce terms. The knowledge industry will be the primary industry, as agriculture used to be in the pre-industrial age, the machine industry in the industrial age and the service industry in today's developed countries. Recently Japan invited 300 experts to write a book called *Predictions for Science and Technology in the Year 2020*, which says the volume of knowledge will be doubled between 1993 and 2003, and, after an explosive breakthrough between 2004 and 2010, it will be three or four times today's level between 2011 and 2020. We can see part of our future situation from these points.

(3) Technological development in the area of information-transmission speeds up the arrival of the knowledge age. We must pay more attention to the development of multimedia technology, and to the Internet. Not only does this technology change the structure of the economy rapidly, it also has a significant effect on human work and life, speeding up the arrival of the knowledge community.

(4) The connotations of 'capital' and 'mode of production' will change. In a traditional industry, the primary forms of capital are buildings, machines, stocks, inventories, and so on, but incorporated forms of capital, such as talents, tactics, information and views of value, are more important today. In the future the real value of industry will not be in products, commodities and other visible capital items, but in databases, talents under their own control, programmes, information and internalised views of value.

The traditional mode of production, in which all production factors work together, will change, and it will be replaced with a divided, small-scale mode of production. Most workers will work at their homes instead of going to their offices. Traditional cities, which have a large number of inhabitants, will dissolve and people will work and live in their communities.

(5) The world economy will become more of an organic whole, not because of the development of transnational corporations but because of the transmission and use of information and knowledge. Today, nothing can stop their movement across national borders and no country can close its economic borders to information.

(6) Economic change will bring cultural change.

This is our hopeful future. China is a developing country, and its market economic system is developing. In today's world China will not only develop itself, but also make due contribution to the world economy as a whole.

13.5 Concluding Remark

China is planning to establish a preliminary socialist market economic system by the year 2000. In thirty years of reform (1980–2010), China wants to solve one problem: it wants to finish its transformation from a traditional planned economic system to a modern market economic system, so that the Chinese economy can function effectively as a market economy in the twenty-first century. In 2010, this reform will be finished and a relatively complete socialist market economic system will have been set up.

The GNP of China in 1990 was double that of 1980. GNP in 2000 will be more than twice GNP in 1990, and in the year 2010, GNP of China will again have doubled that of 2000, so that China will approach the level of the secondary advanced countries in the world. Today China is trying hard for this objective.

Further Reading

'Service Trade into Noble Trade System' (1994). *New York Times*, 15 April.
'Post-Capitalist Society' (1993). *Financial Times*, 4 February.
Sichuan Academy of Social Sciences (1994). 'Reference to the Study of Social Sciences' (leaflet published monthly).

14 The New Centre of the Future Society: Prosperous Villages in India

NANDINI JOSHI

14.1 Alternative Development

When I received a letter from Professor Yamaguchi about this seminar, I found its theme—reviving the village as the centre of society—very interesting. More interesting still for people in India is the fact that even a rich country, a highly developed country like Japan, is emphasising the importance of the village, even to the extent that it regards the village as the new centre of the future society. It wants to revive the village as the centre of the community; to take systematic steps in that direction. Moreover, the organisers of the conference represent three main constituents of this society: a university, a newspaper company and the governing body of a village.

For some years, there has been an interest among intellectuals in alternative technology and in alternative development. A new debate has begun to focus on progress that can consider not only one aspect of a situation but the entire situation in its totality. It is felt necessary that progress should be compatible with safeguarding environmental balances. Progress is meaningful only if it is sustainable.

It is appropriate to underline a point in this context: alternative development can take place only in an alternative society. We want to get rid of our present ills and evils, but also to keep the socioeconomic system, preserve the *status quo*. This is absurd. It is inconsistent. And the absurdity of this contention must be exposed. Fundamental revolution demands fundamental changes. At present, our society is confronted with a vital choice; a choice between sticking to present cities and creating new villages.

In this choice for the future, on the one side there are increasingly more crowded, complex, crime-ridden cities, threatened by galloping inflation and unemployment. On the other side there are lustrous, prospering, free villages, bustling with useful commodities, professions, talents and artistic abilities.

Economists have so far built theories that economic progress involves the migration of population from villages to cities. Professor Simon Kuznets systematically structured these theories, and even won a Nobel Prize for his work. However, scholars now recognise the opposite view—that, in the future, economic progress will involve the migration of population from cities to villages.

The future of the world community lies not in its huge, congested, violence-threatened cities, but in thousands of small, prosperous, peaceful village republics. The problem that arises, however, is that at present the condition of the villages is disastrous.

14.2 The Role of Science and Technology

We are, therefore, confronted with an agonising set of questions. Are our scientific and technological achievements being used to strengthen a system that seeks power, profit and patronage rather than the progress of the people? Is science leading to development or to destruction? The advances in science and technology were aimed at alleviating poverty, reducing inequalities and enabling societies to be self-sustaining and sovereign. What has happened, however, is just the reverse.

Despite the fact that India has planned intensively for economic progress through harnessing modern technology, approximately 400,000 villages out of a total of 600,000—which account for as much as 75 per cent of the country's population—do not have an access road during monsoons. Of these, about 200,000 do not have an access road for the rest of the year either. About 450,000 villages do not have a post office. About 540,000 villages do not have a telephone. It is impossible to reach the remote villages.

Still the initial hope that poverty will be eradicated with the use of even more advanced technology is being nurtured, and arguments are being put forward to support this view. In fact, even in the industrially advanced countries the growth rate of production is decreasing. The technological blizzard that swept the rich to the dazzling heights of gloss and glamour is now raising doubts about its ability to sustain, let alone promote, prosperity. Worse, it has brought about chaos and crisis in the rich countries (Sezler 1987).

Contrary to its objective, therefore, modern technology has not delivered the desired results even in the industrialised countries—capitalist as well as Communist. For the first time since the 'industrial revolution' we are now thinking of the possibility of growth without high technology.

14.3 Unemployment

Chaos and crisis are in-built in modern technology because it not only produces goods on a mass scale but also creates mass unemployment. Therefore, it ultimately kills its own customer. To be able to produce is not sufficient; it is also necessary to be able to sell. If production cannot be sold the result is a loss instead of a profit.

Through modern technology a society can produce more goods and services, but it simultaneously destroys its ability to buy these goods and services. Modern technology is, therefore, unsustainable.

Unemployment created by modern technology results in poverty and starvation, in the lack of relevance of the educational system, in the maltreatment of minorities, in boredom for the rich and destitution for poor, in drugs and crime, in terrorism and violence.

The evils of modern technology arise from the fact that those very few who own or control the modern automatic huge-capacity machines also consequently control the employment, income and livelihood of the masses. Technology that increases production without increasing employment is, therefore, a fraud to enslave the masses.

It is not that our forefathers did not know how to invent machinery: they avoided it on the grounds that it would lead to the material and moral degradation of society. Machine-based industrialism, which has been ushered in and supported for two centuries by modern science and technology, is, as Mahatma Gandhi warned, 'going to be a curse for mankind'.

14.4 Reviving Traditional Sciences and Technologies

In this respect, traditional sciences and technologies can play a significant and effective role to counter modern culture. Until relatively recently, prior to the industrial revolution in the late eighteenth century, Indian sciences and technologies had elevated Indian villages to such heights of prosperity and progress that the British, the French, the Dutch and the Portuguese vied with one another to enter the country, and Columbus set out to reach this land (but hit upon America instead).

The revival of the traditional sciences and technologies, therefore, would entail the revival of the village as the centre of the community; that is, *Gram Swaraj* (village home rule). How could this be achieved given the fact that the villages are fatally poor at present?

14.5 Village Home Rule

The revival of villages would require a revival of production there and of the consequent work opportunities for the village people. How could the people find work opportunities? Today the lack of work opportunities in villages is not due to the lack of money, as is usually believed; it is due to the lack of a market. As a result of poverty, there is no significant market in villages at present. However, there is one major exception—cloth, which everybody inevitably has to buy and for which, therefore, there is already a large and permanent market in every village. So the production of cloth could be undertaken in villages and thereby the latent energies of the people could be revived.

Moreover, since enough cloth for a village community could easily be produced by about 10 per cent of the people there, the other 90 per cent of the people could then undertake the production of other commodities and services to exchange for the locally produced cloth. This key to our traditional heritage is missing at present because the mill cloth from outside the villages can be bought only with cash. But if the cloth were produced in the village itself then it could be paid for in kind instead of in cash. A village population, usually between 2,000 and 4,000, could provide a sufficiently large market for all residents to undertake local production for the local market. So following on from cloth production, anyone could undertake the production of other commodities and services useful to the village community.

The revival of the production of the large number of commodities and services in the villages could then be ushered in by revitalising our rich treasure of traditional sciences and technologies.

14.6 The Pivotal Step

The pivotal first step towards achieving this objective is the revival of village-based cloth production. So the catalytic role is to be played by the spinning wheel and pitloom (not the *Ambar charkha* of the Khadi Commission, which, and also the slivers for which, cannot be made in villages).

If one analysed the economy of a village in a country like India, one would find that, despite dire poverty, the village people have to buy cloth. Of course, food is more essential than cloth; but foodgrains grow in the village, so one can get them by working on a farm. For cloth, cash is necessary. Even though per capita expenditure on cloth in a village is low, when added up over the entire village population the total expenditure turns out to be very substantial. It is the village people's biggest cash expenditure on any single item.

To earn cash, village people have to sell off their farm produce. If, however, they started producing the cloth they use, and other industries began after the textiles, the village people's need for cash would be drastically reduced. Then they would not be forced to sell off their produce at any low price. In that case, they would be able to use their produce according to their own will and choice. Then they would be able to use their natural resources for their own progress. The spinning wheel can open up this opportunity for the villages.

At present, however, despite growing all the raw materials the village has to beg the government and others for even its basic necessities.

Further reflection would reveal that, if the village people got back their spinning wheels and pitlooms and started producing cloth and subsequently other commodities, the city would hardly have anything that was indispensable for the village. On the other hand, the things the village supplies to the city are essential for the city. The foodgrains, milk, butter, oil and vegetables that the village provides are vital to the city. Urban industries also depend on villages for their raw materials. Thus cities are totally and continuously dependent on villages. In reality, the village is the provider, and the city is a bunch of beggars. The village sustains the city, while the city exploits the village.

The spinning wheel shows the way for thousands of villages to regain their freedom. Through the spinning wheel the villages can utilise their abundant human and natural resources, which are currently being wasted, and can attain both prosperity and peace.

It is not possible to produce anything else in a village before cloth, because the people lack purchasing power as a result of their poverty. So even if some other thing were produced there, it would have to be sold outside the village. That would necessitate entering into competition with big companies, and the millions of village people cannot survive such fierce competition. But cloth is the only commodity that everybody in a village has to buy from outside at present despite poverty. So cloth already has a market within every village, a wide and permanent market, among the unemployed people themselves. Furthermore, village people can produce cloth without requiring money, or any other help.

This self-contained system of local production and a local market is a precondition for starting production in a village. Only cloth production using the spinning wheel can meet this precondition. Once some people in a village started to produce cloth, the rest would then start producing other commodities and services, in order to save their own major expenditure on cloth by bartering for it, and to utilise the time they waste at present. These commodities and services could then also be bartered for grain, milk and for one another. Thus, the spinning wheel could usher in a new industrial revolution in thousands of villages.

14.7 Advantages

Since the simple spinning wheel is usually criticised as a slow instrument with low productivity per person, it should be pointed out that it is the only cloth-producing instrument that brings into use the time of the old, retired and disabled, who have no productivity in the present system, and short-staple cotton, which can be cultivated on waste land, as opposed to the long-staple cotton required by mill machines, which can be cultivated only on highly fertile land using fertilisers, pesticides and irrigation facilities. The spinning wheel and pitloom require no other inputs for producing cloth, and therefore the commodity that accounts for the largest chunk of national expenditure could be produced through only two inputs, the time of the elderly and the disabled and short-staple cotton, which are wasted at present.

Moreover, the other village professions that could follow on from the hand spinning have very high productivity, even with simple tools of production. For example, an artisan could produce 800 roof tiles, or 1,500 bricks or 18 kilograms of cooking oil per day, or block-print ten dresses, or give health care to a large number of persons—all of which have very high price-tags in the present market.

In addition, the village-based production and sale of cloth and subsequently of other commodities and services could eliminate all the tremendous costs currently necessitated by modern technology: management, offices, factories, machinery, transport, warehouses, middlemen, distribution chains, shops, advertising, promotion, banks, monetary institutions, bureaucracy, governments, and defence and armaments-production.

As a result, the traditional technologies could help to produce goods at very low cost. To take just one example, a shirt that costs sixty rupees or more in the market could be produced in a village from just the equivalent weight of raw cotton, namely 300 grams, costing only six rupees. On the other hand 600 million village people are forced at present to shell out a monumental amount of cash to buy clothes. Traditional technologies could, therefore, help tremendously in relieving them from slavery and poverty, in retaining the monumental amounts of cash among the cloth producers in villages, and, consequently, in creating markets for the rest of the population to produce other goods and services.

14.8 Building Prosperous Villages

Thus, traditional sciences and technologies could usher in the production of cloth and subsequently of an unlimited number of commodities and services in every village by a judicious use of its resources and skills to fulfil the needs of its people. They could revitalise the limitless capacity of our villages to build on our traditions in order to ensure a full and enriching life to all. This vision of Mahatma Gandhi, *Gram Swaraj*, could be realised by a revitalisation of village-based cloth production through the spinning wheel and loom. Such cloth production would automatically revive other forms of production in villages since it would induce the other people in the village to save their money and to gain employment by producing something on the strength of the local cloth production. It follows therefore that we should focus all our energies on launching cloth production in villages.

Contrary to the common belief that the spinning wheel is a negation of industrialisation, it is in fact the only harbinger of rural industrialisation. Instead of the present city-based industrialisation through modern technology, it could usher in village-based industrialisation through traditional technology. As the 'spinning jenny' ushered in the industrial revolution, the outcomes of which are unemployment, crime and wars, the spinning wheel could usher in a non-violent revolution in thousands of villages, the outcomes of which could be prosperity, human dignity and peace.

14.9 Global Impact of Knowledge

The development paradigms that emerged after the 'industrial revolution' to serve the machine-based society are now increasingly turning out to be bank-rupt, if not destructive, in their various formulations. They have not delivered the desired results, even in the industrialised countries—capitalist as well as communist—that nurtured them, advocated them and transported them to the rest of the world. They are proving economically unsustainable, inadequate to serve as a framework for culturally enriching growth, detrimental to ecological balances and counter to the fundamental human values of freedom, non-violence and justice.

Despite being opposed ideologically, both the capitalist and communist models of development are based on mass production through mega-automatic power-driven machines, and therefore on centralised control over ownership and production and consequently over the employment, incomes and livelihood of the people.

In the capitalist system this power is gained by the industrialists, while in the communist system it is gained by the state. In both systems the power becomes centralised in the hands of a few people. It is this centralisation of power that is disastrous to growth and exploitative of the people, no matter whether it is in the hands of industrialists or of the state. The real issues, therefore, are left out by a discussion limited merely to the pros and cons of only these ideologies.

Not long ago, prior to the industrial revolution in the late eighteenth century, the cultures of the so-called 'underdeveloped' countries of the 'Third World'—India, China and other Asian countries—set the pace for the rest of the world. But with the sweep of the industrial revolution across the world through mammoth technology combined with aggressive international trade, and with the consequent ascendancy of colonialism and imperialism, these countries lost their creative initiative. Their Western-influenced elite began to believe that the paradigms of industrialism were better and changed the national economic patterns.

But now all countries are seeing through the illusions, contemplating the failure of contemporary economic paradigms to meet the needs of the majority of their populations and searching for a new philosophy of development.

In this respect, India has a responsibility in effectively countering the modern culture. The spinning wheel can be the key to turning from centralised to decent-ralised production, from top-down to bottom-up changes and from automatic technologies to those utilising hands, head and heart. In the spinning wheel, India has a remedy for the unemployment and poverty of its people, and also a message for the shattered world economy.

14.10 A Future Reality

The spinning wheel is all the more relevant for the future because of two major outcomes of the present economic system: widespread unemployment and galloping inflation. Since cloth-production on the spinning wheel does not require money, machinery, infrastructure, government or even organisation, it can be taken up promptly by the unemployed.

In the contemporary context of escalating inflation, the spinning wheel and the consequent production methods will become so highly and increasingly rewarding to the unemployed masses that they will become a global reality in the not-too-distant future. Within the very short span of the last two to five years, the commodities that account for the major expenditure of the masses, such as cloth, building materials, groceries like oil and sugar, and so on, have become so expensive that similar hand-made commodities can be produced at less than one tenth of their market prices. Allowing for inflation over the coming years, this comparative advantage will continue to increase, rendering the high-technology products unviable and inducing unemployed people to take to cottage industries. Since textiles are the pivotal industry, the spinning wheel will pioneer these changes.

Once cloth production in the village is under way, the village-based production of other commodities and services can be taken up at a very fast rate. In order to save their large cash expenditure on cloth, village people would want the locally made cloth that they can pay for in kind instead of in cash, and would themselves produce a commodity or a service to give in return. Many roof tiles, bricks, colours, medicine tablets, ornaments, shoes and toys can be made in a day, even with simple tools, and many saris can be printed and dresses tailored. Thus plenty of other goods, highly priced in present markets, can be offered for cloth and for each other without money. This gives a tremendous incentive for cloth production. The spinning wheel thus removes the constraint of money and opens up the way for the village people to achieve prosperity and freedom.

As Gandhi forecast, 'I claim for the spinning-wheel the honour of being able to solve the problem of economic despair and unemployment in a most natural, simple, inexpensive and business like manner' (Gandhi 1921). He visualised that there will be no poverty in the world of tomorrow, no wars and no bloodshed.

The future of the contemporary crisis involves not chaos but construction.

References

Gandhi, M. K. (1921). 'Indian Economics', *Young India* 8 December: pp. 405–7.

Joshi, Nandini (1992). *Development without Destruction*, Ahmedabad: Navjivan Publishing House.

Sezler, Richard (1987). 'The Seer's Catalogue', *Omni*, interview with Marion Long, January: pp. 36–40, 94–100.

15 Community Development and the Futures of Sustainable Communities in the Philippines

CESAR VILLANUEVA

There are no ready-made paths to sustainable communities in the Philippines today since we are continually creating the paths along the way.

15.1 Present and Past Landscapes of Community Development

The greatest challenge to communities in the Philippines today is their capacity to survive. Survival is where Filipinos have always been triumphant against great odds. But this time is different, since it is now the very life-support systems of communities that are being imperilled. Environmental malaises, such as deforestation, species extinction, and marine and aquatic degradation, aside from the regular doses of social and economic ills, have put a severe strain on the capacity of the communities to forge a better quality of life for their peoples. The threats to the communities can be partly attributed to the feeble attempt by the past and present administrations to achieve the status of a newly industrialised country by the year 2000.

But while the environmental and socioeconomic problems take on more alarming proportions each day, there are also emerging glimmers of hope amid the enveloping gloom. The emphasis given to community development through government intervention and private initiative has evolved through the years a more holistic view of development anchored on precepts that are more dynamic, people-oriented, ecologically founded and egalitarian. One dramatic expression of this development paradigm is the phenomenal growth of private volunteer groups with a popular orientation and a clear social development outlook. The growth of such groups and their involvement in the community has vastly reshaped the terrain and contours of the social landscape of the Philippines.

Presently, there are close to 20,000 non-governmental organisations (NGOs) in the Philippines. This growth of private voluntary organisations came about in the democratic climate fostered by the People Power Revolution in 1986.

More than expanding the democratic base, the proliferation of the NGOs pushed the traditional power-holders to recognise the role of the organised sectors in community development. The enactment of the Local Government Code of 1991 actually instituted grassroots participation in the basic development process.

Looking back, however, pre- and postwar community development efforts in the country were basically confined to the traditional emergency relief and civic activities of such organisations as the Red Cross and Community Chest. The motivation was primarily charity and compassion, and the aim was to extend help to those in urgent need. People were usually viewed as passive recipients of assistance.

It was in the 1950s that some private agencies started popularising the community development approach. The government in fact created the Presidential Assistance on Community Development (PACD) to pave the way for rural and urban communities to participate in the national development programme. In the 1960s the Catholic Church's influence in community development became more profound, as seen in the issuance of the papal encyclicals that discussed the social teachings of the Church. Herein, the poor were now viewed as both object and subject of development work. Communities were also made aware of their given resources and the need to organise for self-reliance.

It was in the 1970s that the NGOs started to go beyond community-focused work to actively advocate people's issues, including social justice, agrarian reform and rural development, and batted for policy changes geared towards social reform.

The 1980s saw the NGOs addressing the recurring socioeconomic problems of the country and forging multidimensional approaches to include community organising, co-operative development, capability- and institution-building and the delivery of support services, such as para-legal training, participatory research and non-formal education.

In the 1990s, community development work took on a very strong global component. This was brought about by the worldwide environmental crisis that came to prominence in the UNCED Conference in Rio de Janeiro, Brazil, in 1992. It was imperative for NGOs involved in community development work to redefine and refocus their objectives by taking into account ecological considerations. 'Sustainable development' has, indeed, become a central phrase in the NGO community and is challenging some basic assumptions about community development.

15.2 Sustainable Development or Sustainable Communities?

The popular phrase 'sustainable development' is, however, confusing and carries with it a great deal of baggage. It seems to have been co-opted by everyone for whatever capacity it will serve them in. The basic problem actually arises in its operational definition. What does it really mean in a given local context? It is in this light that we would prefer to refer to this new-found vision as 'sustainable community'. And what does sustainable community mean in the Philippines today?

Community development work can actually lead to a sustainable community if the triple issues of equity, environment and development are addressed. These three concerns are self-reinforcing phenomena in the country, and must therefore be tackled simultaneously.

The equity question is very central in Philippine community life. The majority of Filipinos continue to live in poverty as a result of the highly skewed distribution of wealth and power. To illustrate this phenomenon, take the island province of Negros Occidental. A study showed that 3.8 per cent of the population who own private lands control 72.4 per cent of total private landholdings. Poverty is a natural consequence, therefore, of this inequitable distribution of power and resources. The poor majority lack access to such resources as land, forests and the seas, which are greatly threatened by misuse and depletion. They are also deprived of the power to control their lives because of elite domination in the country's economy and politics. Such elite control has stifled their participation in the decision-making process. It is in this context that an accelerated implementation of agrarian, urban land, aquatic and political reforms has become imperative in developing sustainable communities. These reforms, together with the empowerment of communities and people's organisations, will surely pave the way for the more equitable access of the poor to natural-resource use and benefits, and boost their struggles for a better life and future.

The issue of equity is fundamental to the building of sustainable communities. How can there be sustainable communities if there is a gaping chasm between the few rich and the many poor? It follows that integral development can only happen if the majority of the people, more than having access to resources, possess the power to transcend personal and structural weaknesses and positively transform themselves and their communities.

There is at present an admission among NGOs that community development work in the past has been primarily production and people centred. Although these are necessary elements in creating sustainable communities, they are insufficient in themselves because of their failure to consider the carrying capacity, protection and enhancement of the community's life support-system, which is being endangered by the way people think and by the way Philippine society is organised.

Indeed, the environment has become a crucially pressing issue in the country today. The spectre of an ecological nightmare is haunting local communities from the coasts to the hills and uplands. Seventy per cent of our coral reefs are in an appalling condition, with blast fishing and sedimentation taking their toll. Most of our mangroves, which are essential to the spawning of fish, have vanished. In 1988, only around 140,000 hectares of mangroves remained, down by almost 40 per cent from the 228,000 hectares that existed in 1972. Deforestation has cut a wide swath of destruction through our forests. Before the massive lumber production and widespread cutting and burning of trees by big foreign and local logging companies and *kaingeros* (slash-and-burn farmers), the Philippines had more than 40 million hectares of forests. Today, there are only 1.2 million hectares left.

With the dire lack of opportunities and social turmoil in the countryside, millions of Filipinos have migrated to the urban centres, making the development process go nearly haywire. The metropolitan cities have virtually become smoky, overcrowded and stressful areas of the frenetic mass activity that has come to epitomise the 'mega cities' of the world. This trend has stunted and even rendered impossible the integral growth and development of organic communities in these areas.

The issue of the environment for sustainable communities has both inner and outer aspects. The inner component is a recognition that changing our ways of thinking may be the only chance left for humanity to reverse the process of destruction, violence and inhumanity afflicting the world. It is also anchored on the belief that the only real recyclable resources are our thoughts, and that no amount of structural and developmental change can sustain itself without the corresponding mental change. Here, we must revive the sacred connection between our ways of thinking and our world to help create the pathways towards sustainable communities. What is asked of us is to relearn the cultivation and nurture of positive thoughts, joyful feelings and good wishes in the garden of our minds. Meditation, which is basically the creative use of our minds, becomes central to this call for renewal. A new earth spirituality based on Geo-Justice is a strong challenge and concrete response: thinking clean and doing green under a strong ethic of sharing.

Overall, the environmental component of sustainable communities is both a lifestyle and a strategy concern. The lifestyle issue is self-explanatory but the strategy might need a little elaboration. For sustainable communities it means the integration of environmental concerns into community decision-making. The reform of property rights is also a prerequisite for self-regulation in the utilisation of natural resources. Assigning secure access rights to threatened resources to responsible communities or organisations establishes a lasting tie and a long-term stake in their protection for sustained productivity. Sustainable communities must also work towards the rehabilitation of degraded ecosystems and help establish an integrated system of protected areas. Sustained environmental education of communities and the strengthening of people's participation through constituency-building must be vigorously pursued. Lastly, development must be brought down to the level of the communities, which, in turn, must be made active agents in social and national development.

When we talk of development here, we do not mean something bigger but, more importantly, something better. The kind of development we mean is socio-cultural, economic, political and spiritual. It must be participatory, community-based, creation-centred, and self-determined towards self-reliance. The model of *peace zones* or *life zones* comes to mind. Peace zones are specific geographic areas, unilaterally declared so by their people, within which war and any other forms of armed hostility may no longer be waged. Such a declaration paves the way for the community to initiate a peace programme that addresses the roots and manifestations of conflicts in the community. This has led also to the normalisation of the day-to-day life of the people and ensured the delivery of basic services and development projects for the total well-being of community members. In fact, in the Cantomanyog Peace Zone in Candoni, Negros Occidental, a community reforestation programme has been initiated by 'Eco-Kids'. This is one example of giving children the opportunity to chart their futures.

Some communities, among them the peace zones, have embodied the collective sense of spiritual solidarity among our people. They find strength and vigour in their oneness and diversity, which are being expressed through popular forms of worship, indigenous peace-making, collective prayers and celebrations, and harmonious interpersonal relationships. In a way, they have also achieved a kind of connectedness with their environment, anchoring their lives for generations in the land, the seas and the rivers, the forests, the plants and the animals. Such a sense of spirituality, so intrinsic in the Oriental setting, has made our concepts of and approaches to sustainable communities distinct from the mainstream paradigms.

So, going back to the basic assumption, what is appropriate—sustainable development or sustainable communities? While clearly establishing the distinction, we must not lose sight of the fact that sustainable development and sustainable communities are in the same vein. The basic difference lies in how the terms are applied in their contextual usage. Sustainable development carries a universal perspective and a general paradigm while sustainable communities are the specific and concrete outcome of such a paradigm. Clearly in our context, the forging of sustainable communities must be given primary stress.

These, in brief, are the essential ingredients for sustainable communities. First and foremost, they are people-propelled. Second, they are creation-centred, environmentally caring, culturally sensitive and spiritually connected. These are communities rooted in a strong sharing ethic, and are democratic and participative. Finally, they are globally linked.

15.3 Emerging Trends for Communities in the Philippines

Decentralisation of governance, as embodied in the Local Government Code (LGC). The enactment of the LGC, which aims to devolve power and decentralise decision-making, is considered a milestone in the Philippine political process. The transfer of power and accountability from the national government to its local units has made governance more accessible to communities. The LGC has also instituted sectoral representation as a means of ensuring popular grassroots participation in vital community concerns.

Ecological disasters have forced communities to find alternative ways of living and preserving resources. The recent spate of natural calamities to hit the country, including volcanic eruptions, earthquakes, landslides and typhoons, has displaced communities, forcing them to find other livelihoods suited to their relocation areas. In many communities, such tragic events have galvanised people into being more vigilant, creative and active in protecting and managing their environment. More and more fishing communities, for example, are organising local resource management councils (LRMCs). LRMCs are tripartite bodies composed of government, non-governmental and people's organisations, and aim to empower stakeholders in putting to proper use the natural resources of a given community.

The formation of Basic Ecclesial Communities (BECs) by the Catholic Church in a predominantly Catholic country, as mandated by the Second Plenary Council of the Philippines (PCPII), signals a reinvigoration and redirection of local communities from mere traditional functions towards a more developmental and liberational role. PCPII, which brought together all sectors of the Church, was held in February 1992 to institute reforms and set a new direction for the Roman Catholic Church in the Philippines. Given that Catholics comprise more than 80 per cent of the national population, the creation of BECs, which seek to empower the laity, reflects the progressive thinking and spirit of reform now gripping the Church. Past experience of church-based communities shows that the BECs, on a mass scale, offer a broader alternative path towards sustainable development through their power to direct community action on peace and justice issues in particular.

Displacement of communities by the influx of tourism and development projects. The government's avowed goal of achieving newly industrialised country (NIC) status by the year 2000 has opened the floodgates for huge and unbridled capitalist investments to virtually engulf the country. This situation has led to an 'assembly line' form of development, resulting in the greater exploitation of labour, surplus extraction, land speculation and conversion, and the outright displacement of communities. It has also triggered a superficial boom in the tourism industry, which has taken its toll on both the human and natural resources of communities. More women and children are being victimised by a flourishing flesh trade that relies mainly on the patronage of foreign tourists. In the guise of short-term job-creation and income-generation, hapless urban poor, farming and fishing communities have to give way to tourist facilities and other development projects.

15.4 Contending Scenarios for Communities in the Year 2010

The status of NIC-hood is achieved. Communities are now clustered around regional industrial centres and serve as factory production lines, with each community playing a specific role in the division of labour. Weekends rotate to fall on any day of the week, according to work schedules. Prime agricultural land around such areas has been turned into vast residential subdivisions and commercial and recreational centres. Consumerism is on the rise, and acute commercialisation has permeated the prevailing sociocultural set-up. People begin to worship sports on Sundays.

The Caucus of Development (CODE)–NGO (the network of networks) breaks down. CODE-NGO, which is composed of a majority of the national NGO networks, is committed to the empowerment of communities. However, it slides into an internal squabble for dwindling funds and is dragged into the heated ideological fray between feuding extreme-Left forces. This greatly weakens the momentum for creating sustainable communities, since community projects are identified according to the availability of donors. Worse, the resulting vacuum is filled by business-oriented and government initiated NGOs (BONGOs and GRINGOs). Communities are reduced to being the extensions and contracting shops of businesses. While jobs are created, subcontracting schemes become institutionalised, leading to lower wages and benefits and more violations of workers' rights. Likewise, communities become mere conveyor belts driven by traditional politicos, who dispense favours and patronage and thus further disempower the people in the communities. Since there are numerous experiments and initiatives in creating sustainable communities, the result of the breakdown is even less co-ordination among the NGOs and mass confusion among their community partners.

Empowered, federated and bioregional communities push for their own development agenda, based on equity, sustainability, participation, spirituality and good works. Communications and netweaving of community stories and achievements become a vital way of life. People here anchor their life on solidarity and consider social and environmental relationships as their greatest resource. They exude the confidence to say no to any kind of development that imperils or destroys community harmony, the environment and its carrying capacity. Community work is now directed towards the common good. Trade between sustainable communities comes to be based on ecological surplus. People believe that the ultimate aim of development is the enhancement of the life-support systems of the community, with themselves as the primary agent of change. Communities' NGO partners strengthen their networking capabilities and mainstream the NGO-managed fund mechanism of official development assistance (ODA). A new partnership between donors and communities based on 'complementarity' is thus developed.

In conclusion, building sustainable communities in the Philippines will always be an exercise of upholding life, of weaving the fabric of genuine human solidarity into the tapestry of our community life. At the very least, NGOs and people's organisations must sustain creative community experimentation towards forging sustainable futures.

Summing up our hope for a future worthy of our children, let these words from Robin Broad and John Cavanagh inspire us:

In this decade and into the twenty-first century, old and new Philippine movements with novel ideas and a battery of strategies will be creating sustainable development alternatives that are exciting and challenging not only for Filipinos but for all people seeking new ways to hold the earth together while making life better for its inhabitants. The catalyst: fragile ecological limits that have been passed. The actors: one of the most dynamic citizen's groups in the world, building on decades of activity. Key ingredients: enormous amounts of vision, of hope and commitment. The result: one of the most fertile countries in the world for experiments based on a different kind of people's power. (Broad and Cavanagh 1993: 157)

References and Further Reading

Broad, Robin and Cavanagh, John (1993). *Plundering Paradise: The Struggle for the Environment in the Philippines*, Berkeley and Los Angeles: University of California Press.

Catholic Bishops of the Philippines (1988). 'What is Happening to Our Beautiful Land', A Pastoral Letter on Ecology, 29 January.

Conlon, James (1990). *Geo-Justice: A Preferential Option for the Earth*, San Jose, Calif.: Resource Publications.

Council for People's Development (1992).*The Covenant on Philippine Development: A Primer*, Manila: CPD.

Development NGO Journal 1(1; 1992).

Economy, Ecology and Spirituality: Toward a Theory and Practice of Sustainability (August 1993). c/o David C. Korten, The People-Centered Development Forum, 14 E. 17th St., Suite 5, New York, NY 10003, USA.

Handout of the Think Clean, Think Green Movement, an environmental project initiated by the United Nations Association of the Philippines (UNAP).

Keough, Noel (1992). *Sustainable Development? Sustainable Communities!*, Calgary, Province of Alberta, Canada.

Ragrario, Conchita (1993). 'Sustainable Development, Environmental Planning and People's Initiatives', *KASARINLAN, A Philippine Quarterly of Third World Studies*, 9(1): pp.36–7, 47.

Philippine Institute of Alternative Futures (1993). *Sustainable Development Compilation*, Manila.

Villanueva, Cesar (1990). 'People's Initiatives at Peace Zone Building: The Case of Sitio Cantomanyog in Negros Occidental, Philippines', paper presented at the World Conference of WFSF in Budapest, Hungary.

16 Micronesia Futures in Asia and the Pacific

DIRK A. BALLENDORF

16.1 Micronesia

There are several definitions of the term 'Micronesia'. Geographically, Micronesia includes the Marianas, the Carolines, the Marshall Islands, Kiribati (the Gilbert Islands) and Nauru. Culturally, Micronesia includes generally the same groups, although there is a heavy Polynesian influence at Kapingamarangi Atoll, which is near the Equator south of Chuuk (Truk) and Pohnpei (Ponape), and a Melanesian influence at Tobi Island in Palau. Some ethnographers have considered Tuvalu (the Ellice Islands) to be culturally Micronesian.

Politically, until very recently, Micronesia has been thought of as being synonymous with the Trust Territory of the Pacific Islands (TTPI). This does not include the island of Guam, which is an unincorporated territory of the USA governed under the 1950 Organic Act of Guam, which also made all the local inhabitants (or 'Chamorros') US citizens, but without the right to vote in national elections.

Guam is an important part of the Micronesian region. However, the main focus of this chapter will be on the modern emergence and development of the other island groups, which did make up the TTPI, but now form four new political entities: (1) the Republic of the Marshall Islands (RMI), formerly the Marshalls district of the TTPI; (2) the Federated States of Micronesia (FSM), formerly the districts of Chuuk, Yap, Pohnpei, and Kosrae; (3) the Republic of Belau (Palau), formerly the district of Palau; and (4) the Commonwealth of the Northern Mariana Islands (CNMI). The first three are 'freely associated states' of the USA; the fourth, the CNMI , is a commonwealth of the USA. The freely associated states are entirely new political arrangements for the USA as well as Micronesia. The CNMI has, of course, a closer relationship with the USA than the freely associated states have, and this is because the people of the Marianas wanted it so.

16.2 Overview of Postwar History

During the period of US trusteeship, US assistance and tutelage varied. Initially there was considerable benign neglect of the islands. This was followed, during the early years of the Kennedy Administration, by policies promoting the fastest possible self-sustaining economic growth.

Throughout the 1970s and into the 1980s, however, it became clear that the fastest possible development was not the same as self-sustaining economic growth. The external assistance from the USA that flooded the islands from the mid-1960s to the late 1970s had a tremendous effect. Between 1962 and 1972, US appropriations for Micronesia amounted to $366,779,000 for a rounded average of $36,678,000 per year for the period. By the late 1970s yearly appropriations from all sources in the USA exceeded $70,000,000. Capital construction financed by the USA caused the ratio of investment to GDP to rise spectacularly, from slightly more than 7 per cent in 1960 to almost 67 per cent in 1970. Looking back now on this US federal government appropriations 'book period' of the 1960s and 1970s, the investment had only scant bearing on productivity but immense bearing on a continual rise in budget to support all the added infrastructure and also a wage–price spiral. Some observers say now that the new Micronesian states look like they will have high-wage economies well into future, depending for their consumption levels upon continual US subsidies under the Compact of Free Association. Tourism may offer some hope for a better balance-of-payments picture in the future, and considerable investment is currently being made in this area; however, it is still difficult to see clearly how much income this industry will generate for the islands. If US subsidies are to be reduced, or even stabilised, during the period of the compacts, budgetary receipts must grow equally with the expansion of industries. The amount of monies that would be involved here is very large. Self-sustaining economic growth, even without maximum Micronesian participation, seems improbable for a long time.

In recent years, the US administration of Micronesia has come under critical scrutiny by a number of authors. This chapter contributes to the scrutiny by examining the US presence during the first twenty-five years. This period was a formidable one inasmuch as it saw the transition from war to peace, from war-spoil to Trusteeship under the United Nations, and from a relative unsophistication to a sophistication that has enabled the opening of future political-status talks between the US Congress and the Congress of Micronesia.

From 1944 to the present, four distinct periods in the US administration can be clearly described. The first was from 1944 to 1947, during which time the US Navy was in charge. The UN Trusteeship agreement was singed by President Truman only on 1 July 1947, and from that time until 1951 the US Navy continued to administer Micronesia on an interim basis. On 30 June 1951 authority for US administration was transferred to the Department of the Interior, which continues to be in authority at present. From 1951 to 1964 the budget for Micronesia were very low; wholly inadequate for serious development. The Kennedy Administration dramatically raised the budgets, and these raises continued until the mid-1970s, when the budgets began to fall. Throughout the 1970s the negotiations over future political status continued. By 1978 they had resulted in the formation of four separate new government entities. Each of the entities has its own constitution and each is related to the USA by a Compact of Free Association. Hence, we have periods of administration under US rule as follows.

- Period I (1944–7), US Naval Military Administration;
- Period II (1947–51), Interim Naval Civilian Administration under United Nations Trusteeship;
- Period III (1951–86), Civil Administration by the US Department of the Interior under United Nations Trusteeship; and
- Period IV (1986–present), Autonomy under the Compacts of Free Association with the United States. Palau's compact was ratified in 1993, and since 1978 the Commonwealth of the North Marianas has provided for a close relationship with the USA.

16.3 Government and Decision-Making

The basic unit of government established by the USA in Micronesia was the municipal council. These democratic bodies were led by an elected magistrate at the village level. Above the municipal councils came the district legislature. A number of representatives from each municipality came annually to the district centre for a session. These groups levied some taxes and made appropriations for municipal and district projects from the taxes they raised. These domestic governing bodies were established soon after the war, and their establishment was accompanied by some social confusion on the part of the people.

Traditionally, the clan is the decision-making body in local affairs. Each clan is headed by a chief, and the chief of the strongest clan is recognised as the most important traditional leader in the district. The Japanese often used the chiefs as political leaders, but they also undermined the traditional structure to some extent by creating a separate group of local officials to supplement the chiefs. When the Americans came the situation was upset. The US military governors tended to look to the traditional chiefs for leadership, while at the same time giving certain operational authority to the local officials whom the Japanese had trained, since they were more competent in the handling of certain bureaucratic affairs. In some cases this created administrative vacuums.

Traditional decision-making in the clan was accomplished through consensus of opinion. The US administration, however, did not make decisions in this way, and paid little heed to the task of blending the traditional methods with the imposed ones. This has been, through the years, a continuing source of misunderstanding and disagreement. Some US officials have clearly spoken out against the consensus process of decision-making. In 1968, the Commissioner of Administration for the Trust Territory said, 'I personally do not believe in administration direction by consensus; at some point the decision must be made and cannot be postponed because it might go crosswise to the beliefs of one of the people.'

From the beginning, the US administration operated under a centralised plan. The main headquarters were located in Hawaii, and field headquarters were first at Guam, and then at Truk in the Eastern Carolines, which was situated roughly in the middle of the territory. A liaison office was established at Guam after the field headquarters was moved to Truk. This centralised plan was the cause of much inefficiency. Scattered over a geographic area larger than the continental USA, and provided with inadequate means of transportation and communications, the Americans moved slowly in a cumbersome structure. A management survey of the territory completed in 1951 recognised this situation as a problem, and made some suggestions for solutions:

[One of the problems] of government personnel is the small amount of time spent in direct contact with the islanders and work on islanders' problems. A tremendous amount of time is required for the support of the administrative district itself. A reduction in the numbers of American personnel, the improvement of physical facilities, and the elimination of many administrative directives and orders, should release the Civil Administrators from many routine, duties now required. This will make it possible for them to spend more time on the governmental and economic aspects of their jobs, which is the basic reason for their being in the islands.

In 1964 the Congress of Micronesia was established and it held its first regular session in July 1965. The Congress was patterned after that of the USA and brought the idea of representative government into sharper focus for Micronesia. Senators and Representatives came from each district to make laws and appropriations from their base. The taxes were drawn mostly from businesses. The importance of the Congress grew rapidly and a sense of growing nationalism was seen to develop where there was none before.

16.4 Economy

With regard to the economy, subsistence agriculture and fishing have been basic all through the history of the Micronesian people. Most of the islanders had to revert to them after the war, when the Japanese were repatriated, but they had always formed the economic underpinning for the people. An early assessment of the economic situation made by the Americans is as follows:

The natural resources of the islands are meagre, though they will sustain the local island peoples reasonably well. There are limited opportunities for future expansion and development. Furthermore, [the] islands cannot be expected to be self-supporting in the sense of producing public revenues for the maintenance of necessary administrative and welfare service at levels satisfactory by modern standards. In this latter respect, the islands are a liability and an inevitable charge on the national purse. The United States, of course, gains compensation benefits in terms of national security.

This is a very revealing summary because it indicates that the USA has never been economically very interested in Micronesia. It therefore helps to explain why there was only minimal economic progress during the first three administrative periods discussed here.

Since the mid-1960s, tourism has been seen as the greatest potential money-making industry in the Territory. A number of luxury hotels were built an Guam, and several were planned for Micronesia as well. In the late 1960s, Continental Airlines, which serves the Trust Territory, planned to construct six luxury hotels as part of their service contract. Not all the people in Micronesia, however, wanted this development. The Yap Legislature passed a resolution at their 1968 regular session expressing general dissatisfaction with the whole idea, and indicated that they did not wish to see a luxury hotel built on their islands. To this day, none has been constructed.

US business was not encouraged to establish itself in Micronesia. Land is protected and can only be leased, not sold. Moreover, there was no infrastructure to support modern business, and the tax situation for sending goods to the US mainland was not good. In short, there was little economic incentive for any business to come to the islands.

16.5 Diversity and Fragmentation

In the early 1970s, when it became increasingly clear in the Trust Territory that the people of the Northern Marianas wanted a relationship that aligned them more with Guam than with the rest of Micronesia, some people were not at all surprised. There were a number of natural causes this encouraged this split. Perhaps the main reason was the greater similarity of culture, even though, locally, many people consider the Chamorros of Saipan and Guam to be very different.

Nine distinct languages have been identified in Micronesia by linguists. In addition, there are many dialects within the language groups and differences in pronunciation. People from the Northern Marianas do not understand Carolinian dialects readily, nor do they understand Trukese, Yapese, Pohnpeian or Kosraean. It seemed natural, and even inevitable, that the people of Saipan, Rota, Tinian and elsewhere in the Northern Marianas, would choose to associate more closely with Guam than with the rest of the Micronesian islands.

A wide cultural diversity exists in Micronesia. While the overall character of the many cultures is fundamentally similar, there are great differences in cultural personalities, and these are important. Although it takes only a couple of hours to get from Saipan to Truk, the cultural changes are very significant; the food is different, the manners are different, the way people fish is different, and the tolerance of strangers varies.

The ethnocentrism of islanders is another cause of the fragmentation in Micronesia. Islanders look at their home islands as a kind of 'mother cow' that will take care of them in times of need, and for which they have very warm feelings. Outsiders, although not entirely unwelcome, are simply 'outsiders'. While the concept of regionalism is understood and appreciated, at least intellectually, in Micronesia, it is a long time before people are comfortable enough with it to practise it in their everyday life and relationships.

There are also some political causes of the fragmentation. The US administration in Micronesia was very slow to establish the institutions of democratic self-government. This is a point over which there is considerable disagreement; however, critics say that the USA should have allowed the establishment of a national Congress in the islands long before it actually did.

High Commissioners in Micronesia were political appointees and they, in turn, usually brought in people with whom they were politically comfortable. This caused numerous changes and inconsistencies in the implementation of policies and programmes over the years.

A certain educational fragmentation also took place in Micronesia as development progressed. At first there was only one public high school in the islands, Pacific Islands Central School (PICS), which was located at Truk and later moved to Pohnpei. Xavier High School, run by the Jesuits, was the only non-public high school in the early days. Hence, students from all over Micronesia came to study at these schools and became classmates. They learned together, grew up together and were able to better co-operate because of this familiarity. The establishment of high schools, both public and private, on other islands and eventually on all the islands was very good from an educational standpoint, but not as good from a unifying standpoint. No longer did Micronesians have as ready a chance to associate with one another in the formative years of personal development.

The process of fragmentation in Micronesia was a long one, mixed in with many positive motivations that were intended to create unity but actually had the opposite effect. There were many factors contributing to it, and the understanding of the fragmentation has become a very complicated business.

16.6 Towards Independence

From the very beginning of its implementation, the Trusteeship Agreement for Micronesia was interpreted ambiguously. The USA said that it did not have sovereignty over Micronesia, but at the same time the US Representative to the Security Council maintained that the USA 'intends to treat the Trust Territory as if it were an integral part of the United States'. This ambiguity spawned claims to Congressional authority for Micronesia under the territorial clause in the US Constitution. But the power of the US Congress to legislate for the Trust Territory also comes from the Trusteeship Agreement.

The problem arose as to where to best situate Micronesia within the US constitutional system. It had, after all, an unprecedented political status within the US political scheme. It was not technically or practically a 'territory' or 'property' of the USA, but it could not be conveniently treated otherwise.

In 1951 President Truman placed administrative jurisdiction over Micronesia within the Department of the Interior. This department, which had jurisdiction for other territories, seemed a logical place given its experience; it also seemed to indicate a domestic position for Micronesia. Over the years the Congress has extended many laws and programmes to the Trust Territory that were designed and intended for the US mainland and its territories. Some examples are the Elementary and Secondary Education Acts of 1965 (and as subsequently amended), which provided tremendous amounts for aid to education and compensatory education, including the Headstart Programs. Another example were the Economic Opportunity Acts, which provided for all sorts of loans and business enterprise support.

But, at the same time, the government has also frequently treated the Trust Territory as a foreign area, particularly in the matter of Customs and Immigration. In 1966 it extended the Peace Corps to the region and allowed them to mount the largest programme ever in their history (on a per capita basis, there was one Peace Corps Volunteer for every ninety-one living Micronesians in 1967).

One of the most significant educational benefits that has been extended to Micronesia is the programme containing the Basic Educational Opportunity Grants (BEOG), or 'Pell Grants' as they are currently called. This programme provides for government scholarships, amounting to around $4,000 per person per year, to be given to Micronesian students qualifying for participation in US higher education programs. Some estimates currently put the total yearly cost of this programme at over $15 million, which is above and beyond the regularly allotted Trust Territory budget.

The negotiated Compacts of Free Association contain some similarities to the Trusteeship Agreement, as well as some differences from it. However, the strong defence and security interest sections have led some observers to indicate that the compacts are nothing much more than an extension of the Trusteeship Agreement outside the aegis of the United Nations. While there are similarities, the differences are marked, especially in terms of the vital parts of the agreements.

As a legal agreement, the Trusteeship was signed between the USA and the United Nations Security Council. The compacts are agreements between the US government and the people of the new Micronesian states. Actual termination of the compacts can be accomplished only through mutual consent, whereas the termination of the Trusteeship Agreement, or any changes to it, could occur with only the consent of the USA.

In the matter of defence and security, however, the compacts and the Trusteeship Agreement are essentially the same: in both cases the USA ensures defence, albeit with consultation.

It remains to be seen whether this history of ambiguities in the administration of the Trust Territory by the USA will carry through to the implementation of the Compacts of Free Association.

The question of the independence of these new states often arises. These new states are not independent. They are separate from one another (and are in that sense 'independent' from each other), and they are autonomous and self-governing under their own constitutions.

In some cases the people have changed the names of their island to reflect more clearly the traditional pronunciation. Ponape has changed its official name to 'Pohnpei', which means 'stone alter' in the local language. Kusaie has changed its name to 'Kosrae', to conform more closely to the way the people there say the name of the island. Palau has been changed to 'Belau', and Truk has become 'Chuuk'.

There are a number of other suggested changes of name in the offing in

Micronesia, and we can expect to see this happening over the coming years. There is often lively discussion in the islands as well as in Washington over the advisability of these various name changes. Without a well-developed orthography for the Micronesian languages, there is always a disagreement over spelling. The US Coast and Geological Survey, which is responsible for the maps of the area, has been known to spurn the changes made because of the expense involved in revising and re-revising the maps. However, the wishes of the people have gradually prevailed, and we can see changes readily made that should be honoured.

The 1980s saw the compacts adopted by the people of Micronesia, new state constitutions adopted for self-government, and various name changes made within the island groups. The people of Micronesia have been clearly expressing their rights to self-determination.

16.7 The Future for Micronesia

Fisheries development is potentially a tremendous future economic resource for Micronesia, although there a lot of basic research still needs to be done to understand the migrations of the fish. At present the Micronesians collect licence fees from South Korea, Japan, Taiwan and mainland China. This, of course, will continue, and perhaps important service facilities to support fisheries will be constructed on the islands.

However, when the present Compacts of Free Association are terminated in the year 2001, the USA and Micronesia will review their political arrangements and negotiate for extensions or perhaps for entirely new ones. The amount of money provided by the USA will be reduced, and the Micronesians will have to make up any differences with investment and development from elsewhere.

In the future, the regional powers of Korea, Japan, China, Taiwan, the Philippines and other countries will play much larger roles than they presently do. The amounts of economic assistance provided in all forms by these nations will have to increase, and investment by these countries in the islands will also increase. For the involvement of the other countries of the region the future looks bright. However, the serious economic and social problems in Micronesia will also be inherited if these countries become involved.

By the beginning of the twenty-first century, the new freely associated states of Micronesia will have to renegotiate their political status with the USA. In some cases, these may be renewed; in other cases, they may be changed by mutual consent. Future projections of Micronesia's economic growth, including scenarios for alternative political statuses, as well as for the present statuses of 'free association', require the generation of considerably more data than are now readily available. For such a task, outside economic consultants with expertise in econometrics will be needed. Much of the data for such studies may be available in Washington, in the US government agency reports and assessments of the new freely associated states.

Preliminary indications, and the experience that has been recounted above, show that Micronesia is not yet making substantial progress towards economic self-sufficiency under the Compacts of Free Association, and that dependency on the USA has increased instead of decreased. On the other hand, clear political progress—internally in creating institutions, and externally in foreign relations —has been made by the new freely associated states in Micronesia. The reduction of US–Soviet tensions has altered some of the basic politico-military assumptions of the Compacts of Free Association. The change, along with the failure of sufficiently impressive economic progress in Micronesia, makes it worth reconsidering alternative political statuses, notably a decentralised federalism within the Federated States of Micronesia, or the fragmented independence of some of the states under the provisions of the compacts.

These general conclusions, however, are highly tentative. The issues and choices that the new freely associated states of Micronesia face are too complex for quick analysis.

Micronesians will continue to have greater control over the course of their own development, and they will have to exercise patience and caution in future investment implementation. The other countries of the region will have to study the cultures of Micronesia more seriously than they have in the past. We can expect a considerable amount of educational, social and cultural exchange to take place.

The future will be dynamic and exciting and should be contemplated and welcomed by the Pacific Rim countries and the Micronesians alike.

Further Reading

Ashbolt, A. (1977). 'U.S. Colonialism in Micronesia', *Arena* 49: pp. 44–63.

Bertram, G. (1986). 'Sustainable Development in Pacific Micro-Economies', *World Development* 14: pp. 809–12.

Carano, P. and Sanchez, P. (1964). *A Complete History of Guam*, Vermont: Tuttle.

Cloud, D. S. (1988). 'End of Session Tempest Leaves Palau Twisting', *Congressional Quarterly* 26 November: pp. 3398–401.

Gale, Roger P. (1979). *The Americanization of Micronesia*, Washington, D.C.: University Press of America.

Gerston, L. N. (1989). 'A Tale of Two Cultures: The Conflict Between Traditional and Modern Institutions in Palau', proceedings of the Pacific Islands Political Studies Association conference, Brigham Young University, Hawaii.

Graves, H. (1987). 'Compact Pending in Washington', *Pacific Daily News*, 15 September.

Hempenstall, Peter (1988). *German Rule in the Pacific*, Canberra: ANU Press.

Hills, Howard (1984). 'Compacts of Free Association for Micronesia', *The International Lawyer* 18(3): pp.583–609.

Isley, P. A. and Crowl, P.A. (1951). *U.S. Marines and Amphibious Warfare: Its Theory and Practice in the Pacific*, Princeton, N.J.: Princeton University Press.

Johnson, G. (1987). 'Back to the Ballot Booth for Palau', *Pacific Islands Monthly* July: p. 26.

King, V. (1986). 'U.S. to Finalize Pacific Fishing Treaty', *Pacific Daily News*, 13 November: p. 3.

McHenry, Donald F. (1975). *Micronesia: Trust Betrayed*, Washington, D.C.: Carnegie Endowment for International Peace.

Manhard, P. W. (1980). 'The United States and Micronesia', *Journal of Labour Research* 1: p. 207.

Marshall, Mac (1979). *Alcohol in a Micronesian Culture*, Palo Alto, Calif.: Mayfield.

Nevin, David (1997). *The American Touch in Micronesia*, New York: W.W. Norton.

Peoples, J. G. (1985). *Island in Trust: Culture Change and Dependence in a Micronesian Economy*, Boulder, Colo.: Westview Press.

Rampell, Edward (1966). 'Power Plant Fall-Out Leaves Islands in Debt', *Pacific Islands Monthly*, August: pp. 12–15.

Trust Territory of the Pacific Islands (1961–4). *Annual Reports*, Washington, D.C.: U.S. Department of the Interior.

United States Congress (1985). 'Approving the Compact of Free Association . . .', House Report of the Committee on Foreign Affairs, 99th Congress, first session, 1 July.

U.S. Government Survey Mission to the Trust Territory of the Pacific Islands (1963). Also known as 'The Solomon Report', vol. 2 [copy available at the Micronesian Area Research Center, University of Guam].

Weisgall, J. M. (1985). 'Micronesian and the Nuclear Pacific Since Hiroshima', *SAIS Review*, Johns Hopkins University: pp. 41–55.

Wooten, A. (1984). 'The CIA Spy School at Saipan', *Glimpses of Micronesia* 24: pp. 24–6.

17 Interconnecting Local Communities Globally: An Australian Perspective

TONY STEVENSON, INGRID BURKETT AND SAN SAN MYINT

17.1 Communications and Information Technologies

In the past few years, the infrastructure that facilitates human communication across the globe has undergone unprecedented change. This has been the result largely of the replacement of analog electronic signalling with digital modes, the development of fibre optic cable in place of the copper twisted pair, and the convergence of computing with telecommunications. As a result, people around the world are able to communicate faster, more cheaply and in higher quality text, sound, graphics and visual images than previously.

The advent of digital video communications (DVC), the ultimate in inter-active, integrated communications and information technology (C&IT), has the potential to reach out and influence virtually every level of our society and culture—from our homes to the workplace and schoolroom—in manufacturing, health care, education, transport and entertainment. Any listing of the effects on the way we live, work and play would be seemingly endless. 'DVC has the ability to further extend human capacity, for it can make visible the invisible, such as allowing surgeons to see inside a patient's heart. It can also help see things closer and sharper and allow us to see things otherwise impossible. Thus, it alters reality for good or ill, for example in allowing scientists to visually model the molecular world to design new life-saving drugs or in making danger or violence more graphic and explicit through high-quality resolution' (Free *et al.* 1992: 1).

As DVC matures commercially, later in the 1990s, it will offer the combined power of moving video images and the intelligence of the modern computer, all hooked into the fast-expanding global telecommunications network of optic fibres and satellites. It will significantly enhance human interaction across the globe, allowing not just reception of images about far-away places but increased participation by local communities in the global interchange. We are beginning to see significant displacement of what we now call mass media by the so-called intelligent broadband network, the largest contrivance ever to be constructed by humanity. The new transnational broadband network will have the ability to carry the relatively larger capacity needed for full-motion, full-colour video signals.

Apart from its awesome reach and grasp, this C&IT contrivance will be able to connect people both more selectively and interactively. It is already technically possible for someone to watch a tennis match or consult a retail catalogue, in fully moving colour, in the high definition possible with digital electronics. And it is possible to record it for sending forward in the network to a friend. In addition to this increased selectivity, it is possible for people to discuss the images in real time and even alter them. There is a blurring of the conventional distinction between producer and consumer. The individual, at home or school, who once was only on the receiving end of mass-media messages, has the capacity to become a producer of images in the network. While such selectivity and interactivity are now possible, it is economics that inhibits their widespread use. But as more and more people hook into the C&IT contrivance, the costs should come down, as has happened with traditional technologies now in widespread use, such as analog television (Stevenson 1993).

17.2 Balancing Economy and Ecology

This is all happening at a time when the world is 'approaching or exceeding critical thresholds in the balance between economic development and population growth on the one hand, and resource conservation and environmental quality on the other' (McNeill *et al.* 1991: 195).

It is a time of increasing local and global problems, including economic and social inequality and injustice, crippling debt, rising unemployment, increasing social disintegration, ecological disasters and disenchantment with politics and political leaders.

To meet such crises, futurist and alternative economist Hazel Henderson (1989) has proposed that the traditional formula of production be replaced. In the traditional formula the inputs are land, labour and capital, where the output has produced a cul-de-sac: mental games of infinite regress terminating in a logical double bind. Her 'future formula' for a 'minimum- entropy society' would have capital, resources and knowledge as the inputs, while the outputs would be healthy people and healthy bio-regions on a peaceful, healthy, equitable and ecologically viable planet. Korean futurist Tae-chang Kim has suggested that we need a shift from knowledge of ruling to knowledge of healing.[1]

Japanese futurist and information economist Kaoru Yamaguchi (1990) is more optimistic. He sees that the capitalist market economy is already being replaced by an economic framework of self-management and information-sharing. As services and information become globally traded goods, new economic structures are emerging based on globally networking eco-share regions made up of ecologically knit habitats where people share traditions and cultures. Yamaguchi proposes a MuRatopian economy as the new social design of the information age, characterised by village support systems and stewardship of the local environment.

---

[1] Personal discussions, Bangkok, 8 August 1993.

However, not all people are as optimistic as Yamaguchi. New technologies have a habit of presenting a paradox. Janet Lippman Abu-Lughod (1992) has shown how communications revolutions, from printing to the telephone, have routinely permitted the decentralisation of some elements of society while, at the same time, tending to concentrate others. She proposes that the consolidation of the absolutist nation-state was assisted by the ability to codify regulations and directives from the centre to the peripheries in print. Simultaneously, in Europe, itinerant printers diffused common knowledge and made possible printed production for specialised market niches.

The new C&ITs present a similar potential to centralise and decentralise. If the technologies are used to further centralise control in such institutions as big business and authoritarian government, the problems brought on by the industrialist command economy could further threaten equity and ecological harmony. In fact, it could hasten the onset of a largely artificial world. On the other hand, there is promise that interactive networks will enhance the opportunities for co-ordinating decentralised communities in collaborative global networking, as suggested by Yamaguchi.

17.3 Telecommunications and the City

Regardless of whether the new C&ITs end up centralising or decentralising power, or both, they stand poised to alter the shape of the ubiquitous form of human settlement, the city, which in the form of the metropolis, Syed Rahim (1992) claimed, is under pressure to accumulate wealth and power.

We have been warned that population pressures and their associated ecological impacts will make current forms of human development unsustainable. Jim McNeill, John Cox and Ian Jackson (1991) claimed that within most developing countries, and increasingly in industrialised countries, debilitating poverty and extreme wealth—often the root causes of environmental degradation—are coming to be increasingly concentrated in cities. Yet it is the economic, social and cultural dynamism of cities and metropolitan areas throughout the world, in both developing and industrialised countries, that is fundamental to a development process without which most economies would not survive.

Much of this dynamism comes from the networking of human settlements, which makes possible the allocation of investments and the sale of goods and services. C&ITs, in the sense that they offer potential for decentralisation, promise a solution to this very problem of cities buckling under environmental, economic, political and demographic pressures by networking smaller, decentralised communities. However it would first be necessary to buck a trend that is most spectacularly demonstrated in the developing world, where Peter Newman (1993) estimated that the trend to urbanisation would soar from 4 per cent of the population in 1900 to about 40 per cent in 2000.

In both industrialised and developing countries, it is not surprising that villages and small towns have become the targets of revitalisation programmes to make them more appealing for retaining local residents and attracting people back from the cities (Fujimoto 1992).

In 1962, the first *zenso*, or National General Development Plan, was introduced in Japan to reduce the differences between cities and villages by industrialising regional centres (Fujimoto 1992). But by the fourth *zenso*, a quarter of a century later, such policies had failed. Socioeconomic, industrial and political power was concentrated in Tokyo. Protests about the resulting pollution had turned policy away from a 'single- minded industrial-age objective': the pursuit of productivity and profits, and, according to Kaoru Yamaguchi and Hiroyuki Niwa (1994) the emphasis had gradually shifted to a healthy environment. More recently there has been a movement to restore self-reliance to local communities and restore cultural heritage. As Isao Fujimoto (1992: 17) put it, 'Community revitalisation is about harnessing the creative energy of people [rather] than about making a thing.'

In Australia, decentralisation and regional development has been an issue for at least the past hundred years, largely because of the concentration of the population in the state capitals and provincial cities, virtually all of which are along the coastline or relatively near it (Powell 1988). Certain attempts at decentralisation have sought to disperse the population beyond the state capital cities. Growth areas have been established in several locations far beyond the state capitals; yet, today, the main population persists near the coastline. An example of enforced population shift occurred just after the middle of this century, when virtually all Commonwealth Government departments and agencies were relocated in the national capital, Canberra, on a planned site southwest of Sydney. Canberra is still one of Australia's fastest growing areas, but so, too, are the settlements along the sunbelt in southeast Queensland, concentrated around the Queensland capital, Brisbane.

Decentralisation of Australia's population has not been a complete success. Even the Commonwealth is now relocating small units of some of its agencies back to capital cities, to put them closer to where the action is. It is the isolation of Australia's Commonwealth public officials in Canberra, and their consequent lack of knowledge of Australian life beyond, that has brought widespread criticism of their inability to make policy for the rest of Australia.

Australian parliamentarian Senator Margaret Reynolds (1991), who lives outside Canberra at least while the Australian Parliament is not sitting, sees Australian cities as sprawling, impersonal clusters of housing controlled more by real estate profit estimates than by deliberate public policy planning. She has advocated that Australia's urban environments, where 80 per cent of Australians live, be accorded the same priority given to unique wilderness and coastal areas. Cities make increasing demands for land, housing, water, food and energy and are a key element in the debate to protect the global environment. In reshaping the urban environment, Senator Reynolds says that it is essential to consider a return to the old village concept where neighbours were supportive and a genuine sense of community-belonging prevailed.

17.4 Alternative Lifestyle Communities

At the latest estimate, in 1986, about 60,000 Australians were living in alternative lifestyle communities. Our research estimates that there are now about 100 such communities in Australia. Alternative lifestyle communities are 'microcosms, small scale societies and social experiments in which many social processes can be studied and from which we can learn about the possibilities for new forms of social organisation and the practical limitations of these new forms' (Kantor 1973).

In a study of an Australian alternative lifestyle community at Maleny in southeast Queensland, we identified nine broad philosophical underpinnings of its members' lifestyle:

(1) The value of diversity. One women interviewed at Maleny stressed that 'diversity keeps the community vibrant'. Diversity is needed in community processes and participation to maintain open relationships and to generate further innovation (O'Connell 1991).

(2) The need for fluid, open relationships. There is a need to address conflict, develop and maintain open communication systems and maintain synergy in relationships.

(3) The importance of oral communication and 'folk wisdom'. Whereas in formal organisations the written word has ultimate authority, the spoken word is of prime importance in the community. Both formal and informal meetings are important in Maleny, as are workshops, festivals and gatherings. People value story-telling, art, fantasy and poetry as integral parts of the communication process and this is made obvious especially through the diaries published by one of the co-operatives. As Singh (1992) said, 'just as natural scientists are fascinated by the diversity of the natural world and alarmed by the disappearance of species, so people involved in community arts are both intrigued by and protective about the diversity of human expression'.

(4) The use of intimacy and conviviality as the major form of communication and interaction. Closely related to the notion of oral communication and folk wisdom, this idea was expressed by a woman interviewed about what community meant to her: 'It is a lot of people living in the same area, but somehow it is more than that . . . the whole is greater than the sum of the parts. It involves certain kinds of communication between people and a feeling of belonging.'

(5) The value of innovation and change. Maleny seems to thrive on innovation and change. Open organisational structures allow energy to spread, which, in turn, creates further innovation.

(6) The importance of place. It is the nature of the locality, its geography, ecology, history, culture, demographics, formal systems and location within the wider region that dictate the forms of economic and social

activity (O'Connell 1991). Maleny has a LET (Local Energy Exchange) system of bartering, which uses the Bunya (a local nut) as its unit. This system illustrates the importance placed on local energy, as Skrandies (1991) remarked: 'with Bunyas, you obtain other values that money cannot buy—particularly a sharing of a common interest in wanting to see our region flourish in a healthy way—not just in a material sense'.

(7) The importance of self-organisation, self-responsibility, enterprise and ownership. 'The process used in economic community development emphasizes the power of the individual and encourages ownership on the part of the participants. The passive student becomes an active, self-managed information seeker, and the unemployed alienated young person passively receiving welfare becomes the owner of his/her own creative enterprise' (O'Connell 1991).

(8) The importance of empowerment rather than power. Related to self-management and enterprise, empowerment is central to community organisation, replacing the more traditional power factions that dominate decision-making and other community processes.

(9) The value of community participation. The atmosphere in Maleny is reflected in the views of one woman interviewed: 'I believe in being involved and I believe in what we are doing.' According to Singh (1992), Maleny 'is a town noted not only for its cooperatives—many of which cater for alternatively-minded people—but for an extraordinary number of service clubs and organizations. Thanks to the commitment of many people over many years, there is an ethos of empowerment, of nurturing locally while thinking globally.'

17.5 Local–Global Connections

The economic, social and ecological imperatives that have encouraged some to return to community-style living have global dimensions as well as local implications. Globalisation, in part facilitated by C&IT, has spawned changes that flow right through to local communities, who now must make international connections to contend with local problems.

And, conversely, there are examples of community revitalisation programmes in Japan, for example, where communities attempt to reach out not only to their own area and region but beyond Japan to the world, suggesting implications that go beyond Japan. Isao Fujimoto (1992) has said that rather than one global village, we have the makings of a globe of villages, each vital, dynamic and having something unique to offer.

If local and global actions are interconnected, it seems appropriate to place local development in a global framework and 'to look for practical ways to make direct international connections between community groups struggling with local events which have international origins' (Kelly and Chanon 1993: 1) and local change that has global implications. It seems to follow, therefore, that emerging C&ITs have a role in such local–global interconnections.

Doug Cocks (1992: 269) proposed that social technologies, in particular, where people are the tools for achieving such linkages, need further exploration to ensure that people do not become the tools of further social control. He defined social technologies as recipes for increasing the effectiveness of a class of interactions or transactions between people. Examples include the alphabet, credit cards, a national constitution and taxation.

New social technologies, as social innovations, are not always easy to locate or invent in the traditional Western framework of science. In this framework, the answers to many of contemporary society's problems lie in the accumulation of yet more knowledge and, then, the imposition of more rational, specialised solutions. This involves what Watzlawick (1980) called *first-order* change, or 'change which occurs within a given system or frame of reference but which does not change the system itself'. In other words, Western science seeks the answers within a Cartesian paradigm that subscribes to principles of rationality, quantifiability and objectivity. Prigogine and Stengers (1984: 79) suggested that we have two options: we can either 'accept science with what appears to be its alienating conclusions' or we can 'turn to an anti-scientific metaphysics'. Berman (1981: 23) went further. He proposed that, unless we adopt some kind of participating consciousness and a corresponding sociopolitical system, we will not survive as a species. What, then, is the alternative?

Second-Order Change

According to Berman, we need a 'dramatically altered perception of reality'. He was saying that we need to change the way we see change. We need to learn that the solutions proposed by Western science for social problems are in fact the problem. We need second-order change or 'change which is directed towards the frame of reference or meta-level' (Watzlawick *et al.* 1980: 15). In effect, second-order change is applied to the attempted solution since, from this perspective, the 'solution is conceived of as the problem'.

According to Bateson (1972), the type of learning needed to create second-order change is what he called 'Learning III'. This contrasts with Learning I, which characterises first-order change. Learning I relates to problem-solving within the context. Individuals learn through positive and negative reinforcement, trial and error. For example, individuals learn that if they put more into the recycling bin, and less into the rubbish bin, they can reduce their local taxes. In Learning II they discover the nature of the context itself: individuals 'learn to learn' (Bateson 1972: 249). Thus, for example, people begin to understand the overall context of recycling in alleviating the problem of waste build-up and thus change their attitudes and behaviour towards recycling. Learning III is the synthesis of second-order change where individuals realise the arbitrary nature of their own paradigm, or Learning II, and go through a profound reorganisation of personality as a result (Berman 1981: 346).

This is more than the traditional notion of self-realisation, since it is an integral aspect of the search for community not 'merely a personal ecstatic vision'
(Berman 1981: 273). Thus, Learning III is the development or redevelopment of
a 'participating consciousness', whereby one becomes part of a greater social
communion and adapts a form of thinking that allows one to 'break out of the
mental traps of our cultural conditioning to see and understand the way others
perceive their world' (Stevenson 1989: 7).

Learning III allows us to see the link between individual, local and global
change as inherently natural and necessary. The result is 'an emphasis on
community rather than competition, or individuation rather than individualism'
(Berman 1981: 275). Such a link follows five principles: (1) the preservation of
diversity—in all aspects of relationship and thought; (2) an emphasis on power
within rather than power over; (3) an emphasis on local rather than central; (4)
sustainability rather than usability and destruction; and (5) an emphasis on
evolution (especially co-evolution) rather than fixation.

It is this final point that may provide an answer to how to begin the process of
linking individuals to local and global change.

Lewis Carroll illustrated the absurdity of the question of beginnings in *Alice's
Adventures in Wonderland* when he said, 'Begin at the beginning, and keep going
until you reach the end.' In evolutionary processes beginnings are always difficult to determine precisely, as is obvious from the search for the point at which
humans became human. Perhaps the concept of beginnings is too rational. We
may risk being stifled by the very paradigm we seek to change if we see the
process as a 'fixed procedure or set of techniques' with precise beginnings and
endings (Morgan and Ramirez 1983: 20). Perhaps we need to redefine how we see
beginnings and move from being tied to a fixed notion of beginning to one that
is fluid, open and evolving. Thus the earlier question of how the process starts
may be less important than saying 'let the process flow'. The process should be
dialectical, simultaneously individual and social, conscious and unconscious, a
beginning and an end.

17.6 The Local/Global Netweaving Program

The Local/Global Netweaving (LGN) Program begun in 1993 at the Communication Centre at the Queensland University of Technology, Brisbane, Australia,
can be used to illustrate some of these notions.

The LGN starts with the vision of a world where self-managed communities
and other social organisations network and learn freely through sharing ideas,
goods and services globally. Its aim is:

To develop an action research process for studying the potential for facilitating inter-
connectedness across regional and cultural boundaries which enhances relationships
characterized by equity, creativity, fun, understanding and ecologically sustainable economic development for individuals and groups.   (Communication Centre Report 1993)

It is intended as a meta-network for the study of human networking—or, in our terms, netweaving, which makes it more descriptive and avoids the mechanistic connotations of the word 'network'. It is founded on the importance of four main principles: (1) *connection* to local communities and between local communities to global processes using such social technologies as netware[2] and C&IT software and hardware; (2) *participation* in local, regional and global processes, in democracy, in visioning and in innovation; (3) *communication* to share, connect, participate and act; and (4) *Action* to achieve and sustain the first three principles in a practical way. These principles are not seen as discrete, but as integral, as will be shown in the following discussion, where each will be examined.

Connection

Underlying LGN is the assumption that individual, local and global 'interconnections are fundamental to the paradigm of human coexistence' (Communication Centre 1993). This calls for a view that we are in 'an ecological, systematic, permeable relationship' with the world around us to the extent that we then 'necessarily investigate that world when we explore what is the human consciousness and vice versa' (Berman 1981: 149). That world includes ourselves, our relationships with others, our communities, our regions, our environment and, ultimately, our globe. We are related in a meaningful way to all these processes. Thus LGN will involve change at all these levels so that the connections can facilitate the exploration of individual, local and global problems in ways that will not lead to further problems or situations where the solution becomes the problem. Take Bangkok as an example. Surely the solution to the city's dreadful traffic problem does not lie in the building of yet more roads, even in the form of freeways, since that solution only confounds the traffic problem by encouraging yet more traffic. Bangkok needs such a second-order change as public transport or decentralisation of the city, at the very least.

Strategies from Learning III are necessary in order for individuals to step outside the offending system—their competitive, individualistic framework—to see it for what it is and reorganise their ways of thinking to incorporate more humanitarian frameworks emphasising individuation and participation. From the level of the individual this process needs, then, to be translated to the community level so that communities can adopt the principles of Learning III to facilitate a 'more wholistic view of the globe' (Yamaguchi 1990: 1025).

Participation

LGN is founded on participation and holism as organising principles. Participation is seen not only as taking part, in the dictionary sense, but also as giving part and sharing whole. Participation is seen as weaving together the processes of

---

[2] A term coined in the Communication Centre by Paul Wildman to describe the processes in social networks mediated via C&IT.

giving, taking and sharing. This advocates a holographic framework where individual participation is a necessary part of wider social change. Social change is located in each individual, and each individual is located in the social change. Therefore, again, LGN involves Learning III, since individuals and communities change their perceptions of reality from non-participation, competition and control to participation, co-operation and holism. At the individual level this represents a process of self-realisation, as described earlier. Individuals move from being passive observers to sensuous participants in the surrounding world; from being organised to self-organising. If the aim of LGN is to be met, each participant in the programme must embark on a journey to redefine the self, a journey liberating that participant from the individual's cultural bias and the Cartesian paradigm. This does not come easily. To remove a mask once thought of as part of one's real self can be a deeply disturbing experience, as Kierkegaard said (quoted in Rogers 1961: 116).

At a group level, participation demands recognition of a group mind that transcends individual minds, allowing the group to see itself as a whole that is greater than the sum of individuals in the group. For a group in the LGN programme, then, this means there would be no control by individuals or imposed decisions but rather a degree of self-determination in decision-making. It would mean that variety and diversity in the membership would be valued as enhancing the process of the group. Communities involved in the programme would need to develop the ability to transcend local customs, while still inherently valuing them, in order to see and appreciate the contexts of other communities facing similar problems and issues.

Participation, then, requires a recognition and an appreciation of the connectedness of personal, social and global changes in a way that inspires understanding and action. It cannot be forced, but we believe that individuals and groups may be empowered in ways that allow them to begin the process of self- and social realisation.

Communication

The realisation that each one of us is inherently connected to the world and its processes demands a major shift in perception for most of us, particularly in Western societies. Even so, if meaningful change is to result from participation, then realisation alone is not sufficient. We must begin to communicate about our connections, to share them and act on them. Herein lies the value of such a programme as LGN, which aims to link people (individuals and communities) 'to facilitate social, cultural, business, industrial, scientific, educational, sporting, trade, marketing, economic and welfare liaisons' (Communication Centre 1993: 5), not to forget spiritual liaisons, in ways that are meaningful at a local level but also have relevance on a global level. The programme is cross-cultural and involves people from widely diverse backgrounds. The hope is that people will be encouraged to think of solutions to problems from a variety of perspectives, advocating the adoption of Learning III principles.

The LGN programme aims to use interactive C&ITs (for example, tele-conferencing, including video-conferencing, audio-conferencing and computer-conferencing or electronic mail) to facilitate communication between people irrespective of economic background, race, gender, geography or other characteristics (Communication Centre, 1993). In using technology to assist such communication, we consider it necessary to place a framework of use around the technology that sustains the values emphasised in this chapter and avoids what Lilienfeld (quoted in Berman 1981: 285) called a 'globalist culture'. This was described by Berman as a 'world knit closely together by a system of computerized mass media and information exchange', leading to 'the end of diversity and freedom, a homogenization of the globe under man's domination—or rather, under the domination of a small, powerful elite'. Von Bertalanffy (quoted in Berman 1981) went further, saying that computer technology makes the systems idea another, indeed the ultimate, technique for shaping humanity and society even more into the mega-machine.

The LGN programme needs to develop a view of C&IT and its use that would avoid this frightening, alternative future.

Action

The LGN programme is fundamentally an action-oriented endeavour. It is based on the premiss that 'each and every one of us learns through action' and, thus, that 'action is the means through which we engage reality' (Morgan and Ramirez 1983: 10). Within this framework, action is thought to link, inherently, subject and object, conscious and unconscious, mind and nature. In addition, the action-orientation of LGN means that it goes beyond the collection of information and the expansion of knowledge, since it is 'guided by a concern to develop capacities for people to investigate and understand their own situations' (ibid.).

17.7 Conclusion

The action principle of the LGN programme, then, ensures that the principles of connectedness, participation and communication are enacted in practical ways to facilitate appropriate social, economic, technological, ecological and global change, in new designs for living, working and learning.

However, whether it is practical, given the command nature of most of our politics and economics, remains to be seen.

Here, at Goshiki-cho, we invite local Awaji communities to connect with Australian communities, such as Maleny, or communities in other countries, in order to explore the advantages of local–global netweaving. We hope we can establish connections, here, this week.

References

Bateson, G. (1972). *Steps to an Ecology of Mind*, London: Intertext Books.

Berman, M. (1981). *The Reenchantment of the World*, Ithaca, N.Y.: Cornell University Press.

Cocks, Doug (1992). *Use with Care: Managing Australia's Natural Resources in the Twenty-first Century*, University of New South Wales Press.

Communication Centre (1993). *The Local–Global Netweaving Project Proposal*, unpublished report, Brisbane: QUT.

Free, Les, Stevenson, Tony, Mandeville, Thomas, Hearn, Greg and McKenzie, Andrew (1992). *Australian Service Industries: Public Policy Issues and Service Industries Opportunities for Australia in Digital Video Communications*, Canberra: Australian Government Publishing Service.

Fujimoto, Isao (1992). 'Lessons from Abroad in Rural Community Development: The One Village, One Product Movement in Japan', *Community Development Journal* 27(1): pp. 10–20.

Henderson, Hazel (1989). 'Eco-feminism and Eco-communication: Toward the Feminization of Economics', pp. 291–4 in R. Rush and D. Allen (eds.), *Communications at the Cross-roads: The Gender Gap Connection*, Norwood: Ablex.

Kantor, R. (1973). *Communes: Creating and Managing the Collective Life*, New York: Harper & Row.

Kelly, A. and Chanon, G. (1993). 'Community Development Practice in a Global Economy', unpublished paper written for the Social Work Practice Centre, Taringa, Queensland.

Lippman Abu-Lughod, Janet (1992). 'Communication and the Metropolis: Spatial Drift and the Reconstitution of Control', *Asian Journal of Communication* 2(3): pp.12–30.

McNeill, Jim, Cox, John E. and Jackson, Ian (1991). 'Sustainable Development: The Urban Challenge', *Ekistics* 348(May/June): pp. 195–8.

Morgan, G. and Ramirez, R. (1983). 'Action Learning: A Holographic Metaphor for Building Social Change', *Human Relations* 37(1): pp. 1–28.

Newman, Peter (1993). 'Cities and Development: An Emerging Asian Model', *Development Bulletin*, 27 May: pp. 20–2.

O'Connell, Margi (1991). 'Community Economics: A Creative Approach to Employment', *Social Alternatives* 10(3).

Powell, J. M. (1988). 'Decentralisation', pp. 967–70 in *The Australian Encyclopedia*, Terrey Hills, N.S.W.: Australian Geographic.

Prigogine, Ilya and Strengers, Isabelle (1984). *Order out of Chaos: Man's New Dialogue with Nature*, London: Flamingo Press.

Rahim, Syed A. (1992). 'Communication and the Metropolis: Economy and Identity', *Asian Journal of Communication* 2(3): pp. 1–11.

Reynolds, Margaret (1991). 'Urban Sprawl: The Need for Reform', *Social Alternatives* 10(2): pp. 23–4.

Rogers, C. (1961). *On Becoming a Person: Therapist's View of Psychotherapy*. London: Constable.

Singh, L. (1992). 'Black Possum: An Experiment in Community Publishing', *Social Alternatives* 11(4): pp. 35–44.

Skrandies, J. (1991). 'Local Energy Created out of Unemployment', *Social Alternatives* 10(3): pp. 15–18.

Stevenson, T. (1989). 'Communication Strategies for Facilitating Networking in the Pacific', workshop presented at the WFSF Pacific Basin Conference, Nagoya University of Commerce, Aichi, Japan, 20–23 November.

—— (1993). 'Anticipating Policy Issues for Emerging Communication Technologies', paper presented at the 'Censorship Issues: Law, Technology and Effects' conference Brisbane, May.

Watzlawick, P., Weakland, J. and Fisch, R. (1980). *Change: The Principles of Problem Formation and Resolution*, Beverley Hills, Calif.: Sage.

Yamaguchi, Kaoru (1990). 'Fundamentals of a New Economic Paradigm in the Information Age', *Futures* December: pp. 1023–36.

—— and Niwa, Hiroyuki (1994). 'New Thinking on Japanese Community Development in the Information Age', *Technological Forecasting and Social Change* 45(1–XX): pp. 79–92.

Part IV

Sustainable Community Projects in Awaji Island

18   A Community-Wide Medical Network System

MITSUGU SAITO

18.1 Goshiki-cho Town

Hyogo Prefecture has designated Awaji Island an 'island-wide park in the international community'. I would like to talk about the direction that the Goshiki-cho town government has been working towards to position Goshiki-cho within this overall plan.

Goshiki-cho has an area of 58.14 km^2 and a population of 10,600—10 and 6.7 per cent of the entire island, respectively. Located on the west coast of the island, Goshiki-cho receives the full force of the winter winds and has an average winter temperature 1–2 degrees lower than the island's east coast.

With the rapid economic development of postwar Japan, this area has steadily lost population to the cities, while the age of our citizens continues to rise. At present we have four centenarians in the town, the oldest of whom is 106 years of age. Her sister is 94, and thus their combined age is 200. Today they both reside in a home for senior citizens established by the town, and live in good health, even helping others who are in need.

18.2 Health-Oriented Policy and the
Integrated Circuit (IC) Card System

I have been mayor now for fourteen years,[1] and during this time have promoted the concept of health in community-building. Until now our administrative efforts have focused solely on people's mental and physical health. Yet I feel it is time that we extended the concept of health to cover healthy living conditions; that is, protection of the natural environment and the provision of facilities that allow the residents of the area to live in health and security, with the ability to help each other and to enjoy a green environment.

Another type of health is economic health. The lack of work opportunities and a struggling economy have resulted in a decrease in population. For these

---

[1] *Editor's note*: Mr Saito served as a mayor for sixteen consecutive years and resigned in July 1995. This chapter is based on Mr Saito's community presentation at the First World Futures-Creating Seminar, 16 August 1993.

reasons our administration has been promoting economic health as part of our health-oriented policy.

Let me now report on the efforts we are currently engaged in. First of all, we could not move ahead with our health-oriented policy without an understanding and awareness of the policy among residents. Therefore, in 1980 we issued the 'Town of Health' declaration. The eleventh day of every month was designated a 'Health Day', a day on which extended families are encouraged to sit down to dinner together and talk about health, their children's future and other topics to improve communication within the family. We began to build our policy on health while working to raise awareness of health issues among residents in this way.

To provide a facility for mental and physical health and welfare, we enlisted the co-operation of the then-governor of Hyogo Prefecture, and over a period of 10 years built Kenmin Kenko Mura (Goshiki Health Centre for Hyogo Citizens). We also secured highly skilled professionals to run the centre, which now has five medical doctors. In a 'greying' community it also becomes important to secure public health nurses, home helps and others who are able to give local assistance.

In addition to promoting such a health policy, one fundamental issue is whether we are able to understand the real living conditions of the residents of Goshiki-cho. That is to say, a system is required that gives the government the ability to understand the health conditions of each individual.

First, to find out how healthy the children of this town are—long before they become subject to the diseases of adulthood—we conducted a health survey of children from the fifth to ninth grades, with the co-operation of the Hyogo University of Teacher Training. In addition, we conducted town-wide health checks and also health checks every five years for those aged 40 and over. The data for each individual amassed from the survey and checks were entered into computer files, paying special attention to the complete protection of privacy. These data were then incorporated into a public health medical-information network using an IC card system.

This system was designated a 'model system' by the Ministry of Health and Welfare, and was set up under the guidance of the head of the prefectural hospital on Awaji Island. The IC cards can hold up to 8,000 characters, allowing them to record both living conditions and health information. When a card is presented at any of the town's medical facilities or at the prefectural hospital, the doctors are able to call up the patient's data to aid in the diagnosis. The system was inaugurated in 1989, and today there are 4,600 card-holding town residents.

Two types of card are issued, one valid from birth to 20 years of age and the other from age 20 on. At present, software is being developed to allow the card to store information about a person's social activities and welfare. In today's ageing society, we cannot divorce social welfare issues from medical treatment and public health if we hope to provide security and maintain a stable population in the community. After one year of studying software possibilities, we decided to allocate one-tenth of the capacity of the adult card (800 characters) to information of this type.

18.3 Medical Information Network through CATV

We live in an information age where major world events reach us in near-real time; yet we often lack access to information close to us. For example, an elderly person living alone dies without asking for help from anyone and is not discovered until several days later by neighbours. Such events may start to increase as the number of senior citizens in society grows.

In this type of situation we see how important it becomes to provide localised information and to obtain accurate information to support neighbours and build a local community whose members can help each other. One of the primary projects of the Ministry of Home Affairs developed in response to this situation is the introduction of cable television (CATV).

This system is now being implemented in Goshiki-cho and will provide interactive capabilities in the future. Its goal is to utilise the medical information that is stored on a person's IC card via an interactive link through CATV to medical clinics. This will provide support for nursing and home care of the elderly as well as allowing the transmission of information for assistance in the event of an emergency at the home of a person who lives alone.

Perhaps the most serious problem facing Japan and Goshiki-cho today is the decreasing number of children being born, and consequently the lack of manpower to support an ageing population. The birth rate has currently dropped to around 1.5 children per woman. Not enough youthful energy is available to take care of the growing care needs of the elderly.

At the same time, efforts are being made to reduce the annual number of working hours to 1,800 in Japan, a country known for its extended working hours. The national government has established a ten-year plan to deal with Japan's ageing population, and is calling for more homes for senior citizens and for more people to work as home helps. Who, though, will support and run these facilities? If the goal of 1,800 hours is met, not enough labour will be available to revitalise local regions.

When a large portion of society becomes senior citizens, special facilities alone will not be enough to handle the demand for nursing care. At-home care is one possible solution, yet the basic lack of available workers and the difficulty families face in taking care of the elderly at home remain as major obstacles. For these reasons we are building a support system that utilises the interactivity offered by the new medium of CATV.

At present, medical clinics in Goshiki-cho are trying out a 'home hospice care' system. Six elderly patients whose lives hang in the balance receive love in a warm home atmosphere, while receiving visiting nursing care and medical treatment. To be surrounded by one's own family towards the end of one's life is surely preferable to being confined in a hospital. Lending a hand through media technology is one response to the problems of the ageing society that we will be faced with in the twenty-first century.

Through the CATV link, a doctor at the medical clinic can see the facial expression of a patient and can gauge the patient's condition while referring to IC card data to make a diagnosis. The doctor can then give appropriate guidance to the visiting nurse. When a specialist's opinion is needed, the data can be sent to the main prefectural hospital and advice received in a short time. We intend to have this system functioning fully in two years.

18.4 Conclusions

By these means we aim to establish a town that people can live in without fear of old age, as well as a community with a stable population. No matter how much effort the town government puts into measures to deal with ageing, though, we cannot accomplish what needs to be done without volunteer efforts. Each person must be ready to contribute—to help others in true volunteer spirit—in order to keep our town healthy in the twenty-first century.

This 'World Futures-Creating Seminar' is an event heralding genuine international co-operation and exchange here in Goshiki-cho, and it is my hope that the seminar is able to help the people of Goshiki-cho to expand their horizons, cultivate a rich acceptance of the people of the world and contribute to building a co-operative local community.

19 A Comprehensive Health Care and Welfare System in Goshiki-cho

TAKAMARO MATSUURA

19.1 The Introduction of the IC Card System

Against the background of a rapidly ageing society and a decreasing birth rate in Japan, the establishment of a comprehensive health and welfare system covering all stages from childhood to adulthood and old age, has become a priority. Within such a system, an important problem will be how to link organically health-promoting activities for inhabitants of the community with public health and medical care activities, and with welfare policies.

Goshiki-cho, Tsuna-Gun, Hyogo Prefecture, is a small town situated almost in the middle of the west coast of Awaji Island, facing the Seto Inland Sea. It has a population of approximately 10,600, of whom over 25 per cent are aged over 65.

The town has experimented with a comprehensive health-management system for its residents—a system that combines public health, medical care and social welfare using an integrated circuit (IC) card. After one year's field trial, the IC card system was put into operation in April 1990 with the distribution of cards to all town residents over 60 years old. This system is now known nationwide as the Goshiki-cho 'Health Card System'—the most advanced IC card health-administration system in Japan.

In addition, the 'Health Card System for Children' was established in April 1992, covering the paediatric field from newborn, to infant, to school child, and the cards have been distributed to all the children of Goshiki-cho between 0 and 6 years of age. To the Health Card System, has been added the 'Welfare Information System', thus completing Goshiki-cho's comprehensive public health, medical care and welfare information-management system. Now an effort is being made to extend the age coverage to adults under 60 and to children over 7. (In 1995, more than half of the residents of the town were card-holders.)

The most important feature of the IC card system of Goshiki-cho is that an advanced hardware information system (including the IC cards and computer

This paper was written in collaboration with Professor Shingo Katsuno and Professor Junko Nagai, Department of Epidemiology and Health Education, Hyogo University of Teacher Training. In addition, the Editor supplemented it by incorporating documents provided by the Goshiki-cho Health and Welfare Centre.

networks) has been put in place to support the linking of local administration, public health, medical care, welfare and education for residents. In other words, not only is the IC card used for its electronic memory, which makes it possible to manage, maintain and call up information on individual health and welfare; it is also being utilised a means of organising administrative bodies and medical institutions and as a support system for public health and medical care. Furthermore, this IC card system has been positioned among other network systems of public health, medical care and welfare, all performing an educational function in improving the health-awareness of every member of the town.

19.2 Components of the IC Card System

Health Card System

The Health Card System consists of seven institutions: the prefectural General Hospital, which is out of town in Sumoto City, two town clinics with beds, three practitioner clinics without beds in the town and the Goshiki-cho Health and Welfare Centre. The host computer is installed inside the public health centre of the Goshiki-cho Health and Welfare Centre. This computer holds all the basic, individual data and all the health-screening data of every resident. Each medical institution that is a member of the system is equipped with a computer terminal and a reader/writer. The lines between the host computer and the terminals are only 'turned on' with the insertion of an IC card.

The types of information held on the card are shown in Table 19.1. These items of information are prepared for the IC card, and input and output at the computer terminals by means of a card-reader/writer. Fifteen kinds of information on medical examination history can be shown simultaneously on the terminal. In addition, the pattern of the examination results can be shown in time-sequential graphs on the terminal for twelve chronic diseases, including hypertension, myocardial infarction, diabetes and chronic hepatitis.

For the protection of privacy and confidentiality of information, the access of card-holder and operator to the contents of the card are restricted. In other words, only the full name, date of birth and sex of a card-holder are printed on the card, together with a photograph of the holder's face, which allows identification of the card-holder.

Furthermore, every card-holder has his or her own pass number, and the system cannot be activated unless this number is input. Operators are classified into four branches of the medical profession (namely, administrator, ambulance man, nurse or public health nurse, and physician) and every operator is given an official operator card. Without this card, access to the system is impossible. Furthermore, the level of access is determined by the kind of operator card, and only a physician is allowed to have access to all the information input and output.

Table 19.1. Information held on the IC card

Information items	Description
Basic personal	ID, name, address, health insurance card code and number
Emergency	Blood type, past record of adverse reactions to medicines, allergies
Present disease	Disease name, hospital name, date of development
Past history	Disease name, age
Family record	Past medical record of parents, brothers and sisters
Medication	Date of prescription, number of times, medicine name, usage, doses per day, dosage
Medical examination	Date of examination, type of examination, data obtained from various examinations
Medical examination history	Date of examination, type of examination

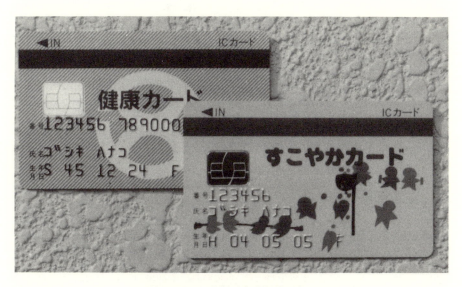

Figure 19.1. Health IC Card

Health Card System for Children

The Health Card System for Children is tailored to the specific needs of paediatric medicine in the variety of health-check items it covers. These needs change
with the growth of a child from newborn baby, to infant, to school child in terms
of the importance of acute diseases and allergic diseases and dental information.
Moreover, confidentiality measures have also increased in complexity as a result
of the expansion of the system to include school teachers for handicapped
children as well as the medical profession.

This card system is much the same as the Health Card System in terms of its
appearance on terminal screens, but has also adopted other, child-specific screen
images.

Welfare Information System

The Welfare Information System has been provided to store individual welfare
information for every inhabitant in a previously reserved space on the health
card. The aim is one of organically linking such physical data as health conditions, medical care information and welfare information. This system also
registers the amount of time spent in volunteer activities. This information is
stored in order to establish a system whereby the results of volunteer activity will
be compensated in the future.

19.3 Home-Care Support System Using the
Two-Way CATV Network

To make it possible for the sick to continue to receive home care as long as they
wish, what is needed is a comprehensive care system in which the public health,
medical care and social welfare trinity can grapple with the complex problems
confronting home patients and their families. With the increase in the number of
aged households, a growing number of elderly people are looking after their
spouses. This situation gives rise to numerous problems. In recent years, the
number of patients who say that they wish to go home earlier and prefer to
recuperate in their own homes, despite the fact that they need hospital treatment,
has been rising steadily. The physical and psychological burdens shouldered by
family members supporting the sick person may be heavier than medical service
providers assume.

CATV System

To confront these problems in an ageing society, we thought that the introduction of a two-way CATV network would be of great help. Town-wide CATV
began to operate in Goshiki-cho on 1 April 1994. It is based at the Goshiki-cho
Information Centre, and its coaxial cable extends 240 km, with an optical cable

installed to accommodate the heavy traffic between the centre and a TV receiver. The services consist of two channels of town programmes, nineteen channels of commercial re-broadcasting, town-wide free cable telephone services, a home-care support system and an emergency call system. Around 6,886 access ports have been established, and 2,983 homes (or 94.2 per cent of the town) subscribed to the CATV at the time of its initial operation. Each home has two cable junctions, one for CATV and the other for the home-care support system. The application fee of 40,000 yen was waived for those who applied a year before operations began. The monthly subscription fee for CATV is 1,500 yen, while the channel for the home-care support system is free.

Home-Care Support System

A year after the start of the CATV service, on 10 May 1995, the home-care support system and emergency call system were put into operation, making the most of the two-way capabilities of the town-wide CATV network. Since then, home patients and their families have been linked to the hospitals and Goshiki-cho Health and Welfare Centre. Visiting nurses and health carers are now able to consult physicians on-screen, as the occasion demands, without a trip to the hospital from the patients' homes.

Two services are provided under the support system. First, those patients who are seriously ill and request home hospice care can be given timely advice and improved nursing, care guidance and mental support through a *fixed* two-way CATV terminal and a vital sensor installed in the home. In this way the support system also alleviates the burden of their families. Of course, even under this system, house visits and home care are available as before.

Secondly, home helps, town clinic nurses, public health nurses and physiotherapists regularly visit the elderly in Goshiki-cho who are in poor health or require nursing at home. When they find something abnormal with a patient, they show the condition to the doctor through a *portable camera* and a CATV terminal, and consult with him over the proper course of action, thereby contributing to the improvement of home-care quality. The photographs in Fig. 19.2. show this home care service.

To protect the privacy of patients under this system, as with the IC cards, dialogues, images and other information running through the support network are automatically scrambled by encoding devices.

Emergency Call System

For elderly people living alone and for those who might need to make emergency calls, pendant alarms are provided, so that they can call doctors anytime by simply pressing a button. These emergency calls are carried by the telephone cable system and managed at the Goshiki-cho Health and Welfare Centre. The calls and medical advice are simultaneously recorded for the re-examination and improvement of the system.

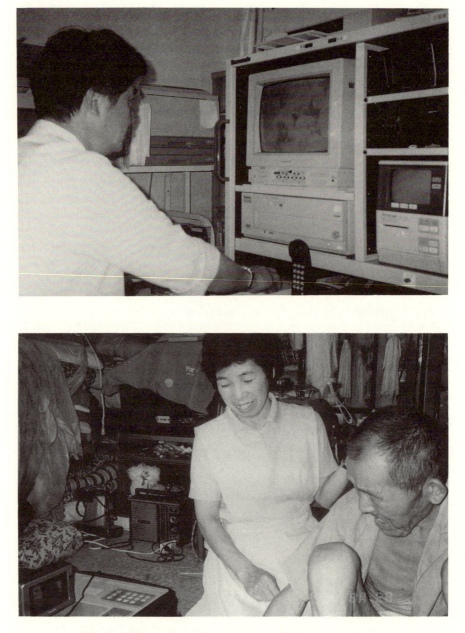

Figure 19.2. A portable camera and CATV terminal
in operation between the centre and a patient's home

19.4 Conclusion

The public health, medical care and welfare system of Goshiki-cho, which encompasses all the life stages of the town's residents, was completed in 1992 and is now in operation. Under this system, a method of utilising the information stored on IC cards for the administration of the town's health services as well as for comprehensive epidemiological studies has been adopted that respects individual privacy. Alongside this system, a CATV network covering the whole town has been established and, by means of the two-way channels, a linkage system between home care, home welfare, emergency information and medical institutions has also been put into operation. These measures now make the home-care support system more comprehensive and solid.

The population of Goshiki-cho town is not large and hardly fluctuates. The health awareness of the inhabitants and the balance of medical institutions provide appropriate conditions for undertaking an experiment in a comprehensive health and welfare system and for evaluating its results. The project under way in Goshiki-cho, where the proportion of elderly people in the population is high, will be a model for a comprehensive health and welfare system in the ageing society in Japan as a whole. It can, therefore, be concluded that the Goshiki-cho project demonstrates the proper scale of community-based development for the organic operation of such a system in the information age.

Further Reading

Department of Health and Welfare, Goshiki-cho (1992). 'Goshiki-cho Guidelines for Health and Welfare Work'.

Matsuura, Takamaro (1996). 'On the Installation of the Home-Care Support System Using Two-Way CATV and its Operational Evaluation' [in Japanese], *Journal of the Japanese Association of Rural Medicine* 44(5): pp. 689–96.

20 Establishing a Higher Institution for Future-Oriented Studies

KAORU YAMAGUCHI

20.1 Future-Oriented Studies

We are now at the turning-point in history from an industrial age to an information age. Yet we are still confronted with many serious socioeconomic and environmental problems caused by the industrial age. We cannot solve these problems with old-fashioned industrial-age approaches. We need new, holistic solutions based on future-oriented studies. In this belief, dissatisfied with the industrial-age paradigm in economics, I have been actively involved in future-oriented studies since 1988, through such organisations as the World Futures Studies Federation and the World Future Society. This involvement has given me a good opportunity to consider what future-oriented studies are and why they are also needed in a traditional field such as economics, with which I have been familiar for many years. To my disappointment, this opportunity gave me a headache rather than a clear image of future-oriented studies. Nevertheless, this headache of several years turned out to be worth suffering for a social scientist like me who was trained in a narrow academic field. I am now in a position to state my own understanding of future-oriented studies and why they are needed. I will then make a proposal, on the basis of these arguments, for establishing a higher institution for future-oriented studies.

The future is wide open to everybody. Consequently, everybody, even the novice, is qualified to be a futurist without professional training. This means that any field of studies, even science fiction or subjective beliefs, seems to fit into future-oriented studies. Indeed, the futurist organisations mentioned above are associations of people with backgrounds as diverse as science, professional life, politics and writing. In this sense they are very different from other established scientific and professional associations. Because of this inter-professional diversity, the academic activities of futurists have seldom been regarded as academic by traditional scientists. And, to tell the truth, I myself, as a professionally trained social scientist, once felt shy to identify myself as a futurist. What makes future-oriented studies look non-academic, then?

(1) Future-oriented studies are similar to ancient philosophy, which covered

This chapter is based on Yamaguchi 1992.

almost all possible areas of science, including mathematics, astronomy and medicine. As scientific knowledge advanced, many areas of philosophy became independent scientific fields, leaving almost no room for philosophy *per se*. Future-oriented studies seem to have been following the same path in the last two decades. Since the late 1960s and early 1970s, when the need for future-oriented studies was realised, those areas that were able to apply newly developed scientific methods of statistical inference and estimation, forecasting and computer simulation have adopted future-predicting studies into their own research fields. These future-predicting research areas, however, have not been regarded as independent fields of future-oriented studies, but as mere extrapolations of their own traditional enquiries into the future. In this way most fields of scientific research have developed their own counterpart to future-oriented studies, and no room seems to have been left specifically for future-oriented studies. In other words, from the viewpoint of scientists and professionals, no extra research area remains that needs to be further covered by a new branch of science called 'future-oriented studies'. Hence, future-oriented studies are, by definition, non-academic to them.

(2) Since future-oriented studies are regarded as non-academic, no efforts are made to establish their own scientific methodology or futurology. Consequently, no scientific paradigm is established on which futurists are able to build their own models and communicate with each other. Moreover, there is no textbook with which students can be professionally trained and evaluated. Where are future-oriented studies, then? Obviously they are not included in academic curricula, for which textbooks are essential ingredients. The only areas in which no paradigm, and hence no textbook, is required are science fiction, story-telling and scenario-writing, in which writers and politicians can attract people with their own subjective visions of the future.

These two points have made future-oriented studies irrelevant to the educational curricula in present-day higher-education institutions. Those institutions are established on the basis of the scientific methodology of the industrial age; that is, the whole consists of parts and the individual and independent analysis of its parts inevitably leads to the understanding of the whole. Accordingly, they are destined to specialise only in scientific education in the parts, under the many different names of departments and faculties.

Interrelated Wholeness and Wisdom

If future-oriented studies are interpreted as extraneous and non-academic, there is obviously no room to establish them as a new or alternative science. But are they? Let me consider wholeness first. Modern science has gradually revealed that the whole is an inseparable and organic entity and that mere analysis of its individual parts is not enough to understand it. In other words, almost all socioeconomic and environmental phenomena are gradually coming to be understood as mutually interrelated at the deepest level, as if Mahatma Buddha revealed the fundamental cause of all of our afflictions. Typical presentations of this new way of looking at the whole can be found in the Gaia (Lovelock 1988), chaos (Gleick 1987) and complexity (Waldrop 1992) theories. This new view makes the traditional division of scientific research areas entirely powerless to cope with the socioeconomic and environmental problems we now face, because a solution obtained from one separate branch of research, applied independently, might cause another new problem somewhere else. Thus, what has been missing in industrial-age scientific research, and hence in the academic curricula of present-day higher institutions, is a study of interrelated wholeness and interdependence. This study is not merely interdisciplinary, as used to be believed among futurists, but a totally new synthesis of individual analyses at different levels of the whole, depending on the objectives of our scientific enquiry. My work is a small, but first step towards this new synthesis at the level of economic life (Yamaguchi 1990).

Let me now turn to wisdom. The future is uncertain. Yet we have to make decisions today, in preparation for this uncertain future, on the basis of our future visions or beliefs (Yamaguchi 1993). In this sense, the future only lies in our present decisions about the future, and hence in our mind. But can we envisage what kind of future our mind wants to create without knowing our mind itself or ourselves? Envisioning the future implies self-awareness. In other words, self-awareness is a prerequisite for better decisions about the future. Through an effort to attain self-awareness, a relationship between ourselves and our environment is eventually revealed; that is, an interrelated wholeness of which we are a part.

Self-awareness is not knowledge but wisdom. Wisdom cannot be sought through knowledge, partly because it is of a personally acquired nature and thus hard to accumulate like knowledge and to pass interpersonally. This is why it is not taught at a school based on scientific knowledge. Thus, Zen meditation has been practised in the East independently of industrial-age school systems, because it is believed that wisdom can only be sought through the endeavour to attain self-awareness. It is now time to change the worn-out approach to schooling. The search for wisdom can be a scientific learning process within a new holistic view of science,[1] though a scientific paradigm, in the traditional sense, and textbooks based on it are not yet available. In short, we absolutely need wisdom for decision-making or future-oriented studies.

To conclude, a study of interrelated wholeness and the search for wisdom are what have been entirely neglected in the industrial-age methodology of science, and hence within the present-day higher institutions based on it. In fact, these two things are the most essential fields of study for creating a better future in the twenty-first century. Given the nature of these fields, it is right to regard them as essential constituents of future-oriented studies. Future-oriented studies can now be defined in principle as a new holistic science that consists of the following two major fields: (1) a search for wisdom through practice to attain self-awareness, and (2) a study of interrelated wholeness and interdependence.

---

[1] For the integration of religion and science within a single consistent worldview, see Sperry 1991.

Five Inseparable Fields of Study

Higher institutions in the industrial age have failed to provide future-oriented studies. This is why we urgently need to establish a new higher institution that focuses on the future-oriented studies defined above. What kind of specific areas should be covered, then, within future-oriented studies? From the definition of futures studies above, we can derive the following five major fields, which constitute *an inseparable whole*:

(1) Wisdom and Self-Awareness Studies

- training for self-awareness and enlightenment through meditation
- ecological awareness and a new holistic philosophy
- medical training for well-being

(2) Future-Oriented Methodological Studies

- a non-linear paradigm based on chaos, evolutionary and complexity theories
- mathematical programming, statistical inference and time-series analysis
- computer programming, simulations, scientific visualisation, artificial intelligence and virtual reality

(3) Human–Nature Interrelationship Studies

- ecologically sustainable natural and organic farming using effective micro-organisms
- creation of new ecoshare regions and communities based on natural habitats
- holistic solutions for such environmental problems as global warming, acid rain, depletion of the ozone layer, tropical deforestation and endangered species

(4) Human–Technology Interface Studies

- renewal of traditional technologies, for example making tofu and soy sauce
- use of clean forms of energy, including solar, tidal and wind energies
- new ecologically sound orientation for such high technologies as info-communication, biotechnology and new materials

(5) Inter-Human Networking Studies

- new information and network economics, beyond market economics
- renewal of traditional and diversified cultures and histories
- networking of economies, cultures, technologies and the environment

Having identified these five inseparable areas of future-oriented studies, it is strongly recommended that a working team of professionals from these areas be formed to construct a new synthetic paradigm that covers these five areas holistically. The objective should be to write a textbook of future-oriented studies on the basis of the new paradigm.[2]

In order for the holistic study of these five areas to be effective, it is desirable that students of future-oriented studies have a comprehensive and professional background in one of the five areas. Hence, a higher institution for future-oriented studies should be aimed at the graduate level.

20.2 A Higher Institution for Future-Oriented Studies

Towards a New Participatory Democracy

Let me consider further why we need such a higher institution for a sustainable future. An industrial-age system of representative democracy has three pitfalls: (1) it is not a form of democracy in which all members of society participate—participatory democracy; (2) no future generations (for example, children yet to be born) are allowed to represent themselves; (3) no other living beings—animals or plants—are allowed to represent themselves. It is not too much to say that many of the socioeconomic and environmental problems we now face have been caused by these pitfalls underlying industrial-age democracy.

To make a democracy a better system for wiser decisions, future generations and all living beings have to be equally represented. A new democratic system in the twenty-first century will have to allow these new voters to represent themselves by introducing, say, a quota system in which one third of votes are reserved for them. Since it is technically impossible for them to vote by themselves, they will have to be represented by someone else. Who, then, can vote on their behalf? Those who complete future-oriented study programmes will be qualified to represent them and cast the reserved votes in all decision-making processes that affect them, because future-oriented studies have the specific aim of making wiser decisions for a sustainable future. In this way a higher institution for future-oriented studies will prepare people to play an important role in the new standard of participatory democracy in the twenty-first century. This is another reason why such institutions are urgently needed for the next century.

The Network University of the Green World

Awaji Island, located in Osaka Bay, is part of Japan's Inland Sea National Park. The island presents itself as a future-oriented place for the following reasons. First, its beautiful environment of green countryside has been conserved despite its proximity to such big cities as Kobe and Osaka. Second, according to an old legend, it was the first island in Japan to be created by the Gods, and thus

---

2 The 'Future-Oriented Complexity and Adaptation Studies Seminar', which is mentioned below, has been organised with this specific objective in mind.

traditional village life and ancient culture have been preserved well on the island. Third, it has better access to an international airport than Tokyo: Kansai International Airport, opened in Osaka Bay in September 1994, is just thirty-five minutes away by boat. Fourth, when the longest bridge in the world, connecting the island and the mainland of Japan, is completed in 1998, Awaji Island will become not only a tourist spot but also a place to rethink the relationship between environment and technology. The bridge will also give islanders direct access to large cities, including Kobe, Osaka and Kyoto. Finally, the island will become a symbol of *network and communications* for the twenty-first century, as New York used to be a symbol of *liberty* for the twentieth century thanks to the Statue of Liberty donated by the French government about a century ago. France's second monument, symbolising communications, will be donated in 1998 and set atop a hill on the Awaji side of the longest suspension bridge in the world.

On the basis of these features, Awaji Island seems indeed to be an island of the future, and in this sense a good place for newly establishing a higher institution for future-oriented studies. Fortunately, there is good co-operation among the island people, as well as those in WFSF, WFS and the Future-Oriented Project of UNESCO, in realising this idea. The institution will serve as a networking campus to create an ecologically sustainable green world for the twenty-first century, as envisioned above. It will, therefore, be appropriate to call such a new institution 'The Network University of the Green World'.[3]

The Future-Oriented Complexity and Adaptation Studies Seminar

To disseminate worldwide this idea of establishing the Network University at the beginning of the next century, in 1993 Goshiki-cho, one of the ten small towns on the island, with a population of just 10,600, began to sponsor the annual summer 'Future-Oriented Complexity and Adaptation Studies (FOCAS) Seminar'.[4] 'Go-shiki' literally means 'five colours'—a good coincidence indeed with the five colourful areas of future-oriented studies defined above. The town, though small in size, is known throughout Japan for its 'Declaration of Health', which includes the use of Japan's first system of electronic medical cards to store the townspeople's medical records so that they can be utilised efficiently at the

---

3 The URL of the Network University homepage is http://www.bekkoame.or.jp/~ k_yama/.

4 The seminar used to be called the 'World Futures-Creating Seminar'. Following the second seminar, a residential workshop was held for three days (11–13 August 1994) to discuss the further development of the seminar and the Network University project. The participants were twelve lecturers from the second seminar: Steven R. Bishop, George Cowan, Nadegda Gaponenko, Jerome C. Glenn, Jerome Karle, Pentti Malaska, Kazuo Mizuta, Linzheng Qin, Tony Stevenson, Terushi Tomita, Theodore J. Voneida and Kaoru Yamaguchi. On the last day of the workshop, all agreed that the seminar should be renamed to reflect what we want to pursue—what is described in this paper. Thus, a new research field was born: Future-Oriented Complexity and Adaptation Studies. FOCAS aims to (1) understand the interrelated wholeness and interdependence of future-oriented complex phenomena (such as the environmental, socioeconomic and natural), which cannot be *linearly* predicted, and (2) use our brain and technology so that human beings, societies, communities and individuals are able to become well adapted to these phenomena.

time of treatment. In April 1994, to promote this medical health-care system further, a town-wide fibre-optic medical network system was installed with the aim of allowing the townspeople to obtain medical advice from doctors interactively at home via video screens. Fortunately, the same network system can also be used for CATV conferences. In other words, teachers and students staying with host families in the town can communicate with each other or hold a meeting at any time, at home. The town is thus capable of becoming a network campus without any further investment in communications. Considering these possibilities, the town seems to be a very good place to establish a network campus. The campus need not be an ugly complex of concrete buildings as in the industrial age. Instead, the campus of the future will consist of small and eco-logically sustainable solar houses, networked together in a lovely pastoral area. Goshiki-cho is indeed fully capable of fulfilling this potential. I am personally very grateful for this opportunity offered by the town. It is we the futurists who will turn this opportunity into *The Network University of the Green World* at the beginning of the twenty-first century.

References

Gleick, James (1987). *Chaos: Making a New Science*, New York: Viking.

Lovelock, James (1988). *The Ages of Gaia: A Biography of Our Living Earth*, New York: Bantam Books.

Sperry, Roger W. (1991). 'Search for Beliefs to Live by Consistent with Science', *Zygon* 26(2): pp. 237–58.

Waldrop, M. Mitchell (1992). *Complexity: The Emerging Science at the Edge of Order and Chaos*, New York: Viking.

Yamaguchi, Kaoru (1990). 'Fundamentals of a New Economic Paradigm in the Information Age', *FUTURES* 22(10): pp.1023–36.

—— (1992). 'Creating a Higher Institution for Future-Oriented Studies', in Richard A. Slaughter (ed.) *Teaching about the Future*, proceedings of a seminar organised jointly by UNESCO and the Canadian Commission for UNESCO, Vancouver, Canada, 21–23 June.

—— (1993). 'Information–Decision Structures and Futures Research', *FUTURES* 25(1): pp. 66–80.

Index